From Chains to Change

by

Glenn Johnson

Chicago, IL

From Chains to Change

Second City Books
1935 S. Plum Grove Rd., #349
Palatine, IL 60067
www.secondcitybooks.com

Published in the United States of America

First Edition: January 2011

ISBN: 978-1-935766-10-0

Library of Congress Control Number:
2010941470

Poems "Childhood Years" and "Walk On"
have been printed with permission by Kristen Elizabeth Rymarcsuk

Cover Design by
Wendy Barrett

I want to encourage you to turn the pages of this book in a slow and thoughtful manner.

There are many people in pain, whether it be physical, emotional, or spiritual. Perhaps you have exhausted everyone's patience and given up the hope that anyone cares or understands. I encourage you to take the journey with Glenn and become an overcomer just like Christ.

In John 16:33, Jesus says, "These things I have spoken unto you, that in me you might have peace," (Things may look dark, but everything is under control; Trust God and believe); "In the world you shall have tribulation but be of good cheer; I have overcome the world." He did this through the cross so we too can be overcomers when believing and trusting in Him!

As you reflect on Glenn's words in his book you will see that his journey is not so much about waiting for the storm to pass, but about learning to dance in the rain.

Joy and Blessings,
Pam Wool

***From Chains to Change** is an eye-opening book. It is a personal look at the struggles of inmates behind bars. Glenn Johnson was faced with danger, discouragement, and sometimes daily setbacks as he adapted to prison life. This is an inspiring account of a man dependent upon God. A man who called out for forgiveness and protection. A man who received the love of God in a climate not many people will ever experience. May you be as blessed as I was reading this book.*

Dawn Parker
Pastor's wife

"To my Father,
three-in-one."

Contents

Prayer and Reflection for Resolution

When I was spending my time in county jail and eventually prison, the downtime that I had gave me the time to reflect on all the things I did that lead to my time there. I used this time to pray to God to give me another chance to contribute to his glory, gain, and benefit. I found that for me it was difficult to just pray within my thoughts. Instead I choose to write them down, giving me more reinforcement when I prayed. I wrote all my prayers in a notebook for future reference and to remember what I needed to pray for. In writing them down I was able to put into words my inner thoughts.

The important thing that my journey can accomplish is to give anyone who is dealing with a conflict, addiction, or looking for a renewal the ability to read the prayer journal I've written, and that the introspection and reflections of what I went through will encourage you to search your own heart. My hope is that you would start your own journal of prayer, and start giving God an earful, asking questions along the journey so that you will get an answer—an answer that you might not like or weren't expecting, but that is how God answers us, in his time not ours. With God, patience is essential, and believe me, He will answer.

The journey that you will take will last a lifetime, and I know in my heart a journey that you will never regret. The journey will be scary to take, there will be bumps in the road. However, God has the most wonderful way of answering and assuring us that the journey will be fruitful and will give you blessings along the way.

I'm hoping and praying that you enjoy my journey in prayer
and begin your own.

G.

Forward

At a time when the Spirit of God desires to move people from brokenness to wholeness in Jesus, he raises up people to stand in the 'gap.' We need men and women who are willing to rise above the status quo. To place their journey to healing and restoration, even though difficult and transparent, into the hands of those who desperately want to know true freedom. Glenn is one of these people.

I will never forget the day Glenn came to East Gate Christian Center and sat with me for more than an hour. In this time he revealed his heart, journey, and need for discipleship. It is with sincere honor and love that I responded to this level of vulnerability.

We have worked together closely in church and restoration ministries, and have become brothers. We have spent hundreds of hours together since that first meeting, and to God's glory, this book has been the fruit that has been created.

Working as a jail and police chaplain for about ten years caused me to have great concerns and to look for real answers. The true need was not throwing more money into systems which were not working; the real need was for men and women to provide real tools to help bring opportunities to overcome dysfunction. This book, and the true life's answers it presents, coming from Glenn's experiences with God, is one of these tools. It has the breath of God on it.

You will not get anything from this book if you are looking for a simple one, two, three. But if you are looking for practical, godly steps, to a lifelong opportunity of walking in the freedom that comes through Jesus Christ, then I recommend this book without reservation.

From Chains to Change, has the ingredients needed to drive you into a change in your life which will break you free from any type of behavioral addiction. May God bless you as you pour over these pages!

Steve Barr
Senior Pastor, East Gate Christian Center
Freeport, Illinois

To God Be the Glory

January 1

Father in heaven, I pray that your strength makes me powerful and strong, and that I may fight those doubts that the evil one plants in my mind. You are my refuge and strength, my peace and rock I stand on. That is the strength that will get me through oh Lord! I am weak yet you get me through that weakness. I have doubts yet your presence gets me through. I battle the evil one constantly, he plants those seeds of doubt. I need you. Please comfort me Lord! Fortify me Lord let me have peace knowing that your power is my strength. I know that the Holy Spirit watches over me providing me with all that I to fight my battle. As your servant, Job was made to suffer, so have I been brought low. I know that everything happens in your time and I know that I would rather surrender to your glory then give into the evil one.

I pray for the evil around me to be taken away. I pray that I am able to spring the traps that are put in my way. There is no peace unless you are there standing beside me. Father I thank you for every day I'm given, for your love for me. You are always there, you will never leave me, for you are eternal life and I am only dust in the wind. Love me Father. You are all I ever need in my life.

G.
Psalm 137:23

January 2

Father,
Lord I have sinned, I have broken your laws, I am unclean and not worthy of your forgiveness. You gave us your son to pay the price for our sin. I thank you Jesus, for your sacrifice for me. I know my sins are forgiven through you Lord. I know that with your gift of sacrifice I have eternal life. Thank you Jesus! Thank you Father!

G.
John 10:11

January 3

Father,
It's Monday night the 3rd of January, 2005. I am scared about my future, such as it is, I'm hoping that you have enough control over my life to guide my steps the rest of the way. I know that my way didn't work so let me do it your way and I won't have to worry. It is amazing the different thinks that you think about being in prison. Things like, how many days to go, how to fight for self respect as the system brings you down to new lows in ones' life. Some people would like to say that prison is a place of rehabilitation, that is the biggest laugh here in prison Lord. Prison is a place for, control and punishment, very few people are concerned about the rehabilitation of a prisoner. There is no love lost between the correctional officers and inmates. The officers know that 72% of the inmates will be back within 2 years of release. Lord I can never come back I don't think I will survive if I was to return. The cost would be too high it would mean that I would have let everyone down again. I know that if I forget you Lord and your plan for me I'm doomed to fail so I need to get myself right. I know that Satan will try his best to get his hands on me again and I can't let that happen. Help me Jesus, you are the answer and I have heard the call. Let me serve you and my fellow man with the best of my abilities for the glory of your kingdom.

G.
John 15:9,10

January 4

Father,
I have a question not so much for you Lord but for me. What is my life without Jesus? I feel like it is an empty void and a longing for that void to be filled. I in the course of my life searched for all forms of escape most of which was evil. I brought down all that I loved. I surrendered to Satan's way and I was weak and found wanting. Nothing I did Lord ever really brought me true happiness and all I ever tried or did brought me down. Yet Jesus is always there Father, and He gave me everything, He gave me life by His death on the cross. He gave me the gift of eternal life, His blood for me. He knows my deeds, He knows my shortfalls and yet with love He surrendered his life for me. I struggle every day of my life over the sins I committed and ask that my sins be forgiven Father. I am no better than anyone else, even those who choose to condemn me for what I have done, however I forgive their weakness. We all can learn if we come to you Lord. Father I pray through Jesus that He grants me the gift of eternal life. I Love You! Amen.

G.
Psalm 63:1

January 5

Father,
Lord in my darkness you have brought me light. Lord you have held court and giving me a trial. Lord you have convicted me of my sins. Lord, sentence me to a lifetime of serving you. Lord, take control of my life and allow me to sing and praise you. Lord, keep my thoughts clean, and take out the trash that I have built up over my lifetime. Lord I know that my sins have been forgiven and yet I still feel guilty. I know now that only you Lord can get me through what is ahead in my life. Lord, I need to know how I might serve you. Lord would you give me the answer? I know Lord that everything happens in your time, I will wait. I just want to know what to do. I love you Lord and want to serve you.

Your loving son,
G.
John 12:26

January 6

Father,
Looking at the list of my sins I can easily say that I have broken every one of The Ten Commandments. I have worshipped others before you. Father I have idolized things other than you. You are the only one I love. I have used your name to curse others, and used your name wrongly in general conversation. I have not always given you the time you have asked for. Father I have not always honored my parents even to the point of wishing them ill will. I have not listened when I should have. I have been a thief, taking things which don't belong to me, from family, work and places of business. Father I have wished people harm or wished hey would die. I have probably killed the enemy in war. I have committed adultery, in thought, words, and deeds. I have made up lies and gossiped about others. I have wished for my neighbors' wife, wanting to be with her. I have wished to have things that my neighbor had. For all these sins I repent and ask for your forgiveness. I will try not to break them and keep you Holy. I will always try to be aware before I act. Father, forgive me, your loving son.

G.
Matthew 19:17

January 7

Dear Father,
I have written down my thoughts on The Lords' Prayer and here they are. Father, hallow be your name: We come to you with thanksgiving, that you would have us as one of your children through our Lord and Savior, Jesus Christ. We thank you Father for always being with us, weather we know it, or not. For taking the lead and guiding us along your path that you have given us, that you comfort us and see our needs, and provide for us. That you heal both our physical and spiritual body, that you allow us to shout your name to the heavens. I'll give you with my next thought tomorrow.

G
Psalms 119:9,10

January 8

Dear Father,
May your kingdom come and will be done on earth as it is in heaven. I pray Father that whatever you want me to do until your return will be done according to you will. Father I further pray that all men, women, children, family and friends do what you want. I pray that the body of believers, and our earthly shepherds, follow your perfect plan. Father I pray that all over the earth, nations bow down to your will and perfect love.

G.
Proverbs 3:6

January 9

Father,
Give us this day our daily bread. Father I pray that when I come to you, that you will nourish me, body and mind. Father I pray that when I come to you in prayer I will be shown what to feed on to receive your nourishment. I will try to pray constantly and let you renew and refresh me. I pray that I work earnestly serving you and others. I pray that the fruits of my labor are given to you first. I pray that I continue to grow stronger in praying to you.

G.
John 4:34-38

January 10

Father,
Forgive us our trespasses as we forgive those who trespass against us. Father may I ever be forgiven for all of my sins that I can remember or the sins I have forgotten. Father I pray that I might be able to forgive those who have sinned against me and ask that you forgive them and take care of them. Father as I go about my daily life I will always try to remember to think of your love before I act.

G.
2 Chronicles 7:14

January 11

Father,
Lead us not into temptation and deliver us from evil. I pray Father that I be given a pure, soft and repentant heart. Father please teach me your love and caring so that I may be obedient to you, so I can come to you in prayer in times of temptation and disobedience to your will. Father! Please give me your protection and strength so that I do not need to be put through the fires of hell in my disobedience. I pray Father that I may make my life better walking down your path. Father! Please protect those that I love and let them not be tempted as I was.

G.
James 1:12-15

January 12

Father,
For yours is the kingdom and the power and the glory, forever and ever. Amen! Father I pray that I worship and glorify you every minute of every day of my life. Father I pray that through the blood of your Son Jesus and the presence of the Holy Spirit I might share in your kingdom. Father you are all powerful and have authority over me, and authority over all people, that there is nothing in this world as powerful. I pray to you my King that I may bow down and sing your praises, forever and ever, Amen.

G.
Jude 24,25

January 13

Father,
Lord when I study your word it gives me comfort. I ask you Lord to give me clear understanding. I see in your word that loving you is not rocket science. Father your Word says, "No one can come to you without first accepting your Son Jesus and the price he paid, "that in honoring Him we will see your Kingdom." John 14:6. Father I want to thank you for your

Son, Jesus. There is a rite of passage from death to life and that Jesus is the answer. Praise Jesus! I can't understand why anyone would choose death over life, permanent separation from you, the alterative is not good, not good at all? I pray Father that all people including the inmates here would come to you and understand your love and receive your gift.

G.
Revelation 21:6,7

January 14

Father,
Lord I feel weak and that I'm under attack by Satan. I pray to you as my heart beats fast and my hands shake. Father I need your comfort. I need you Lord to be here with me and keep me protected from what I am going through. I know that I am weak Lord and can seek refuge in your arms. Please Lord, let my thoughts be your thoughts not mine. I know that Satan is strong but you are stronger. Lord as I go through my struggles to overcome my weakness, please be there for me.

G.
John 14:30,31

January 15

Father,
Today was another rough day Father Satan is still attacking me. Lord I am being tested and evil people are being put in my path. I am constantly being asked to do things that would put my time here in prison is in jeopardy, the thought of losing time and staying longer scares me. I am not strong or knowing in how to play all the angles that are played here in prison so I need your help. How can I be saved from this madness? I pray Lord that you will protect me and solve my problem, stop those who choose to cause me harm.

G.
Psalm 118:14

January 16

Father,
Thank You! Praise Jesus! Father it seems that the crisis is over, that the threat to my safety and well being is gone. The inmate who was causing the trouble has been removed from the cell unit I'm in. It seems like he was acting out with the corrections officer and was sent to segregation. Lord you are so wonderful, and you do answer prayer. Why did I ever doubt you?

G.
Psalm 6:8-10

January 17

Father,
I feel so unworthy of your love, for all the sinful things I've done. I know Father that I'm forgiven, yet I still feel ashamed. Forgive me Father for feeling this way, I do my best. I try to overcome my demons and it is so hard, that's why I'm coming to you. There are times Father that I feel you desert me and I sometimes get angry. I lust after things I shouldn't and those things are not what I want, I just get mad and then I fail miserably. Please Father, hear my prayer and help me. I love you Lord and fear you wrath, you know I'm trying. Why Father must I suffer so? I know that everything is for my benefit and yet I fail. Please Lord let your Spirit work within me. Father you know my heart and you know my sorrow please give me peace and love. Father, please guide me down your path of righteousness. In Jesus name I ask, Amen.

G.
John 5:24

January 18

Father, Lord it is mid-morning and the inmate in the next cell is causing trouble, giving the whole cell block, his thoughts on life. He rambles on his ideas of what men are like, not making any sense. Father I don't understand why he is doing this? In the world he creates it's every one, for themselves. There is no relationship with you Lord he has given up, that is the sadness of this ranting. In this cell block the agony is so unbelievable, there isn't much hope,the inmates turn to every form of perversion possible for their comfort except you Lord. There is not much going on that would include you being in the cell block Lord. I think it is the shame or the lack of hope. The inmates take the easy road to obtain the things that they need or want. Father I pray for healing and understanding Lord, show yourself too these men. Father what is the key that will open their door? I would say that it is nothing but the blood of Jesus that can open their door and loose the chains. I pray for that peace here today and every day. My challenge is that I let the Holy Spirit work in me and prepare me for the work I will be doing in your Kingdom. Lord I pray for your guidance.

G.
Psalm 6:2

January 19

Father,
Lord it is Saturday and thing here in the cell block are fairly calm. Thank you Jesus! I guess that boring is better than putting up with the child like antics that the inmates show on the gallery. LJ is getting his hair cut tonight so hopefully that will keep things quiet in the cell for a little while, at least I hope it will. No letter today so I'll have to wait until Monday. Today for lunch I had "Mystery Meat," only you Lord and the cooks' know what it is, I sure don't. Tonight the dinner that was "Soy Burger Steak," at least I won't gain any weight. Maybe I'll get a surprise and get a visit and that would be nice. I love you Lord and thanks for being with me, your son,

G.
Psalm 66:1-3

January 20

Father,

Lord in the middle of the night there was a shakedown and the correction officers' found illegal, homemade hooch. My cellmate and I were taken from the cell and LJ put up a fight, he didn't win. We were put in a holding cell for three hours, in our underwear out in a cold hallway, with broken glass windows to let the air in from the outside. The worst part of this situation is if I am charged with this offense along with my cellmate I stand to lose one year across the board if I am found guilty. I pray Lord that my cellmate stands up and takes the heat for this violation, but there is no way of telling which way LJ will go, I pray Father that you help me out of this situation. Father, I know that you are with me all the time and I need you.

G.
Psalm 69:1-3

January 21

Father,

Lord thank you for a new cellmate, D is 1 year older then I am and he's white. D just told me he has 12 yrs. Left on his bit, he will be 72 yrs. Old when he gets to go home, D has done 18 already. Lord I just am thankful that I am not in his place. Father I pray for relief in the position I'm in with these charges hanging over my head. I do not want to spend an extra year in here. Lord I know that only you can take care of this problem, only you have the power. The Chaplain came by today and brought me some self-help books to study to help me understand what I did and how to overcome. Lord I thanked the Chaplain for her time and gave her a blessing. So Lord, here I am, in another cell, another Cellmate, and probably have another year hanging over my head. What can I do besides prayer and waiting on you? Lord I pray that you watch over me, and that I might surrender to your will and wait on your timing.

G.
Hebrews 13:6

January 22

Father,
Lord today I got my Parole Board hearing results back from Springfield. I was denied my complaint and won't get out of Stateville segregation until June 21st. Filing the complaint was a waste of time but I did get to see how this system works. Lord I can't understand why you couldn't have helped me out, everything in your time, right? I have another problem Lord. My cellmate hates you, and rejects your teaching. D. is cursing your name constantly, this hurts me so much. What should I do? I praise your name Lord, while D. curses your name. Father I will pray for D. and his soul, and hope that he might come to you. I understand that the time for D. has been long and he has 12 more years to go. I will continue to pray.

G.
Psalm 61:1-4

January 23

Father,
Lord I hope that things go OK for me until I get out. I really need to stay unseen. I can't change what will be and I just have to trust that you have my back. Protect my Father! I know that you are all I need. Father I prayed that you cast out the demons that are inside of D. Lord he hates you so much. What do I need to do? I wish I wasn't so weak and able to stand up to D. It's been 3 days since I had a smoke, I could use one right now. I'm going through withdrawal so I've been sleeping a lot and that seems to help so I don't think about smoking. I just read a great newspaper, "The Sword of the Lord." This is a Baptist newspaper and has some good teaching. One of the truths that it lays out is that we should stop thinking about all the bad things that are happening to Christians' and more about the good things and that we would see the happy side and not the sad side. Father what is the best way to be a Christian? Please answer Lord.

G.
Proverbs 1:33

January 24

Father,
Lord to my question about being a Christian. I think you gave me some thoughts? To be a Christian is to be willing to talk and pray all the time and think about Jesus, to help bring new souls into your Kingdom, that salvation is the only way, and that this commitment will give eternal life. I have a limited group of people to talk too so I will just keep these thoughts for later. The only things that they want to hear are the positive things not things that might change their direction. I believe I'm saved and I know there is so much more to the life of a Christian. I know that I have to do the work with all my heart, and let you Lord, work in me. I will write later Lord, talk to you soon.

G.
Philippians 1:11

January 25

Father,
Lord I am ashamed of the way I've acted towards you. I've known about you since I can remember but I never thought you that important in my life. The dark side of life might be fun for a while, unfortunately my highs only lasted for a while and I needed a bigger and bigger high each time. I really could never obtain or sustain the high. Lord you know my heart and who I am. I feel more positive about my faith and love for you. Lord you are the greatest high I ever have had. Father let me stay in your love.

G.
Psalm 9:1,2

January 26

Father,
I come to you today just to give you praise and thank you. Lord, you are everything I will ever need. Amen! Lord I pray for deliverance from the problems I face today and everyday here after. You know why I am asking for your help, for without you I cannot do what needs to be done. Father let me walk in the footsteps of Jesus.

G.
Exodus 3:17

January 27

Father,
Good morning Lord. I know I should not be smoking Lord because it is bad for my health. However, I really need one. I have not had a smoke for a few days and the cigs, takes the edge off, forgive me. D. and I had BBQ Soy for lunch and are expecting cold cuts for dinner. I hate cold cuts, and at least I'm not starving. Father I pray today as I did yesterday to cast out the demons that curse you inside of D. I pray that you give the peace that D. needs. I think that everyone at one or another has forgotten about you Lord, may I ever be faithful. I am finding out that Satan is always attacking and I need to always keep my guard up. I pray Lord give me the strength to fight the temptations Satan places in my path. I love you Lord.

G.
Luke 4:8

January 28

Father,
I have been sweating the charges for possession of alcohol in the shakedown last week. I need you Lord to help me with this problem. I am on edge, waiting for the hammer to drop and put me into a more miserable state then I'm in already. Please Lord! Help!!!!!! Lord this problem is in your hands.

G.
Matthew 21:21

January 29

Father,
So far, so good, nothing has happened yet on my charges. I wonder if the board just likes the inmates to sweat and then drop the hammer. Each day that passes is one more I won't have to spend in this Hell I'm in. I hope to get some mail today it would really help take my mind off of my problems. I wish that I got mail every day, but I also know that people still have things to do that are more important. Life outside doesn't stop because I am here in prison. I didn't get any mail today, well maybe tomorrow. Lord thank you for another day. Lord in case you didn't know we had pancakes and cereal for breakfast, chicken patty for lunch and mystery meat for dinner. Isn't life in prison great?

G.
Lamentations 3:23

January 30

Father,
Lord it sure would be nice to have some decent food for a change, maybe someday. Praise you Lord I finally had a decent meal, Lasagna. The one thing I do know is that dinner will be garbage, of that I'm sure. Well I'm out of squares now, so I'll have to go awhile without, that's OK, it will be good for my health. Just washed my clothes in the sink and that means I won't stink. The cellblock porter just brought me an extra plate of Lasagna. Lord you do answer prayer. Thank you,

G.
Psalm 6:9

January 31

Father,
Thank you for the food I had for lunch yesterday the extra meal was great, however I was right dinner really was terrible. Lord you seem to have answered my prayer with the exception of last night these last few days we have had some fairly decent food. Praise you Lord! Lord I still haven't heard anything from the board and I'm praying constantly. I know Lord that you are there for me. I love you Lord.

G.
Psalm 17:1

February 1

Father,

Lord in heaven I pray with my whole heart let me keep your commandments. Lord, teach me your ways and bless me. I will meditate on your word and respect your ways. I will not forget your word. Lord deal richly with me so that I might see wondrous things out of your word. Let me understand your word so I may give testimony for your gain and benefit. Lord remove from me my lying ways, graciously grant me your favor. I have chosen truth, and your judgment I've accepted with my whole heart. Lord enlarge me heart to obey your word keeping your law. Please Lord let your mercy come upon me. Lord, grant me salvation by your word. Sin had a hold of me because of my wicked ways and having turned from your ways. Teach me good judgment and wisdom. I was sinful and went astray. It is good for me being found guilty, so I can now walk in your light. I pray that your kindness may comfort me as I walk down your path. Lord I ask this all in the name of Jesus.

G.
Colossians 3:9,10

February 2

Father,
I like D. However I wish that RW was back. RW was the first cellmate I had when I got here, I was sad to see him go. RW and I would have great discussions on our faith. RW was open-minded and taught me thinks I needed to get through this time here in F-House. RW and I exchanged information and who knows we might even stay in touch. I wish him well Lord, may you watch over him and protect him, help him to conquer his addiction. Father there are certain people you meet in life and RW was one of them and I wish him well. I'm proud to have known RW. Lord thank you for bringing RW into my life.

G.
Psalm 149:3

February 3

Father,
It is the middle of winter and the cells have very little heat, and it is extremely cold. There is nothing to keep the chill from getting to my bones, this winter seems harsh. I know that coming to you brings me the warmth that I need to get by, thank you Lord for being here with me. I love you so much. I hope that I will do right by you. I know that when the storms come you will protect me and I thank you for that blessing. I have a little less than 4 months to go. Lord I still haven't heard about my charges on the ticket I was to have gotten awhile ago. I sure would like to know what is happening. Lord I pray that all goes right. I love you,

G.
Psalm 107:14,15

February 4

Father,
Lord you know my pain and agony, you know my heart, and you know my weaknesses. Please help me Lord, take these things away. Lord, give me your comfort and peace. D. is doing his exercises and trying to keep himself in shape for his next 12 years here. I am so thankful I don't have that much time to go my 2 plus years is pale in comparison. Thank you Lord so very much. Let me be right in your eyes. The noise here on the gallery is endless, 24/7. I need your peace. Lord you know my pain. I love you Lord,

G.
John 15:27

February 5

Father,
I got some money from the family a while ago and I just found out I might be able to buy a T.V. and have that in the cell with me. I am going to put in a request and try and get this done. I just can't get motivated to write anyone, I really haven't got much to say, I would just depress them anyway, I'll write them when things get better. Today we had mystery meat, cereal and a banana for breakfast, for lunch some type of beef stew, and for dinner I had a soy burger. I get enough food so I won't starve, however I am losing weight, I think I've lost about 20 lbs. I was informed that there is yard tomorrow and if I want to go I can. Yard is given every 10 days and it is 5 hours long it is held out in a secure area. If I choose to go I have to stay for the full 5 hours no matter what the weather. It's February, I think I'll pass. I'm reading the last book I haven't read and I hope I will be sent some books from my family. I didn't get any mail today maybe tomorrow. Lord I love you, without you I am nothing. Thank you Jesus! I know you will help me with what I need. Love you Father,

G.
Isaiah 40:1-2

February 6

Father, I woke today with doubt in my mind planted by the evil one. I sent a prayer to you Lord. Lord you are my comfort, my rock, my refuge and my strength. I rather have you Lord then being separated and apart. I need your living water and nothing of this world I'm in today. The world I'm in here is one of desperation, fear and hate, this world in here was created by Satan, this hell hole is where Satan gathers his legions. Lord there are not many choice here in this prison, one usually follows by what he observes. What I observe are many men sacrificing their souls to get what they want to gain respect and fear from the other inmates. There is a lot of scheming going on and you Lord aren't in these plans, they give up their souls for one good fix. I on the other hand realize that what I need, is you! I realize that you have a plan for me and I just need to listen and follow that plan. I realize Lord that I need to keep my heart open to your will. Lord I will defer to that will and do that which is presented to me. I love you God!

G.
Proverbs 10:2

February 7

Father,
Lord to you be the glory, forever and ever. Lord you suffered and died so that I might live and have a permanent place in your kingdom. I know that you died for me Lord, to save me and give me eternal life. I thank you, a sinner saved by your tender mercy. Lord I'm scared and having a rough time in this hell hole, yet I know that you will protect me and watch over me. I can feel the evil in this place and yet with you by my side I have peace. Thank you Lord! Praise you Father! I've been reading the books I got from my daughter today and this is a great outlet, reading takes up a lot of time and I can ignore what is going on around me. Lord I'll write later, love you,

G.
Psalm 18:2,3

February 8

Father,
I have had plenty of time to observe the ways that men adjust to the situation that their put in. In this cell block are approximately 400 inmates and at no time do they all sleep at the same time. Lord there is no period in the day where it is peaceful. My cell mate sleeps during the day and I sleep at night or should I say, try too. D. is trying to figure out which prison he will be transferred to when his time here is done. D. is classified as an escapee, which means he is transfer to a different prison ever year. There are only 2 other prisons that handle escapees. The two prisons are Menard and Pontiac, D. is hoping for Menard he says there are better conditions to live in then Pontiac. I personally would not want to be in either one. Lord the noise in here is so terrible! I don't know what to do. Please help me Lord! I need you so much to quiet the noise. I'll write tomorrow, love you.

G.
Psalm 3:5

February 9

Father,
I come to you tonight in desperation. I come to you in deep sorrow. I come to you in total pain and suffering, I can't do the time here alone. Father! I am a sinner! I have played games with you, testing your true existence, waffling between what is good in this world and what is evil. I was like the wayward son that you used as an example of returning and giving into the fathers will, to accept whatever the father wanted to do. Lord I can't play anymore games and at this point in my life I can't do anything alone. Lord I am before you tonight naked as the day I was born, stripped of all pride. I ask for you to forgive me in the name of your Son Jesus, who gave his life so that I may be granted that living water, to be able to spend eternity with you Father. I do not want to be away from you any longer. Father I surrender to you will, deal with me as you see fit. Lord I will take any punishment you choose. Lord the only thing I want to do is dedicate my life to your Kingdom, to follow the word that you had

written down as a blueprint for my life and all the people in the world. Let me serve you for the rest of my life. I dedicate my soul to serving that Kingdom. Father whatever you choose for me to do let me do it with joy and love, let my true happiness be in serving you and no other. Father let your will be done and use me for the rest of the time I have left in my life. Lord all I need is to seek the wisdom and understanding you have laid out for me. I ask that you give me your peace. Thank you Lord! Father, mute the noises that is constantly around me, and take away the evil that is here in this pit of hell. I love you Lord Jesus!

G.
Romans 5

February 10

Father,
I'm sit here in my cell at Stateville Prison, it's around 10:30 P.M., I've been hurt throughout my life, but that is nothing like the hurt I'm observing here today. I can hear it in their voices. The agonizing crying that goes on 24/7 from the inmates trying to survive this hellhole. We are living in an ungodly place, a place where there is no compassion or caring, 80% of these inmates have been in prison before; for some of them it's a badge of honor, they try to cover their disappointment at having been caught again. The inmates are always talking about the time they have spent in prison. Lord the sad thing is that they will be back. I've seen many inmates turn to the Bible for comfort, then turn around and continue to do the same things over again. The word just runs off their backs like a duck, right back to the same thing day after day. The inmates talk about revenge, their mistreatment of their woman, and blame everything on their bad luck. They don't want to be accountable for what they did. The language that they use is unbelievable, their reality is there is no escape for their anger and hurt, or so they think. There is no one here to care, the corrections offices only care about keeping the animals in their cages. Lord I know that you are the answer, only you can easy their pain and suffering. Somewhere in their past they were let down by their family, friends and society, or they just couldn't resist the temptations. It's sad to think that you would forgive

them if they only asked, but they don't. Lord I pray those who overcome do well and I will continue to pray for those who don't. Love you,

G.
Romans 6:12

February 11

Father,
I've had plenty of time to look back and try to figure out where I went wrong and the answer is always the same. I fell away from you Lord. I abandoned all I had been taught, all that I was raised on and believed in. Now when I'm with you Lord, I can fell the comfort and peace that you give me and that makes me content. When things were going good I thought like a man and not as a son of God. I pray every night that Satan's demons do not over take me and bring me down, back towards the pits of hell. I know that I've been saved and yet I abuse your grace through Jesus. I thank you Lord for his sacrifice and your mercy. Lord as my life gets shorter day by day I realize that what was important in my past life is not present now. My priorities have changed and I now put you first in my life. Lord I only want to walk in your light, down your path. I'm just a sinner saved by grace. Amen!

G.
Romans 8:1-5

February 12

Father,

Lord I've become addicted to Christ. Jesus is the answer for this world today. I see a small part of what hell is like. I sit here in my cell listening to all the sad souls, souls with no hope except eternal damnation. I hear them blaming the authorities for their being here in prison. I hear them talking about sex, adultery, killing and hurting others. I see them not accepting the consequences for their own actions. I can see where my own actions were immoral and lewd. I see how I was led into those thinks that I did. I see how Satan lured me in my weakness to act sinfully. I see how I turned my back on the things that are right and good. I see how your words have touched my heart like no other. I see that it took the commission of a crime to bring me back to you. I know that through Jesus my sins have been removed. I see that I am harder on myself then you are. I know that there is only one way, and that's with Jesus. I know now what life without you will be like. I know that an eternity without you is worse than being with you. I know that things can only get better with you leading the way. I know to walk in your steps is a daily need. I know not to forget the price Jesus paid for me. I know he has a free gift for me to accept. I ask that you allow me to walk in your footsteps. Love you Lord.

G.

Psalm 5:11,12

February 13

Father,

I did my bible study today, Revelations: Chapters 1-5. I still have so many short comings in my walk with Jesus. I'm so ashamed of the things I've done in my life. Over the course of my life, I have broken every one of your laws'. Forgive me Lord! I have comfort Lord in knowing that you have forgiven me even if others have not, you have given me life. Thank You Lord! It's wonderful to know that I still have time in my life to work for your Kingdom. Praise You Lord! I am lonely here in prison, but that loneliness has been taken away thank to your gift to me. Glory to you

Lord! I know that I need to be ever watchful for the pitfalls Satan puts in my path. Satan will attack me with great vigor, to again trap me in his world, a world of separation from you my Lord. Lord a world without you is no world at all.

G.
Galatians 3:11,12

February 14

Father,
I was just thinking of the stupid thinks I've done to end up in this place. The one thing that gets me through is knowing Lord that you are with me. I find comfort in the prayers I write to you and walking in your grace. Lord let me remain humble before you Father and continue in the wonderful love you have for me. The biggest problem that I have is trying to understand all the evil that surrounds me. Most of the inmates walk away from you, even knowing that you are real. Satan has won the victory in here but my hope is Satan hasn't won the war that rages here on earth, Lord! Keep me steadfast in your love and watch over me. Thank you Jesus for your Holy Spirit and your strength! I love you Father, you are all there is for me, guide me, groom me, and work steadfast within me so I can better serve you. I know you will give me the strength to face the unknown. Praise to you Lord!

G.
2 Thessalonians 3:2,3

February 15

Father,

Today I'm reading a book by Joseph F. Grizone, the book is entitled; Joshua and the City, this book means a lot to me because Joseph F. Grizone seems able to capture God's Love and understanding. The storyline is how Jesus returns to this world as a Carpenter, starts aiding people in need and changing their lives, and the lives of other people who live in a rundown urban setting. The book presents a wonderful blueprint of what can be down to assist, aid and change the mindset of a society that is in desperate need, that when peoples' hearts are changed their lives are the better for it. Father I just want to pray for your help in starting me on a path to help desperate people, people who seem to be beyond hope, people whom society seems to have given up on. Father! I ask that you give me the armor I need to fight this uphill battle. I know that in Ephesians 6 verses 11-17 your blueprint is already written: 11. Put on all Gods' armor so that you will be able to stand firm against all strategies and tricks of the Devil. 12. For we are not against people who are made of flesh and blood, but against the evil ruler sand authorities of the unseen world, against those mighty powers of darkness who rule this world, and against wicked spirits in the heavenly realm. 13. Use every piece of God's armor to resist the enemy in the time of evil, so that after the battle you will still be standing firm. 14. Stand your ground, putting on the sturdy belt of truth and the body armor of God's righteousness. 15. For shoes, put on the peace that comes from the Good News, so that you will be fully prepared. 16. In every battle you will need faith as your shield to stop the fiery arrows aimed at you by Satan. 17. Put on salvation as your helmet, and take the sword of the Spirit which is the word of God. Lord I need to think, will write later.

G.

Ephesians 6:11-17

February 16

Father,
I come to you this day, to give you thanks for my thoughts when I wrote yesterday. What I wrote touched my heart and I needed to think. What I started thinking about was the battle, a battle that is raging today. I know that I can help in the fight and that I am going to needed your expertise. I know Father that when the time comes the Holy Spirit will be there for me and all the others that will stand in this fight. Lord! Please surround me with the right people to fight this battle, let me learn the ways you have set aside to fight the evilness that is in the world today. I will stand shoulder to shoulder with all those who choose to fight. I pray Father that you give me the time to fight. In studying your Word I find comfort and the simple message that you give me. I know that this fight between good and evil is not a movie, that this battle all ready has started, that this battle is in real-time and in real-life. I hope I am ready to lose my life in the fight to stand for your Kingdom. I know there can be no other way Lord! I need your strength Lord. I know that I won't win the war but I will win some battles for your Kingdom. Lord! Strengthen me and let me understand that which I need to succeed. Lord I read, study, think and pray trying to gain knowledge and your strategies for battle, plant these strategies within me. I'm a sinner Lord, I sin everyday even when I'm trying not to. I know that I'm not worthy of your forgiveness and yet through the gift of your Son I am washed clean. Thank you Lord! A humble soldier in your army.

G.
Revelation 2:10

February 17

Father,
Today I did my duty and had a bird bath, it is rough not being able to take a shower. I've washed my clothes in the sink and looked at myself in the mirror, I can see that my hair is getting quite long, I'm starting to look like a hermit. Two days ago chemicals were sprayed on the gallery to wash all the human feces and urine that was thrown from the cells onto the gallery floors by some disgruntled inmates. The chemicals were so strong that it has taken this long for the harsh smell to disappear. Today we are having fish and this is one of the better meals I get. Lord I am waiting on the State Adjustment Board, to see if a can get some of my lost time back, it has been several weeks since I when before them for my review. Lord I hope that there is a positive response when the review results arrive. I know Father that everything is in your hands, thank you. I've given up on the T.V. so I will wait until I get out of segregation and go to my next prison assignment. The time I could have spent watching T.V. can be well spent in the study of your Word. I will write later. I love you Lord,

G.
Hebrews 6:11,12

February 18

Father,

I just talked to the counselor and ask if she could check on the status on the purchase of the T.V. I wanted to get, maybe I'll get some results, sure would be nice. The inmates were just told that we need to put in a request slip for toilet paper. It really sucks the way things are run in here. I know that in all probability I won't be getting the T.V. oh well, I tried. There was no mail today maybe tomorrow. Lord with the time I spend with you, the books I read and the letters I get the time here is doable. I was thinking about LJ Lord and I would pray that at some point in his life he can really get to know you Lord. He told me once that he has been in the justice system since he was 11 and he's only 20 now, so sad. Lord I also pray that his bullet wound heals now that the bullet has been removed. Heal him Father! It is so difficult sleeping here with the constant noise and I thank you for answering my prayers. Since I totally surrendered to your plan for me the noise on the gallery seems to have been muted, thank you. I do not understand this rap music that a lot of the inmates listen to and try to create and sing, there is no love, just hate and degrading of women. The songs talk about selling and using drugs, about killing and fighting anyone who gets in their way. The more I hear and listen to the words, society needs to be worried. Father I pray that you watch over this world, there is a storm of hate coming. Lord watch over, and protect me for the next 31/2 months I have left in here. I know that I will make Father because you said I would. Thank you Lord.

G.

Psalm 11:5-7

February 19

Father,
I have been studying the letters Paul wrote to the seven churches and got to thinking. These letters were on faith, hope, love and encouragement to remain faithful to Jesus and God's word. We need to hope for brighter days. That the Lord will never let us down even in the worst of times. To always remember that all things are possible and that in our relationship with God love will always overcome hate. It is hard to love the men here in prison because of their hate and yet I see a need to do so. I know that had you been in their life, the circumstances would have been different. I know that all things are possible with you Lord. I ask that you soften my heart so I may understand better the suffering of these inmates and to always keep them in my prayers. I ask that I continue to be encouraged to have a strong relationship with you. A oneness with you God, your Son and the Holy Spirit. I ask for understanding and love so I can minister to the inmates and show them a better way. Lord I ask for forgiveness for the times I've doubted you. Let me present to the world the love that you have given me so that others might benefit. I ask this in the name of Jesus,

G.

John 15:16

February 20

Father,
I tell myself only a little while longer and I will be starting a new adventure in a new facility. I can only wonder what that is going to be like. I'm afraid that something might happen here in the next 3 1/2 months here at Stateville. I know I can do that time but if I were to be here any longer it would be extremely hard. Father I'm trying to be strong in knowing that in your arms all things will work out, but I still am attacked by me to doubt you. Lord may I never doubt you, and ever stand fast in that faith. Lord, you are the light in my darkness, you are the rock I can stand on, and with you I can move mountains. Lord I don't need mountains moved I just need you to be there. I Love you Lord,

G.

Mark 11:23

February 21

Father,
Lord there is so much hate and sadness here most of the men here are so young. They think that there invincible. Many of these inmates will be here for a long time and those that get out will be back for another bit. I see that society would rather incarcerate then rehabilitate. I know I do not want to return. Father! I pray for inner peace and comfort Lord for all of us here. I ask that you bind the demons to their master and ease the suffering here. Father let there be a greater understanding by society of the suffering and pain these inmate endure day after day. Lord something needs to be done to inform and educate society what the needs of these inmates are once they are return to that society. I know Lord that when these inmates go home they return to the same situations that brought them here in the first place, that has got to change somehow. The world is fast forgetting that you created all. Lord I see an uphill fight against an enemy that is cunning and attacks mans free will. I know Father that there will be many battles. I know that in the end I will meet you in heaven.

G.
Romans 1:21,22

February 22

Father,
Lord it is a struggle everyday to get by, I don't know where my journey will take me until I'm called home, but I know that I need you to lead me. Lord I just want to give you thanks and praise for all that I've been given. I will hold on to your love and caring for me. It is amazing that you have so many people that come to you and you take care of them (us). Praise you Lord, thank you for being here with me. I think of all the terrible things I've done in the past and yet you never abandoned me. I know you were there protecting me waiting for me to come to you. I know that if I didn't have this time out of being in prison I might not have understood what you can do for people if only they surrender. I know that through all the hard times here I'll be able to get a clearer picture of what you want me to do. I pray Lord that I listen to your plans for me. There has been a

warmer feeling in my stomach since I gave all my pain and agony to you. Lord, guide me and teach me your ways. Lord I ask this all in the name of your Son, Jesus. I can feel the pain of the men here Lord, may they find you Lord to give them comfort. I love you and thank you Lord Jesus.

G.
Revelation 2:7

February 23

Father,
Lord I've been looking back on my prior life. It was a life of knowing you and yet not knowing you. I remember I use to participate in all sorts of church functions and then go out and act sinful and forget about you, I'm sorry Lord for all that time wasted. I know that I shouldn't look back but I do. The one thing about looking back is to take those stains on my prior life and not fall into the same pit I was in. I thank you Lord for being there for me. Praise you Lord! I know that Jesus is the answer for today and the rest of my life. I'm gonna' shout to heaven for all the wonderful things you have given me. Lord I just feel so loved. I am in a new relationship one that will never go away and stand the test of time. I've been waiting for some letters to come and to know that everyone in my family is all right. I'm thinking back to the seedy way I acted in my old life, I am so ashamed. I just thank Jesus for his blood for me. Father I am so looking forward to working for your Kingdom. Lord I pray I don't ignore the signs that you give me for my journey in Jesus footsteps. Lord with you all things will be right. I love you!

G.
2 Corinthians 5:11

February 24

Father,
Lord when I started writing my prayers down I thought it would be tough. I was unsure where these prayers would take me, what path I would take. I had a lot of anger, hurt, sadness and a lot of uncertainty in my heart. Anger at what I had done, hurt for all the people I let down, sad that I would be leaving everyone and everything I had, and uncertain over my prospects while in jail and prison. I have spent almost 10 months being incarcerated now and I have learned so much. With the prayers that I started writing 10 months ago I've been able to come to you and trust that you are there for me, that you will never desert me. The thing that helped me along with my prayers was picking up a Bible and finally reading from cover to cover twice and I'm reading it again. This time that I'm doing has given me time. I had time to reflect, renew and regenerate. I've been able to look back on my life and address that life through reading your Word. To give you the baggage I carried and not look back in a negative way. To use this opportunity to rest and take time to think and spend time with you Lord. This time has given me time to jump for joy, and get excited for Jesus and his blood for me. I want to thank you Lord, I am blessed.

G.
Psalm 23

February 25

Father,
I want to thank you for your Word Lord. I'm learning so much about, who I was and who I am now, just a poor sinner saved by Jesus. Praise you Lord! For me Lord the most exciting two books are Romans and Revelations. Romans excite me because Paul tells what I need to do, and how to live a wonderful life living for Jesus. Revelation is exciting because even with all that will be going on in the future, you win Lord and all will bow down and worship you. I understand now why lots of movies where made about different people and events that took place. One thing that helped me was the arrival of my new Bible. "The Life Application Study Bible" was sent

to me from my daughter. This Bible is written and translated into American English and I can really understand what I'm reading. I personally think that if every person read this Bible, the scriptures would become clearer and there would be a better understanding of what the Word is says to us. This is just my opinion Lord! It's been a long day Lord and the cell is cold and chilly. Give me you warmth Lord, give me peaceful sleep.

G.
Colossians 1:10

February 26

Father,
I come to you to ask that when I stumble and fall on my path, that you will pick me up, brush me off and send me on my way again. I ask Lord that when I am too weak to go on that you cradle me in your arms and carry me. I know Lord that I can't travel your path alone I need a guide, please take the lead and bring me home. Lord your streets of gold and crystal sea are waiting for me. I'm so excited to be with you Lord. Thanks for being my guide. It is still cold in the cell, and February does not show any mercy. I know that I caused my own suffering and a lot of people would say that I deserved what I got. Maybe they are right but with your help Lord I'll prove them wrong. I'm sorry Lord I just got a remorseful thought, keep me strong. I know you will because I asked.

G.
Colossians 1:11

February 27

Father,
February is almost over and I can't wait for the weather to change. I know that this weather can't be good for my arthritis. I only hope that it doesn't get worse. Father I am glad that my hair is coming back and I see in the metal mirror that I have a lot more grey then the day that I was arrested. Father I know that this isn't important to you and it is only my pride talking, sorry Lord. I was just reflecting Lord on the old me vs. the new. I know that the new will have victory over the old. I know Lord that you see on the inside and I have only seen myself on the outside and I thank you for that. Lord I need some better meals, I've lost about 20 lbs., I really could use some more food. I know this is a stupid request but you said I could ask for anything. Lord I love and want to be with you always, keep me in your light and away from the dark.

G.
1 Corinthians 1:8

February 28

Father,
Lord I come to you today in prayer to thank you for protecting me in Viet Nam back in 1968. You know Lord that it was a leap year and I worried that something might happen because of the extra day I had to spend there. Lord you know that I prayed in earnest for a safe journey out of Viet Nam, and you did. I know that it was a long time ago and you were there with me. I got my results back from the State Adjustment Board, they gave me 3 months back on my good time and 3 months back on my out date, thank you for that blessing. Lord in the 21/2 months I've been here I really have learned a lot especially about myself and you Lord. I feel totally free of the burdens, I've carried for decades. I love being in your Word and studying it. I love coming to you in prayer even if it is easier for me to write them down, than to say it in my mind.

G.

February 29

Father,
I come to you Lord in the name of your Son Jesus Christ my Lord and Savior with the Holy Spirit. I pray for forgiveness from my sins because I know I can lay them down in front of you and I am forgiven. I know that through the blood of Jesus as he died upon the cross and paid the price for me I will have a place in your Kingdom. Lord I bless your name and give thanks. I know that I will receive grace and love. I know that you have revived, renewed and regenerated my life. I lift you name on high and say Amen and Amen!

G.
1 Corinthians 1-13

March 1

Father,
In the quite of this morning I am here praying for your guidance. I know that my prayer will be answered in your time and with Love. I am a sinner Lord asking for directions. Lord you know my future, you know my thoughts and you know my deeds and needs. Lord, make and mold me with your love into a strongly convicted man for Christ. Lord let me follow you all the days of my life here on earth. Lord my sins have been forgiven and my shortcomings and pitfalls noted. Help me to do your bidding, show me the way, the light and the truth. Give me your peace, comfort and love. I ask Lord for wisdom too know when to act and not too act, when too stand and when not too. This is what I ask and pray in the name of Jesus, Father thank you for listening to my prayer. Amen and Amen.

G.
Matthew 6:25

March 2

Father,
Dear Lord I've been doing a lot of searching and learning from the Word and other sources and I found an anonymous Prayer that really holds meaning to me. "God is every tomorrow, therefore I live for today, certain of finding at sunrise, guidance and strength along the way. Power for each moment of weakness, hope for each moment of pain, comfort for ever sorrow, sunshine and joy after the rain." Lord it really says a lot about who you are. I know that you are ever present and there is nothing that you don't see or know. I think knowing that fact helps keeps me on the narrow path. I love you Lord and I fail you all the time. I'm trying Lord and I can always use your help. I thank you Lord for listening.

G.
Psalm 16:8

March 3

Father,
Lord this is a prayer I wrote and I present it to you. I've been bruised, but not broken. I've been sad, but not hateful. I've been found guilty, justly. I surrender without hesitation. I saved my soul in my repentance. I know my bruises will heal. I know my sadness will disappear, my guilt will be discharged. I know my freedom will be granted. I know my soul is saved, in Jesus. You have taken my sadness and removed it. You have taken my guilt upon your shoulders. You have given me freedom. You have my Soul. I thank you Father for always being there. I am blessed always.

G.
Psalm 145:14

March 4

Father,
Good evening Lord it's 8 p.m. and I just finished having a wonderful meal: A soy burger that taste like, well I can't describe the taste. I also got an apple at least they can't change the taste of that. I get a little upset over the fact that every meal is cold by the time it get to my cell. I sure would like a warm meal at some point. Today has been uneventful, much like any other day in this segregation unit, I guess that is better than the crying and fighting that usually takes place. I read a novel today and it's only the third time. I do crossword puzzles when I can get them and that helps the time go by faster. When I keep busy with these things my eyes get tired and I can sleep. I have a slip for the health care unit, and I go tomorrow, I wonder what they want. Lord, again I just thank you for the peace that you are giving me. The one who trusts in the Lord will have living water. Praise You!

G.
Matthew 6:33

March 5

Father,
Lord it is hard to have faith when everything around you smells of evil. I get attacked all the time with thoughts of doing something stupid, things that might get me in trouble. I turn away from those attacks because I know that you are with me and that's the best feeling in the world. I know that I can make it with you in my corner. I thank you for your Holy Spirit and his protection. I think about all the wonderful things that have taken place in my life, and that gives me hope for the future. Lord you are the only one who knows what will happen tomorrow. I need to remember that I should wait for what you want me to do in my life. I've got to be patient. Speaking of patients, I went to healthcare today, and all that they wanted to do was draw more blood. I have given more blood in the last 10 months to last a lifetime. When I first got into the Department of Corrections, I went through a complete physical and they drew blood, when I went to

Mt. Sterling, they drew blood two times and when I came here to Stateville it happened again. I hope that is the last time, I feel like a pin cushion. Lord may I ever work for the advancement of your Kingdom. I love you.

G.
Matthew 8:25

March 6

Father,
Lord I feel a little better today, my daughter sent me a book by Rick Warren, "The Purpose Driven Life", as I started working through it, I could feel the love that Rick Warren put into the book. I feel the love you created for me. I just hope I have the courage to uphold my end of the commitment I made to you a month ago. I am alone in my cell and yet not alone I can feel you with me all the time, you are the only one I can turn too. Right now my mission is two-fold, to get myself right in my thoughts and stay right with you. I am here being tested like Paul and Silas. I have tried to be quiet and invisible, not wanting to create waves. I find that even if I try to be invisible those around me don't and that causes me problems. I understand that they are not my problem but I wish that their problems wouldn't be my problems. There is a rebellion in here against the authorities and that causes friction all the time. The joke here is that there is the state's way and the Stateville way. I have only 3 months left here Lord and every day I get closer I just give you thanks for your protection. Love you Father.

G.
Matthew 9:17

March 7

Father,

Lord you have given me this test and I hope I pass, and come through with a better understanding of you and the things you want me to do. The gallery has been on lock-down for a week now so no one can have a shower, or go to the yard. I think of the pioneers and how they had to clean and wash their clothes and try my best to do the same. I'm out of deodorant and that doesn't help much. Right now a lot of the inmates are banging their doors and chuck-hole covers, this makes it almost impossible to think straight. I don't know way this is going on but I'm sure I'll find out soon enough, it really doesn't matter but it is nice to know. The one thing I observed in my time here is you see the weaker side of men, men with little hope. I try to understand and fall short of doing so. Lord I just thank you very much for granting me peace to overcome. I'll write later.

G.
Matthew 14:27

March 8

Father,

I got to thinking Lord, I've been here a little less than 3 months and in that time I have met death-row inmates who were given a reprieve by the Governor of the state. I have met inmates that won't get out for 56 years yet and they are only in their twenties, I've met almost every type of inmate and I see the one thing that they all have in common the need to believe in something, the need for some type of foundation. Some of the inmates find work to do that will give them some sense of purpose, some create problems for the correctional officers, and some retreat into their shell. The thing that I do not see too much of is coming to you for relief and comfort, and for me that is very disheartening. How do I get to them with the message of forgiveness and the love that our Lord and Savior has for them if only they would come to him. There are a few chaplains who visit and try to administer to the inmates but there are over 400 inmates here and they are only here 2 or three times a month and only have 5 hours to minister to the inmates here. The one thing that the D.O.C. doesn't care about is the health of the inmates' soul. It fact I'd venture to say they would say the inmates have no soul. Father! Give me the strength to undertake the mission you have given me, to advance the Kingdom. I know I have my own short-comings and you know what these are so remove them and use me Lord. I had the blessing of getting my cellmate to stop cursing your name around me. I thank you for giving me the courage to ask him to stop. I am always seeing the wonders you are showing me. Father I am just an old sinner yet you have forgiven me and renewed my hope, I thank you humble for that Lord. I'll write soon.

G.
Matthew 14:38

March 9

Father,
Lord I am seeing so much anger in this place, the yelling and screaming that just seems to be endless. One of the inmates took advantage of a newbie, and this new inmate lost the payment for services that he tried to get, he came up empty and now there is a fight brewing. I would imagine that when they meet fists will fly. I'm thankful Lord that the cellmates that I've had I was able to get along with them. I know Father that you have your arms wrapped around me and that gives me great comfort. Praise you Father! My life was so messed up Lord and I didn't know how to get out of that sinful life. You took me, a wretch, a doubter and sinner and washed me clean in the blood of Jesus. Hallelujah! I know that my rewards will come when I come home to you and I don't deserve anything Lord. The one thing I want to do is sing praises to you. Lord you have given me the greatest gift I could ever want, forgiveness and eternity with you and for that I am truly blessed. I Love you Father.

G.
Isaiah 61:10

March 10

Father,
I know that you hold my tomorrow in your hands and I am not to know what will happen, I just have to trust your plan is the best for me. I know that if a had spent more time with you then away from you my life would have been different and I wouldn't be where I am now. I know Lord that you are putting me through the fire to melt the metal of my soul, to cast me and mold me. Thank you! Lord please take this unrefined metal and make it pure. Lord I still need to work on my opinion of black people. I did not have much contact with any black people on the outside, however here the population is about 75%. I know that we are all your children but it is hard especially when you see the actions of the black inmate in here. I have had 3 cellmates that were black and only one was I comfortable with, R.W. I could not relate to the other two because of their hate for white people, apparently the fault is ours for their imprisonment. Lord, give me the strength to judge all the people I meet on their heart and not their color. The sad part is that our society can't get past the color barrier. I pray for a renewal in my heart to accept everyone until proven different.

G.
Galatians 4:26-29

March 11

Father,
Lord as I write you today I was thinking how wonderful it will be when I can come to you in prayer with my thoughts without writing them down. I hope that one day I will be able to pray openly for people and with people, to be a prayer warrior for you. I know that day will come when I'm ready, until then I'll keep writing you if you don't mind. The health department has decided in their wisdom to start giving me medication for T.B., because I had a positive reaction back when I first arrived in the system 7 months ago. I tried to tell them that I had a reaction back when I was in grade school and was treated at that time, they wouldn't listen so I get to take pills for the next 6 months, Yuk! There are certain times when we are

treated like children and when we receive medication both the nurse and corrections officer stand and watch us take our medication, checking the inside of our mouth to make sure we took them. I thought I'd get a letter today, maybe tomorrow. Lord it's time to study.

G.
Psalm 6:7,8

March 12

Father,
My Lord, looking at the world today I feel that your return might be pretty soon. The world I live in Lord is falling away from you, it seems like you are an after-thought, that just not the case you are everything Lord. I hope and pray that this is not the case because there are a lot of souls to be won for you. I have had just a little touch of what hell must be like being here in this place and I know that hell will be worse, so please Lord not yet. I thank you for the mercy that you show all of us in the world today, it would be so easy for you to end it all right now. Father for all those people who don't know you Lord may they someday be brought in to your fold and for those on the fence let them hop off and come to you because Satan owns the fence. Father I thank you for the love you have for me and all those in your Kingdom. I know that when your wrath comes forth I do not want to feel all that pain.

G.
John 4:34

March 13

Father,
Lord I have sailed the world, have explored those things that are good and those things that are bad. I have seen poverty and hunger in this journey. There has been much happiness and sadness in my travels. I know Lord that you were always with me even when I was not with you. I was given many chances to come to you and turned away. In coming to you I have found all that I need or will need. The word need is different than want. I have had the wants and now want the one I truly need, Jesus! Father you are a great God, above all others. Praise you, Father! Hallelujah! Dear Lord my heart longs to be with you. You will be honored and praised above all others. Worthy is the lamb that was given for me. I get chills just thinking about you Lord. Let me continue to worship you all the days I have left on this earth. Amen!

G.
Proverbs 30:8

March 14

Father,
Lord I have come to you with surrender and given myself over to your will, so why do I still feel guilty when I know my sins have been forgiven? Lord I need to get over these feelings and feel the joy and happiness you want for me. Please help me Father, show me how to release these negative thoughts. Lord I give these thoughts to you, let me try to forget that which I have done. I know that there were many things that happened in my past and bringing them to you has been hard I was so ashamed. There are things that happened in my past that I will carry to the grave so I won't hurt people that I care about. I know that you are the only one that knows' what happened and I give that to you, let me not carry the guilt any longer, I pray for you comfort as I give this up to you. I will always love you, may the glory be yours forever and ever. Always your humble servant.

G.
Proverbs 29:8

March 15

Father,
It is amazing to me that in the 11 months I've been incarcerated I have aged about 10 years. My brown hair is gone, and now I have a lot of gray. My weight is substantially less from 220+ to around 180 and although I feel healthy I don't look that way. I can only see my reflection in the water in the toilet bowl, the mirror I have is so scratched up and I can't see much. I am only allowed to shave about once every 10 days when the corrections officer brings a disposable that I can take to the shower with me, when I am done I give the razor back. Great way to exist! I thought Viet Nam was rough but being there doesn't compare. I'm older and I feel it, I get tired faster and just have no energy. Lord I pray that you maintain my strength while I'm here in prison and keep me healthy, I know you will. Didn't get a letter today, maybe tomorrow, I pray Lord for a letter. I have a concern for my dad, concern for his health and age. I know that in the letters that I've gotten everyone says he's doing well I just pray they are telling me the truth. I have concern for my children and all they have gone through since I've been here, I ask you Lord to watch over them and protect them. I pray for the other members of my family, watch over them and keep them safe. I think they all know that I Love them. I know that you will take the lead and be there for all of them. I've rambled enough. Lord, I'll talk later.

G.
Psalm 119:133

March 16

Father,
Lord now is the time for baby-steps. I have very little in the way of personal belongings and no place to call home. Lord I ask that when I get out that you see clearly with the things I need to exist. My list is simple: Clothes to wear, a place to live, a job, a car for transportation, food to sustain me and most important, a good bible church to be fed with life giving water from you Lord. I know it's a lot to ask so I'm giving you plenty of time. Seriously I know that you will provide me with all that I need, thank you.

I pray Lord that you soften the hearts of those family, friends and people I hurt. I can understand the way that they might feel and know that I have to accept whatever the outcome is. Lord, please just work on their hearts, thank you. My resolution for today is to forget the hurts of the past and go on with the new, for I have been made new through you. I love you Lord Jesus.

G.
Psalm 119:153

March 17

Father,
I started thinking Lord about some of the things I want to do when I get out. The first thing that came to mind was to plant a garden. I have always loved flowers and I know a little about planting, so why not. I might even plant some veggies so I can offer them to my neighbors. I don't eat a lot of vegetables. I know that as I sow so shall I reap. I have the longing to fix foods that I like and try new recipes. I think that the one thing I'll fix first is spaghetti sauce, meatballs (Italian) and some garlic bread. I'm starting to get hungry, and oh yeah! I can't forget the fresh grated Parmesan cheese. I know Lord that my life hasn't ended and I will get a chance to rebuild that life thanks to you. I know when I get out that I need to take things slower in my life and spend more time enjoying this wonderful world that is around me. Lord most of my life was used up working, working, and working. I think because of my problem not being able to relate intimately with people I just kept busy. I think that's when my life spiraled out of control, and of course left you on the back burner. I know Lord that my life was nothing without you and I ask your forgiveness. I always say better late than never. I know that I need to use what you provide too make a better life for myself. I know that I will be fruitful and faithful in the walk that I will take with you by my side. I am just so lonely and I know that you bring me peace, thank you Lord. I'll write later, love you Lord,

G.
Psalm 131

March 18

Father,
I wrote down some more things that I want to do when I'm out. I need to spend more time with my kids and grandkids. I know that one of the things I did was to run away from the life I had and avoid all the garbage that came with the complaints I heard from those around me. I was incapable of solving their problems I had enough of my own. I know it was a shameful thing to do. I had an opportunity and I ran. I know now that I can't solve everyone's problems but I can at least offer an opinion and they can use it or not. I know that I can't be a judge and render a solution that is reserved for you Lord. I will try to use the wisdom that you give me to help my family after I've come to you in prayer. Lord you are so fantastic, and can solve any problem that is presented to you. Lord I know that I have to keep my life simple and continue to walk the path you want me to. Lord you gave me a brain and it's time I started to use that glob of mater under my skull. Lord as always, I love you,

G.
Psalm 146:8

March 19

Father,
I pray Lord that I always keep you in my heart. I pray Lord that I always listen to your advice. I pray Lord that I always come to you first before making decisions. I pray Lord that when I mess up and I'm sure I will that I remember that I can come to you and ask for forgiveness. I pray Lord for everyone that doesn't know you gets' that opportunity. I pray Lord that those of us who do know you and the love you have for us, can present that grace to others. I pray Lord that all the beauty you gave this world outshines the ugliness that is in the world today. I pray Lord for the pleasure of working for you in bringing the message of Jesus to as many people I can. I pray Lord that if it is your will, I can help those who have been in prison break the chains and in breaking those chains it will prevent them from any type of life that causes them to re-offend and end up back

in prison. I pray Lord thank you for your son Jesus who gave his lifeblood for all people, and that if they accept Jesus their eternal life is assured. I pray Lord that your glory shines forever in the hearts of all mankind.

G.
Galatians 3:26

March 20

Father,
I thank you Lord for showing me the things that give depth to my soul. I know that working in your word I am learning so much. I am learning about your grand design. You started out with a totally perfect world spoken into existence and then man was created and given free will. I sometimes think that if Adam & Eve didn't have free will things wouldn't be the way they are today, but then again they wouldn't have been human. I know that all Christians want an Eden to live in. It is sad that my (our) way of finding Eden isn't the right way. I know that I allow things that are and were unimportant to clutter my life, if only I could follow you as perfectly as your son Jesus. Lord to me the whole Bible is a revelation, most of all the word gives me (us) a perfect picture of who you are Lord, perfect; perfect in every way, thank you my perfect Lord. I guess being perfect allows you great latitude in deciding the fate of mankind. I know Lord that there have been countless times when you could have put an end to all the evil in this world and yet to bring as many people to your kingdom you let me (us) continue in making up my (our) own mind(s) up. I thank you for all the times you have forgiven me. I know that there is no other God given to men by which I (we) are saved. Lord I just feel like jumping for joy all the time, because you are all I think about 3 in 1. You are a perfect Father, a perfect Son, and a perfect Spirit. I find so much comfort in coming to you, even if is just rambling. I kind of wish you were and English teacher so I could express myself better, this is the best I can do.

G.
Colossians 2:10

March 21

Father,
I am learning Lord, how to be content with what I have and make the best of a less than perfect situation, way less. I also am learning Lord that you are in control of all there is or ever will be. Praise You Lord! I am learning Lord, that in every situation there is a right way, a wrong way and your way. I chose any way but yours and what I got was a small glimpse of what Hell might be, having done everything any other way but yours. Lord let me walk in your ways for all the time I have left on this earth, I know Lord that when I do all things are perfect. Lord! Spring has arrived and I love spring, everything is new and fresh, all the salt has been washed away and the flowers are starting to come to life. I think that my life is now a flower coming to life, I am new and refreshed. I am proud to say Lord that I will bloom in radiant colors for the rest of my life. Praise You my Lord! I only hope that all people take a look at their hearts and realize that their ache is not a heart attack but not having you Lord in their lives. I believe Father! I believe!

G.
Colossians 1:12-14

March 22

Father,
I went out to the exercise yard today to get some wonderful fresh air, was that a big mistake. I went out thinking that with the sun shining and the warmness I felt coming in the cell window, going to yard would be fun. The worse thing about going to yard is if you choose to go you have to spend 5 hours outside. I'm sad to say the warm air only lasted for about 30 minutes. The temperature dropped about 10 degrees. The wind picked up and my noses almost froze, I look like a red nose reindeer. I think the temperature was only 40 degrees when I came in from yard. This was the first time and it shall be my last. Lord I pray to you today to keep me healthy, no chills, and no cold. You know how difficult it is to get anyone to tend to our ills, don't get sick and chances are good you'll make it out

of here. I know that on the lower gallery one of the inmates got sick and it took over an hour before the corrections officer responded, D.O.A. of the guards. I know if I want to go to the health center I need to put in a request and wait for them to send a pass, trust me when I say it might be 2 or 3 days before you can go. The unit has an E.M.T. that comes around at some point during the day to give non-prescription medication for the minor aches and pains. If you're awake you might get some, if not well maybe the next day. To do time here really increases the chances of not making it out of here. I know Lord that I am under your watchful eye, so see to it that I remain healthy, thank you Lord. I love you,

G.
Isaiah 38:16

March 23

Father,
Lord I am learning how to pray more effectively. You know that I come to you all the time. Lord in Ephesians 1:16 that I should never stop praying, that I am to pray constantly. What does this mean Lord? Lord how can I pray constantly? I pray often Lord but I don't pray all the time, so I'm asking how. I know Lord that I don't need to make my prayers long when I come to you I just can't see how to pray constantly. Lord, teach me to pray the way you want me too. I am learning all the time, fill me with you knowledge. I have a lot of time to learn, I'm not going anywhere. I will be out in 17 mos. I'm looking forward to that day. Here we go again the inmates are slamming the chuckhole cover. I think there is disappointment with the meal we just ate. The menu today was some type of lunch meat, some type of potato salad and an apple. I wonder how much planning goes into these meals. I guess just enough to sustain life. I think it's time to get back to my studies Lord, I will talk later.

G.
Ephesians 1:16

March 24

Lord I pray that when I come to you it will be with a clean heart, a heart that is bursting with joy and love, knowing that your son Jesus paid the price so that I might live and be with you in the Kingdom. Praise you! Lord! I am nothing without you. Lord without you I am like a speck of sand ebbing and flowing on the shore of some great ocean. I know Lord that I would not exist without you. Lord you have given me chance after chance to come back to you. I came back on bended knees and felt you Holy presents', as the stars were bursting be for my eyes I knew that you were there, and would be with me forever. Lord never could I have imagined you would show yourself to me. Lord you rescued me from the pitfall of Hell and showed me your' Kingdom. Hallelujah! Glory and Honor to your Holy Name! Lord you are my King forever and ever. I love you.

G.
Ephesians 2:13

March 25

Father,
Lord as I sit here writing to you I am thinking of the sadness my cellmate carries. D. was telling me about how he was robbing a building going in through the roof skylight, that all went well until he tried to get away. He says that there was a cop that had rolled up behind and when the cop got out of the squad he shot the cop without any thought of the consequences. To make a long story short D. got caught and was convicted and sentenced to 60 yrs. D. will get out in 2017. I don't know Lord whether D. ever knew you Lord, but he sure curses you now. I pray Father for D. and all the inmates, that they find their way back to you. I presented you to him, and the decision is his to make. I pray he makes the right one.

G.
Ephesians 2:2

March 26

Father,
Lord I come to you today with a question or two. I was at a "Billy Graham Crusade" back in 1959 at Wheaton College. I was sitting in the bleachers at their football field listening to the Rev. Graham preached on forgiveness, and at the end of the evening anyone who wanted to commit their life to Christ was asked to come down. I was so emotional and in tears I went down and there accepted Christ. My question Lord is what happened after I accepted Christ? I had just turned 12 the month before and this was a powerful awakening, but I had no one to turn too. I think Lord that at 12 yrs. old I could have used just a little help. I remember that the aides told me to talk to my pastor, or a mentor to help me along the way. Lord have you ever talked to a pastor of one of the major denominations? The one thing I know is that their teaching is not the way the Rev. Graham taught. I know that my parents would have been upset that I was looking at a different view of religious teaching. Lord where was the help? I know now 45 yrs. Later how to find the mentoring I need but not back when I was 12. Lord what step did I miss that lead me down the wrong path? Lord I love you with all my heart and I know the answers now I just can't understand where I failed. I love you Lord and we'll talk tomorrow.

G.
Acts 20:28-30

March 27

Father,
I come to you today to ask that you bless my daughter H, today is her birthday and do to circumstances beyond my control I won't be able to be there to help her celebrity. I look at her life and see all the problems she had in the past and yet she is a survivor. H has always done things her way Lord and always lands on her feet. H has managed to have two children at an early age, and still managed to get her H.S. Diploma. I am so proud of her, she could have given up and made other choices, less desirable, she didn't. I thank you Lord for touching her heart and the decision she

made. H has the stick to it attitude. The one think that's hard to get across to her is that you are there for her all the time and will never desert her. I know she love you Lord, she just gets wrapped up in her life and then she forgets about the wonderful blessings that you gave her. Lord please keep a watchful eye over her and keep her in your arms, I know you will. I know that on days like today I get a little teary eyed knowing that I can't wish her a Happy Birthday. Lord put in her heart the love I have for her even though I can't be there. Love you Father.

G.
Mark 10:14-16

March 28

Father,
Lord I come to you today to say thank you for my daughter K. Today is her birthday. I know two birthdays in two days, that's just the way it goes. I miss them both so much. K. came before H. and two years earlier. I tried to make sure that the both had a great Birthday. K. is a little different than her sister. K is a planner and go getter. K. has goals in place and will be able to attain all those goals. Lord give her the wisdom to make right decisions, listen to what you tell and re-enforce the confidence she has. K. has two wonderful girls and she seems very happy in her life. I know Father that she is close to you and loves you with all her heart. I am blessed to have her and her sister to call yours and mine. Lord thank you for these two wonderful gifts. I love you Lord.

G.
1 Timothy 3:4

March 29

Father,

In the fall the wind starts to blow,
The sun starts to go low,
The leaves will fall to ground,
The colors will abound.
In the fall the dew will come,
The signs of winter to come,
The birds fly south with a soar,
The squirrels search for store.
In the fall people get ready,
The thought of winter sure and steady,
The fresh pile the wood will be stacked,
The lighter clothes hung on the rack.
In the fall the signs come with cold,
The same old story of old,
The winterizing has begun,
The deer will start to run.
In the fall the wind steady blows,
The sun starts to go low, the time to hope
The winters not rough,
The new will come soon enough.

Lord this is a poem I tried to write to see if I had any talent. I have never given any thought to writing a poem but these words were in my head and I thought you would like to hear them, I hope you like them Lord.

G.
Psalm 50:2

March 30

Father,
I thought that I would lighten my mood up last night by writing a poem to you. I didn't really read the poem until today. I think it's pretty good, I hope I'm not being prideful, I know that I liked it and Lord I hope you do too. Lord I am finding out that you are a wonderful God. You are above all that exists, the creator of the universe and this earth I am on. There is nothing that can compare to your love and I can only hope to give you all I have, to follow you, and do your work. There will be people who will ask me why am I so peaceful and content? I shall answer that I'm on a journey walking down a path of forgiveness and redemption. Lord my heart cries with happiness that I have never experienced before. You are the one I long to worship and adore. Let me walk with pride and gladness down that path. Lord when I reach the end of my journey I pray I hear: Well done, come on in, my faithful servant. Lord I have enjoyed the time I've had on this earth, but not as much as the time I will spend going forward with you. I love you Father,

G.
Genesis 1:31

March 31

Father,
Lord another month has drawn to a close and I have less than three months left, I'm on the downhill slope. I am just hoping and praying that the two and a half months I have left will be quiet and uneventful. Lord I would like to tell you I'm doing well but I'm feeling down today. Lord I have no reason to be down everything is OK here right now, except the food, the lack of movement and not being able to do much of anything, come to think of it, I guess that would get anyone down, so maybe I'm OK Thank you Lord Jesus for the blood you gave to me from the cross. I cry every time I see a movie where it shows you being out to death. I would like to think that I would be the bearer of your cross to ease your pain. Lord I thank you and adore you, as always

G.
Luke 23:46

April 1

Lord,

I come to you in prayer to ask if you could keep a hedge around L.J. He was acting up tonight in his cell and started his mattress on fire. There wasn't anything done for about 20 min. I know that all this acting up has filled the gallery with a lot of smoke. There is a foggy haze throughout the gallery. The Orange Crush unit has arrived and they are going into L.J.'s cell to extract him. Father I have seen what Orange Crush does and it's not very pretty. The sad part is that there are 20 members here all wanting to get in on the action. There are 6 members entering L.J.'s cell with batons, full body shields, and a video camera. L.J. is putting up a fight, one he won't win. L.J. has finally been subdued and he is being dragged out in hand cuffs and shackles around his ankles. I can see the agony on his face, and the tears from the mace that Orange Crush used. L.J. is being led down to the enclosed cell on the first floor. I know that Satan has a hold on L.J. and not only is he chained for real, he is chained to Satan. I tried Father when we were cellmates to get him to see Jesus and the saving grace he offers. I guess I didn't get through. I pray again that L.J. seeks you and finds out what a wonderful God you are. I will write soon I need time to think about what just happened. Love you Lord.

G.

Proverbs 3:11

April 2

Father,
I want to welcome you back to the lunatic asylum. Lord yesterday was very rough for me seeing L.J. be taken down and put in the maximum security cell on the main deck. I know Lord that L.J. is going to go nuts down there. I heard from the grapevine that he threw urine on the O.C. unit when they came into his cell last night. That will cost him 5 more years if charged and convicted. Lord I still haven't heard about the charges pending against L.J. and myself. Lord L.J. has so much pain. Help him Father! L.J. told me once that he spent a lot of time in church playing the drums and enjoyed that a lot, but then he got involved in selling drugs. L.J. told me that he made a lot of money and had everything that he ever wanted. He told me that he couldn't stand his home life and that he has a father who is a minister and a step mom, and he was clashing with them over their lifestyle and his. L.J. has this great concept—get all that you can and as much as you can. L.J. doesn't care who gets hurt at all as long as he gets his. Lord I'm not saying that anyone is better, just that he is suffering badly. I pray Lord he is steered in the right direction. Carry him Lord! Put people in his way to help him, I pray this in the name of Jesus. Amen.

G.
Isaiah 48:10

April 3

Father,
Lord I come again with a request, ease my burdens about L.J. L.J. has been on my mind so much I can't focus on much else. I feel so, helpless. The only thing I can do Lord is come to you. Lord the human side of me wants to hate him, to be angry at what he did in our cell awhile back, but looking back on the stuff that happened in the last couple of day I feel so sad for him. Lord I know L.J. has a really good heart, and all he has to do is use it. Lord I give my suffering over this to you, I will always care for L.J. and know that he is in the hands of the one he wants whomever he chooses. I hope you are that choice. Father, am I wrong to feel this way?

Am I deserting L.J. because I can't handle this situation? Lord, give me the answer I seek. Lord let me be a better Christian today than yesterday fill me with the Holy Spirit so I have the answers to these questions I asked. You're my God forever.

G.
2 Corinthians 11:28,29

April 4

Father,
Lord L.J. is on my mind, not for the crazy things he is still doing, but about a night when he was talking about the bust that brought him here. L.J. was saying that he was walking along the street in Chicago and was carrying a Mac 10 when a off duty policeman came by. L.J. states that the officer must have seen the weapon he was carrying. L.J. saw the officer get out of the car with his gun drawn. L.J. says that at that point he through the weapon away, and that he was unarmed. The officer then fired at him and put 6 rounds into L.J. body. L.J. says that was the last thing that he remembered until he woke up in the hospital chain to the bed. I would have dismissed his story as want-a-be fiction except he showed me where he was shot. He said that there still were pieces of the bullets still in his body. Lord I was overwhelmed, I had never meet someone who had been shot. Looking at where the bullets entered his body, he is lucky to be alive. I don't think he understands that if he didn't have his weapon in all likelihood he never would have been shot. Lord he has such a hate, take that hate away. I pray again that he may come to you for comfort and inner peace. Lord we all have choices and the choices we make decides what will happen, we all suffer from the consequences. Lord you say that no sis is greater than any other, if you can forgive so can I.

G.
Revelation 16:9

April 5

Father,
Lord in all my life I have never seen anything like I am observing at this moment. L.J. has been carrying on for about an hour, and here comes Orange Crush again. I don't know what they are going to do this time. Watching the effectiveness of O.C., it shouldn't take long for them to subdue L.J. Lord watching what is going on gives me pause to think. Why would anyone want to subject themselves to what will happen? Lord I pray again for L.J., please don't let him get hurt. The situation is under control. L.J. has been chained to the sleeping rack after being stripped. He now is stark naked and can't move any more than 4 ft. I do not understand why these men rebel so much when they know they won't win. Lord I pray for the men here in cellblock F. I've got a calendar started and I'm counting down the days until I get out—71 days left. I am sure glad I can come to you Lord I just need to vent. Coming to you gives me comfort and someone to talk too. Love you Lord.

G.
Isaiah 53:2

April 6

Father,
I promise tonight will be a less stressful gab session. I'm feeling pretty good I had a quiet day no acting out by the inmates. Lord I have called upon you for deliverance, guidance and wisdom, and you have done all three. Lord you have delivered me from those who would try to hurt me, you have guided my steps as I walk down your path, and you have given me the wisdom to view and sort out those things that I need to do towards advancing your kingdom. The one thing that I can do right now in my present condition is to pray. I know Lord that I can pray about all sorts of things when I come to you with pen. I know that someday I'll be able to pray openly without the aid of a pen. What is that which people say; a person needs to get out of one's comfort zone only then will one be able to move forward. I know Lord that I am not quite there yet however I'm

working on this with all my heart. I know that someday I will speak to you without having to write my thoughts down and that will be a wonderful experience. I am just so giddy to have you in my life. I love you Father! God!

G.
Psalm 5:7,8

April 7

Father,
Lord you are the Holy of Holies, the Almighty King, the giver of life, and the one who's sacrifice of death on the cross gave me life. Lord you are the beginning and the end. Lord I pray that your glory and splendor shine in my heart forever. I know Lord Jesus that you suffered and died so that I may have eternal life. You returned to life and paid the price for me. Lord there are times when I lay in my cot at night and weep about all those things in my past life and just praise you for the forgiveness that you've shown me and I thank you for that blessing. I know Lord that I was not worthy and yet you are and were there for me always. I ask that you protect me Lord from all the evil around me and cast down Satan, bind and chain him, please keep him away from me. I need you so much Lord, to be ever in my life. I ask this all in your name Jesus. May I ever praise you Lord.

G.
Psalm 71:19

April 8

Father,
Lord I know that I've been broken of the stubbornness I've had for so long. Lord I was unwilling to change my ways and was lost when I got off the path you had for me. I know Lord that I'm prideful like the drivers who refuses to ask for help in getting the right directions when they are lost. I know Father that being wrapped up in this world has been the biggest problem and I was always letting other things get in the way of a relationship with you. I never thought in a Christ like manner. I never read your word or gave your word much thought until now I'm in your word daily and able to come and call upon you in my times of need. Lord you are my comfort and my passion, you are everything I need. I know Lord that there are good times to come for me, and I know that I will be tempted to forget you in those good times. Lord let me never ever forget to put you first in all that I do. Lord may I ever shout your name as I look to the heavens. I am a sinner saved by your grace and I thank you for your tender mercies. The comfort you show me gives me the peace I need to carry on Lord. I am so blessed and I love you so much. Thank you for keeping me from the pitfalls of Hell, in Jesus' name, Amen.

G.
Psalm 101:2

April 9

Father,
Lord I know that your word says that I will be given no more than I can handle. I know that with all the evil in this place I'm in that it has been a challenge for me. I know that there are times I cry and yet in that moment I know that I can come to you and lay those burdens down before you and you comfort me, thank you Lord. I ask Lord that the guards see your light shining in me and be less harsh then they are. I ask Lord that my cellmate comes to understand that he has his way and I have mine. I pray that Satan's hold on him is broken and that even the many years he's been in prison be put behind him and he is able to start a new life with you. Lord

you have to be the one to change his heart. D. has this book on chess Lord and it's over 1000 pages long, I didn't know there was that much to know about chess. I played him once and was checkmated in 8 moves it wasn't fair, so no more chess. D. keeps to himself most of the time and the time he does talk is spent in trying to figure out where he is going to after his 6 months is done in here. The nice thing about him is he knows all the ins and outs of prison life. D has told me stories of what life was like before the state took back control of the prisons. Lord I'll write later Love you.

G.
Psalm 116:1,2

April 10

Father,
I'm sorry I didn't get back to you last night but D. got to telling me more stories of the things that went on in prison before the state implemented their new system. D. was telling me about the changes that took place in the mid-90. D. said that back then there was a lot of freedom to move around. The inmates had open cells, and the ability to move from one area of the prison to another with little supervision. The inmates were not required to wear any type of uniform and most inmates had regular clothes sent in, the prisoners had control. D said that all change after Bill Curtis exposed prison life with a program he did on T.V. about Richard Speck, during this time two correctional officers were murdered at Stateville. D. said after those incidents changes started to happen. D. said that all the prisons were placed on lockdown so that procedures could be changed. D. said it was a complete overhaul razor wire was placed at the top of the 10' fencing around the prisons, an inside fence was built and placed in front of the outside fence. Razor wire and sensors were placed between the fences. All of the inmates were given the same type of uniforms, blue denim shirts and dark blue stretch pants. The inmates could no longer where street clothes. There where movement times established so no one move unless authorized. Chow was held at specific times and all the inmates were moved in pairs and units at the same time. Prison was no longer a game for the inmates. D said it took away the freedom that the inmates

had in the prison. I know that these are the same procedures that are in place today 10 yrs. later. I know Lord that this is stuff you already knew but it will help me remember how these changes came about. Thanks for listening Lord, as always.

G.
2 Peter 2:19

April 11

Father,
Lord the interesting part of my journey here in prison is the new learning skill. There is a different set of rule if a person wants to get along. There is a different language spoken, like tweeker, that's a rolled cigarette that is very slim with little tobacco in it, a short is halve of a rolled cigarette, a cart is a greeting size card with a line attached to it, it is used for sending and receiving stuff from other cells, the cart is thrown along the floor outside the cell so the guards in the tower can't see. There are just so many interesting expressions, and I might be able to teach them all before I get out. There is a code a person needs to learn and it begins by ignoring things that happen around you, too never see anything, if you don't see anything you don't know anything and you are a lot safer if you remember the code. I know Lord that there is danger even in my cell, there is no way I can predict what my cellmate might do even if he's a nice guy. I know more importantly that you will do what you want and I need to accept your will. I do pray however that you will be watching over me and protecting me. Lord I love you more than any other and you know my life is yours for the rest of my days.

G.
Philippians 4:11

April 12

Father,
Lord I want to thank you for my brother, today is his birthday, Happy Birthday G.! There are some things that I forget in the life on the outside and that is usually every ones birthday. I have always been lax in remembering. I know that I will always try to remember and acknowledge the birth of my friend and family. I am so blessed to have a brother like G. My brother and I have grown closer over the year mostly because of events that happened that were minor problems or full blown disasters, and we supported and helped each other get thru these tough times. When I look back I have to forgive him for getting my 63 Chevy Impala destroyed because someone wanted to get back at him for something he had done, so I forgive him. My brother has been there during all my divorces, and I was there for the birth of my niece after the doctors told him the chances of having a child was very slim, I know Lord that you blessed them and for that I thank you. Praise You Father! I know Lord that for all the arguing my brother and I did we have become close friends as well as brothers. I think that after both of us had come back safely from Viet Nam we shared a new outlook on life. I know that we both knew the frailties of life. I know you protected us Father and again I say thank you. Praise to your name.

G.
Proverbs 18:24

April 13

Father,
Lord my road through the prison system has been well traveled and I know that this is no accident. I know that you are giving me a more complete look at what prison life is really like. I have gained more empathy for the inmates and their plight here in prison. I know Lord that whatever you have for me to do when I get out has to involve the prisoners. Lord you are overloading me with feelings for men I would have ignored prior to coming to prison. I love feasting on the knowledge you are presenting to

me, thank you Father. Lord I pray that for all the knowledge you are giving me that I listen, learn and apply that knowledge. You know all about me and you know where I'm going. Lord may I always work for the Kingdom, some way, somehow. I accept your word and will do what you want, love you Father,

G.
Colossians 1:9-14

April 14

Father,
Lord I was thinking about being a prisoner and the feelings I get are of sadness. A prisoner although a man is not treated like a man in fact he is treated like a child. The prisoner does not have to think all he needs to do is do exactly what he is told, if a prisoner is disobedient the punishment is not pleasant. When men are treated like children they act like them, they cry and whine, and take no responsibility for their action when I see these things happen it makes me angry and sad. My question to you Lord, is how can so many men be repeat offenders with these intolerable conditions they (we) are subjected too? I see that when men are treated like children they (we) act like them, for example if a prisoner needs a guard he has to scream and shout or beat on the door to try getting a response. When the guard arrives 10-15 min. later the inmate is given a lecture on destroying state property. If you need certain items such as soap and toilet paper an inmate better request them a couple of days before they need them. Lord you said that we need not worry about our needs as you provide for the creatures on this earth including us but its' awful rough in here. I'm sorry Lord I know that you provide, the subject just makes me angry. Men are big babies in prison that is true because if these men acted like this on the outside people would walk all over them. I think the age level drops around to that of a teenager; this is my observance of prisoners here. I know that only a select group of people get to see how the prisoners act and people on the outside are unaware of their conditions but that's to be expected because as long as they are locked away it's not their problem anymore, I know that something needs to be done but what? I have learned a lot in

the past 11 mos. Since I first got into the system and I will survive and get by because you are here with me, thank you Father. I know that I will take with me another life experience. I pray Lord that I never forget how things are here in prison and try my best to let people know what it is like to be in chains. Love you Lord.

G.
Psalm 107:10-16

April. 15

Father,
I know you have existed forever and I wouldn't be here if you hadn't given me life. I know that you knew me before I was born and you know my next step. I don't know why I am here but I know that you will give me the answer; my existence cannot be an accident. Lord thru accepting Jesus as my Lord and Savior I know that I have eternal life and I thank you. Lord be gracious and show me my destiny, let me listen to you. I want everything I do to be for your glory and benefit. Lord I know that you will only give me that, which I can handle please pile it on me. I wish to please you Father I want to make you smile. When I am called home I want to see you radiant face, and walk thru the gates with my head held high. I need to remember to follow you commands and let you work in me, this I will do. Jesus you died for me and gave me everything you had, I will try to remain faithful to your sacrifice. Lord I thank you for being the light in my darkness.

G.
John 1:4,5

April 16

Father,
I come to you today with poems written by my daughter along with a letter letting me know how much she loved me. The poems brought joy, gladness and internal weeping. I would like to read you one that really touched my heart.

The poem is entitled "Childhood Years."

> I used to know a man that would sing me to sleep,
> How I miss that when I lie awake that memory to keep.
> I used to know a man that would make time for me,
> Now the time I have far too often unseen.
> I used to know a man that would play ball with me,
> Yes I remember what it was like to be wild and free.
> I used to know a man that would hold me when I was hurt,
> It's been so long since I fell flat in the dirt.
> I used to know a man that encouraged me to follow my dreams,
> And I just kept walking the many balance beams.
> I uses to know my dad so well and I grew up and moved away,
> Yet I will always cherish the good old days.

This poem means so much especially in here. The poem shows how much she really loves me, thank you for giving her too me. I love you Lord.

G.
Psalm 4:7

April 17

Father,
I am in a better mood today and that came about with the arrival of mail. One letter, written by a daughter to her father means more than anything here on this earth. Lord you know I am always praying for letters, and I thank you for placing me in the minds of my family and friends so they will write. K.'s letters give me hope and reinforce your love for me Father. The letters come just at the right time. K. sent me a bunch of books to read about, 16 or so and that will keep me occupied for awhile. I want you to know that you are first though. I sometimes feel guilt when I do something else besides study your words then I remember that you are always with me. I now awake a lot more refreshed ready to start the day. Father forgive me for being a lazy person, in the past when it came to studying your word I was absent without leave. I paid attention to those things that I felt were more important and left you out in all that I did. I am so sorry for without you Lord I am nothing, just a little speck of dust to be swept away during a house cleaning. I just thought about my former boss and his wife and wondered how they are. R. and C. are a very blessed husband and wife, and they complement each other very well. R. is a man who has a heart for the Lord and love for his fellow man. C. is a prayer warrior and singer, Lord I know you enjoy her singing and praising of your Holy name, you gave her an angel's voice, thank you Father. Lord I pray that you continue to watch over them and give them the blessings they so richly deserve. Love you Lord will write later its food time.

G.
John 15:12

April 18

Father,
I am sorry for leaving last night had to eat, what I had wasn't great but I'm alive. I was talking yesterday about R. and C. R. is one of the greatest men I have ever met, we all have heroes and R. is one of mine. R. is focused on the Kingdom and you are first in his life. I know that there were hard times for him with the business he owns and yet he was and I think still keeping lots of people employed and not out on the streets. I started to work for him in 1999 and worked with him until 2003. We parted as friends and Christian brothers, I was sorry to go but the change was necessary. R. needed to get some extra capitol and needed to sell one part of the business, the part I was involved in. I know that it was tough to get rid of this part of the business however business is business. I know that when he sold this part of the business he had one condition that they needed to hire me. Wow! What a blessing. I thank you R. Lord if it be your will let us meet again as friends and Christian brothers. I know that when I was about to be arrested he was there when others deserted me. R. didn't judge just listened, prayed and bought me breakfast. R. went with me when I turn myself in to the Sheriffs Dept. Lord with his comfort and love I got through. Lord as R. serves you let me do the same with all the love that R. has given to you. Father, keep him and his family safe, may we meet again. I love you Father.

G.
1 Corinthians 1:10

April 19

Father,
I have another poem that my daughter sent to me, thought you'd like to hear it.

The poem is "Walk On."

> We walked through the bad, but always got through to the good.
> We walked through our moods and got through those too.
> We go thru life just passing it away,
> Always walking, walking every day.
> Always sharing your life with someone young,
> So they'll be walking on when our walking is over and done.
> We've walked a long way you and I,
> We walked and walked always we reached for the sky.
> We walked through it all hand and hand,
> We walked on enjoying the land.
> We walked and talked from dusk until dawn,
> We walked and walked and kept going on.

Lord I thank you for my poet daughter, she has a great incite and can tear at your heart with such beautiful and truthful words. Lord, give her your blessing as she continues to glorify you in poems. Praise you Lord as always,

G.
Psalm 18:32

April 20

Father,
I got a letter from my brother and he says that my wife A. would not contest a divorce. I guess the honeymoon is over. I know I shouldn't be upset Lord this is just being human. I need to understand that not everybody will stand by me, it just hurts. I know Lord that there is no place in her heart for me, in fact she told my brother that if I'd die today she would spit on my grave. Lord I pray that you take away the hurt and pain that she has over my stupid mistake. Lord let her find a new life, a happier life without me in the picture. I think she will have to wait for awhile on getting a divorce, it's a little difficult to do while I'm behind these prison bars. Lord, protect and watch over A. My brother said he went to pick up my personal items at A's and that she had 6 huge garbage bags waiting outside the house, cold just cold. I'm just sorry that she couldn't understand about why I did what I did. Lord only you know our path, and A and I are traveling on different ones. Lord bless and keep her in your arms, I love you Lord.

G.
Philippians 4:6

April 21

Father,
I learned over the years that there are very few people who remain steadfast and true friends. Lord I have a friend who is just that way, steadfast and true. D and I have been friends for over 50 years. I know that if I need anything, he will be there if it's within his power. We have always been there for each other through thick and thin. I know that when I went to prison he was at a loss, and he still remained a friend. D. and I have always supported and respected each others' quirks. I just wished that I had come back to you earlier than I did. I wouldn't have hurt so many of my friends and family. I realize now that I won't have to walk alone anymore. I thank you Lord for walking my path with me. Lord look after D while I'm away and work on his heart, let him come to you again. I know Lord that he's

been away from you since he was a child and I hope that my stupidity helps him come to realize that you are what he needs. I want to be together with him in your Kingdom. I love you Lord. I know that you have the power.

G.
Colossians 1:19,20

April 22

Father,
What is real love? Real love is a man who would give up his life so that I may live. Jesus I thank you for your sacrifice and giving me a chance at eternity with you in heaven. What is truth Lord? Truth is staying in the Word and accepting the words that the Lord passed down to his people. Blessed be the words from your mouth that you pass on to me. Why am I put thru the fire? I am put thru the fire to find my way back to you or reject you. You have given me free will to chose. I chose you Father. How do I succeed in your ways? I succeed by letting you mold me into the person you want me to be. I know you have a path for me to travel. Lord may I ever walk on your path. How do I resist temptation? I resist by staying the course and call on you when I'm being tested by Satan. Jesus resisted and so should I. Lord when I'm tempted you show me the way to avoid that temptation. How do I know what my mission is? I need to pray for your guidance and to listen to the feeling of my heart. I need to just open my mind and wait with patients. Moses waited for years before he was shown the way. How do I stop feeling guilty when I've done something wrong? I must present myself before you Father and claim the blood of Jesus and ask for forgiveness. I know through all my mistakes you will forgive me. I must lay my burdens at your altar. Lord I don't know if I right in my conclusions but I tried. I know that all these answers will be given to me in your time and while I am working to further your Kingdom. The greatest answer is Love, Love, and more Love,

G.
John 14:15

April 23

Father, Lord when I get the chance to tell others about you, I will tell them that they do not have to suffer like I did. I need to let them know that wasting their time on things that they cannot change will start to free them from bondage. I know Lord that you want the best for us and that you love us dearly. I know they need to believe that you want what's best for us and that your love is there for us to grab on to, that the door is always open. I'll tell them that they need to seek God and you'll find him, knock and he will answer the door, and ask and you will be answered. I will tell others that your son Jesus paid the price by his death on the cross so that we can live eternally with you. Lord I will tell them that I sinned, that I broke your laws, that I was unclean and was not worthy of your love, but through Jesus I now may come to you at anytime and ask for your blessing. Thank you Jesus! Thank you, always with love.

G.
Romans 1:16

April 24

Father,
Lord as I write you today I find it hard to put into words what you mean to me in my daily life. I know Lord that I am nothing without you. I know that you accept me even with all my faults even when I can't see them. I know Lord that without you in my life things seem to go wrong and with you the wrong is gone. Lord when I'm without you my heart aches. Lord how great you are to always be available to talk too. I know that eternity waits and I'll see Jesus at the gate. Thank you for all you gave in doing so I must try to behave. Lord as I run my race towards the finish line I know you'll meet me just in time. I want all those who know and observe me know that I serve thee. With my whole heart I love you.

G.
Philippians 1:6

April 25

Father,
Lord I sit here tonight thinking about X. X is around 45 he has been in and out of prison all of his adult life. X became addicted to crack cocaine in his 20's, and went downhill from there. X has the mind of a child right now, years of constant abuse. We have opportunities to trade merchandise that we have for contraband cigarettes'; this is a way we can get relief for the daily stress. X has no money on the books, so he has nothing to barter with except his food. X has negotiated with the guys in the cell next to me to have his dinners for the next three days given to them in exchange for five cigarettes. He has done this same deal with them on and off for over a month. I can understand exchanging goods for services and smokes I'm not sure. X is just as addicted to smokes as he is to cocaine, anyway Lord I've tried to help feed his habit with extra smokes that I obtained by bartering even though I know that this is wrong. I just can't see him suffering, I can't stand the whining. So who has the greater sin, X for having the addiction or I who feeds his addiction? Lord, forgive me for being an enabler. X has a big problem and I'm just feeding that addiction I'm sorry Lord. Lord I pray for an awakening in X that he come to you for relief, he knows you Lord, but he is not ready to give this addiction to you. I love you Father I will talk later.

G.
Romans 8:28

April 26

Father,
What is the road to salvation? It is a road that takes me to the cross all the time. I must always remember Lord that you paid the price for me, thank you Jesus. I know that if you hadn't paid the price I would be separated from our Father. Lord I know that when I present my sins to you I'm forgiven. I know Father that you erase them and forget them and I thank you. I know it's working Lord because my heart says I can't be forgiven and yet you do forgive. What a great and merciful God you are. I knew

you Lord I just never really came to you to ask for that forgiveness. There is an old saying that confession is good for the soul, thank you Lord, thank you. I hope and pray Lord that I don't forget you once I get out of prison. Lord let me come to you daily and let me stay on the right path. There is one thing I know for sure without you I am nothing, with you I am forever. I like being a new person and the joy I have is the greatest high a man can have. Let me praise and worship you Father that's all I ask. I will talk later.

G.
Romans 10:8-10

April 27

Father,
Lord each of us is a seed that you planted. I need to grow and learn as many things as I can to do your will. Lord, give me the ability to freely use each day to learn more about who I am and what I was created for. I swear from my heart that I want to grow and be as big as an oak tree. I want to be able to grow acorns and set them to seed so they can grow to seed others. I want my journey in this world to forever make a difference in the lives of people. I want to help find the lost and give them a stable footing on slippery ground. I know that the price of a tool has nothing to do with that tools value it's only as valuable as the person using it. Lord, give me the right tools for the job I have ahead of me. Lord let me be a vessel that rescues people from drowning. Lord let me bring them to steady ground. Let me help people find purpose in their life, let me bring them home to you. Lord let people see my heart and see you in me. I know that I didn't deserve your mercy and yet you gave it anyway. I sing praises to your glory. Lord you know my heart. I'll talk later.

G.
1 Peter 1:14-16

April 28

Father,
I praise your name today for all the knowledge that you are feeding me. I am so hungry for your word I can't get enough. Lord I'm having a problem though I can't memorize your verses. I know what they say I just can't quote them. Lord if it be your will help me in this matter. Lord thank you for opening a direct line to you, I just love being able to talk with you like I am. The mind is a wonderful thing and using it to talk to you is great. I know Lord that one of my short comings is racing. I race to get things done all the time. My mind races so fast that I have been known to put my foot in it. Lord give me the patience and help me slow down a bit so I can savor the food I'm being fed. Lord as I read your word over again I pick up more incite and greater understanding, let me continue to feed. I ask the Holy Spirit to keep up as I run this marathon. Lord may I be able to see the good in people and not worry about the bad. Lord your love for me will keep me strong and help me to grow. I'll write tomorrow, we'll talk about my arrest. I love you Lord.

G.
Philippians 2:13

April 29

Father,
Today is somewhat of a milestone and not a good one to remember however I will never forget it. Lord one year ago today I arrived at my house to find several cars parked out front. I noticed that they were from the Sheriff's Department and were in plain clothes. I saw them carrying all my computers out of the house. I knew why they were there and was glad that my suffering was finally over. I walked up to one of the detectives and started to talk to him. He was kind and told me that I didn't have to talk to him if I didn't want to. I needed to talk and get rid of the pain I'd been suffering. After we had finished I felt the whole world lifted off my shoulders, I felt freer then I'd been in a long time. The hard part of this day was losing my wife, my friends and knowing that I would soon be

arrested. Lord I had prayed to you for help and you gave it. I must say though that this was not the help I'd been thinking of; this was going to be a big timeout. The rest of the day and night were kind of a blur. I was very numb and very scarred, I wasn't sure what to do. I contacted the one person that I knew would help me, that was R. We met at a restaurant and talked for a couple of hours. He gave me a place to stay for the night and brought me some toiletries. I laid down and cried myself to sleep, this day opened my eyes for the first time, the anticipation of what was to come beat me down. I will talk tomorrow about my arrest. Lord thank you for being with me during all those rough times.

G.
1 John 1:9

April 30

Father,
Lord it was one year ago today that I embarked on a new journey, a journey that would break me down, strip all the worldly thing I had gained and gave me a new life, a life in this world but not of it. Lord I thank you for that. I know that I needed to go on this path, my life having spiraled out of control. When I prayed to you for help I never expected this type of time out, nevertheless you chose this path for me. I could have hated this path and rebelled, I chose to embrace it and change. I was at my work place when I got a call from my wife telling me that I need to go down to the Sheriff's office and sign some papers. I thought for a moment and couldn't think of what papers they could possible want me to sign. I assumed that they wanted me so they could arrest me for the crime I committed, it turned out that I was right. I told my boss that I had to leave and said I doubted if I would be back, I left and headed to my old bosses place. I met with R. and told him my fear and asked if he would come with me he agreed and headed to the Sheriff's Office. When I arrived I informed them that I was here to sign some papers. One of the detectives who had been at my house came out, he proceeded to inform me that I was under arrest and then he read me my rights, I told him I understood and was asked to turn over all the things I had on me. When he had all

my possessions I was handcuffed and led away to a holding cell. I know that it was at that point my nerves were shattered and I started to shake. This was reality not a television show this was for real. I would now be the property of the State of Illinois. I prayed for your help Lord and you gave me calmness in my soul. Thank you Lord, thank you. The journey I'm on is still ongoing and I know that you are taken every step with me. I know that when I am weak you will carry me forward on my path. Lord thanks again for your Love.

G.
Romans 6:23

May 1

Father,

Good morning Lord, well it's the first day of a new month and the weather should start getting better. I know that with the warmer weather the dampness in my cell will dissipate. I only have a month and a half to go before I get out of this hellhole and go to a new joint, and I am ready. Lord I want to thank you for opening a path for me to become the man that you want me to be. I will listen closely and heed your words. Lord I came before you as a small seed and need to be watered and fertilized to grow. Lord, help me grow strait and tall and be all that I can for you and the Kingdom. I know I'm weak but you are strong, you have what I need to grow. Lord let the change in me be seen and noticed for all to see. Lord let people understand that the old me does not exist I pray for this every day. I know that when I get out a will need to prove I have had a make-over and let that be scene. Lord I still haven't heard anything about the charges I was supposed to be getting and I guess that no news is good news, I just hate that these charges are hanging over my head, the thought of not knowing is driving me nuts. Lord please be there for me in all I do to advance your Kingdom. I love you Father.

G.

Psalm 3:3,4

May 2

Father,
Lord you have given me two commandments which sum up the whole of our being, "Love the Lord God with all your heart, mind, and strength." The other is, "Love your neighbor as you would love yourself." I know Father that when I love you with a true heart you remove the focus on my selfishness, that in focusing on you frees me to love my neighbors. In putting you first everything falls into place. In loving you I have no other Gods. In loving you I will remember to pick a day to rest and worship you. In loving you completely I can trust that you will take the lead. In loving my neighbor it allows me to have respect for my parents. In loving my neighbor I will not kill, steal, commit adultery, testify falsely against my neighbor nor will I desire anything that is my neighbors. Lord love is the most powerful tool I have to advance your kingdom and let me be ever mindful of it. With your guidance I will try to obey the words of law that you have given to me and all mankind. I praise and worship you Lord.

G.
Exodus 20:1-17

May 3

Father,
Lord of all creation I ask that you deliver me from all hate and evil that surrounds me. Father work on my sins as I pray for your deliverance. Lord you are the sun, the moon and the morning star. Lord in my life there is only you, for in you I will have eternity. Lord without you I am nothing I am as dust blown by the wind. Lord I fall short in all that I do without you, and with you I have peace and love. Lord you were crucified for me and raised from the dead and gave me the Holy Spirit. Lord as I stand among the enemy let me stand steadfast in you grace and love. Lord I wake with you in the morning and sleep with you at night. Lord show me the way to walk on your path, be my guide forever. Lord in your name I pray.

G.
Psalm 59:1

May 4

Father,
Lord I was thinking back today about my stay in County jail this time last year. I had no clue as to what my stay would be like and I was nervous to say the least. When I arrived at county jail I was shackled with bracelets around my ankles and hand cuffs on my wrists. The door opened to the garage at the jail and after it stopped I was removed an put in a changing room with glass windows after stripping down naked, my body was searched from top to bottom and front to back the guards didn't miss one inch. I was then given clothes that were uniform with the other inmates, then I was given sheets and a blanket and led to the gallery where I would spend the next 3 and a half months. The gallery area was not very big and there were about 8 cells on two levels, the cell block held about 30-32 prisoners. I was scared and nervous for the first few days not knowing what to expect from the other inmates I didn't know what to expect. I found that the inmate were OK and we all got along, and only then did I start to relax. Lord if I had called upon you for comfort during this new and strange situation I know that you would have had a calming influence, which was to come later when I started to know you and your love. I can say only one thing Lord that fear is sometimes over powering especially when facing the unknown. I do know Lord that you were with me and you protected during my stay in county jail even if I didn't know it at the time. Thank you Lord for being my protector when I needed you most. I love you Lord.

G.
Psalm 57:6

May 5

Father,
Lord 1 year ago today I was brought out of my cell and placed in a room with a bench facing a T.V. monitor with a video recorder facing me so I could observe the judge and he could do the same, when the monitor came on I could see the judge. When I saw the judge my heart sank, Judge J. was a member of the church I attended, in fact more often than not we sat in close proximity to each other, and I became ashamed that I was before him for a bond reduction. I know Lord that he was being professional and all but he didn't even acknowledge me and that just ripped at my gut. I pray Lord that because he's a Judge he had to be observe the rule and show no signs of emotion. Lord I pray that this is what happened, and that sometime in the future we could meet under different circumstances. The one good thing he did do was to reduce my bond from $100000 to $50000. At 10% I couldn't come up with $5,000 so I would have to stay until the conclusion of my trial. I had offers from family members to put up the bond and retain a lawyer but I told them no I just wanted to get it over as quick as possible and start serving my time. I was then assigned a Public Defender, or prison deliverer as the guys in the cellblock called them. I prayed Lord that you would give me a good lawyer, and you did. Thank you Lord. I'll write some more tomorrow.

G.
Psalm 69:16

May 6

Father,
Lord today is my sister's birthday and in the year I've been incarcerated I have not heard from her in any manner. I guess I'm on her pay-no-mind list, that not too surprising though, I only spoke with her when she held Christmas at her house for the family. I also think that she is hurt and ashamed that her brother is in prison, if that's the case I need to understand it. Lord just soften her hurt and lift this burden from her. I still love her and always will till the end of our time here on earth. K. I

still wish you a Happy Birthday. Lord you are my comforter in times of need and this is one of those times, I'm hurt and ashamed also but Lord you know my heart and if I could have done things differently I would have and that makes me sad. Lord I surrender her into your care and protection. Thank you Lord, good night and I'll write tomorrow.

G.
Psalm 69:19

May 7

Father,
Lord as I have been reviewing my time in County I find it interesting that I was able to adjust so quickly and change to a prisoner mentality, that's us against the system. I know that the restrictions were harsh and I had to abide by them, however I didn't have to like them. I also know that I had to get use to these restrictions if I didn't want any trouble. The experience was interesting, I couldn't believe that the windows of our cell were blacked out because women would come by and flash their man and anyone else that happen to be looking. The breakfast consisted of 2 hard boil eggs, a box of cereal, sweet roll, a carton of milk and juice, this was every day. I just had to be thankful that I was getting fed. Lunch was a cold cut sandwich chips and a fruit. The dinner was a hot meal served up cold, a real joke and also a reality check. Lord I was really disappointed with our County Jail. I know that I'm in a bad situation here but prison still gives me better food, I never thought that would happen, I suppose that the D.O.C. has a larger budget. I'm sorry I'm complaining again especially knowing that there are millions of people starving in this world, I'll try to think of that the next time. I love you Lord, I'll write tomorrow.

G.
Psalm 100:4

May 8

Father,
Today is Sunday and I just finished 2 large donuts for breakfast and a bowl of cereal, this is one meal that is halfway decent. Lord after I get done writing you I'll be taking a nap until lunch. I can smell chicken out the open window in my cell, I so hope that chicken is for lunch, I know that I'll get my cellmates chicken so I'll have a double portion, thank you Jesus! I will give my next breakfast to him in trade for chicken that's worth it. I usually don't eat breakfast anyway and D. is more than happy to take it. Last night I was busy making out a list of things to do that will help me re-adjust when I get out of prison, I want to be able to do things that will help advance the Kingdom. I know Lord when I wrote my family and mentioned to them that I was going to try and use my experience being here in prison to help offenders, several of my family members got upset and wanted me to forget about being in prison and not air my dirty laundry. I know Lord that this is the right thing to do. I will not be afraid of what anyone might say, I will do what I know you're telling me to do. I will let you lead me and right now I'll just wait until you give me the word. I feel you so strongly Lord. I am so blessed to have you Father. I would hope that when I get out my family will see and know my heart and I'll have less friction, work on their hearts Lord I need you in my corner. Thank you Lord, I'll get back to you tomorrow.

G.
John 17:24

May 9

Father,
Last year at this time I had the opportunity to meet with the public defender about my case and he told me that the preliminary hearing would be taking place in about a week. The P.D. said that we were going to plead not guilty regardless of the evidence; he said it's all about negotiation. I didn't know at the time that I wouldn't see my P.D. for over a month. Lord I am so glad that I came to you through your word, having plenty of time I was able to study and learn from the Bible the Chaplain gave to me. Thank you for putting the right people in my path. I know it was you Lord who

made the connection. Chaplain B. is fantastic in fact the whole Chaplain group were great. One of the opportunities I had was going to a Bible study with the Chaplain every week. Chaplain B took the lead most of the time and he told it like it was. Get right and get with the Lord and I would have a much easier time of it then if I was away from him. Thank you B. for being brought by the Lord to help teach and guide me. I hope that when I get out we will meet again under better circumstances. Lord, please take care of brother B. and maybe will meet again, if not when I get out when we are called up yonder. I really think that the Chaplains are on the frontline of bring us, the inmates into a relationship with you. Lord you are magnificent! Thank you Lord. I will write soon.

G.
John 12:49

May 10

Father,
I'm thinking about L.J., it's been awhile since I've seen or heard anything about the charges we had over the hooch he had in our cell. I don't see him down on the lower level and was wondering if he was transferred to Tamms Correctional Center. Tamms, is a Super Max Prison. Lord I have been told by prisoners that have been at Tamms that it is not a prison one wants to be in. The conditions are extreme and an inmate is no longer considered to be a human being. One of the inmates I talked to stated that the only daylight he had was when he went to the exercise cell in the middle of the day, and only then could he feel the sunlight coming through the small window above him. Lord I am going thru rough times here but I'll take this over a Super Max. I just pray for the men at Tamms and here in the segregation unit. Lord I know that you can make things better if you chose to. Lord help get the word out about the conditions in these prison facilities. Lord I hope L.J is OK where ever he is. Lord I pray for my cellie D. I pray that he comes to you before it's too late. I love you Lord.

G.
Galatians 5:23

May 11

Father,
In January I was talking to L.J. about the prospects of getting out and what he would do when he did. L.J. said he would go back to the same life he lived only he would do it better and run his own crew so there would be no mistakes. When I argued that this would be no way to live, he said if I couldn't get anything going when I got out that I would do anything I could to survive. I know Lord that for a lot of inmates this may be the case however for me Lord I have you in my corner and know that I will overcome all adversities and succeed. Praise you Lord for your kindness. I know in my heart who I am. I'm a child of yours Lord and pray that I will have you to guide me, I can't go it alone. I pray Lord that this journey I'm on will lead me home. Lord I again ask that my burdens be lifted and that you forgive me for getting angry when L.J. won't listen or try to understand that there is better things out there for him and he doesn't need to go back to the same life that there is forgiveness for him if he comes to the cross.

G.
Ephesians 2:13

May 12

Father,
Good afternoon Father, today is the dog and pony show. One of the things that the Dept. of Corrections does is allow university students who are majoring in criminology a view of what a prison unit looks like, that unit just happens to be the segregation unit I'm in. This group consists of 5 young women, 15 young men and 2 educators. The gallery is now at a fever pitch as the inmates are calling out to the girls with lewd remarks that you know Lord but I won't say. There are even some inmates trying to expose themselves, this is total chaos. I feel that it is demeaning to the inmate to have people come in and stare at them like animals in a cage. This is just so sad and I as a moral human being am extremely discussed. I guess Lord that is why the inmates act up. I know it's impossible for the guard to have any type of control in here at this time. I hope that

on the other side of the cells these students realize that this is very cruel and hurtful too the inmates. Lord I pray that someone in that group of students has empathy for these inmates and their condition some point in the future. Lord I pray that these students receive greater understanding. Lord we are all your creatures and this show is very degrading. I love you Father, I'll write later.

G.
Proverbs 21:1

May 13

Father,
Lord, my mind keeps going back to L.J. and I just pray for his soul. I don't know why this bothers me so much after all he got us busted and I'm still waiting to hear about the charges. I guess it could be that I went through a lot with him and even though we got into trouble is personality is such that I can't help but like him. L.J. had been in the cell for about one week when he started complaining that the spot where he was shot in the leg was turning red and burning and I could see some of the copper jacket of the bullet starting to protrude through the skin. L.J. told the medical technician that he needed to see a doctor to have the darn thing removed. L.J. waited for a week and finally decided to remove the bullet from his own leg. I thought he should still wait but he said that he wanted it out. So there I was taking the fragment of bullet out of the leg of L.J. This was not the smartest thing to do however there has been no help or answer from the medical unit this needed to be done. L.J. and I squeezed the area around the head of the bullet soaking up the blood around it to see what we were doing. This project took all of 15 min. and the fragment was removed. Once we got the piece of bullet out of L.J.'s leg he rested for a moment before he started to kick the door, making noise to get the guards attention. The guard got there only after 30 min. kicking on the door. When the guard arrived he was going to discipline L.J. for making a disturbance then L.J. showed him the piece of bullet and the hole in his leg, the guard said a few choice words and removed L.J. from the cell and escorted him down to medical, thank you Jesus. Lord I just pray that this

young man come back to the fold, that he release all the baggage of his past and present life for you to dispose of. Lord I pray that L.J. may find some help on his path to bring him back to you. Praise you Lord and answer this request, love you.

G.
Proverbs 21.2

May 14

Father,
Good afternoon Father, well we had another group of criminologist students come through, different students same cat calls from the gallery. I guess if you are looked upon like and animal that classifies this place as a zoo. I only have 33 more days left in here Lord, I think I'm going to make it, thank you Lord. I guess it's all about how my time is being used. Most of my time is used studying your word and writing to you, that has been the most redeeming part of this path I'm on so far. Lord let me not be puffed up about these students that are here now. I know that if I was in this class I would want to come to a prison and get a firsthand look at the way prisons run. Lord I still have to work on my human conditioning and be more Christ like. I'm pretty bored right now I guess that's why I'm talking to you. I know you are always with me. Maybe we'll get a banana with dinner I'm sorry Lord I just had to say it. I said it as a joke I know you know. I love you Lord!

G.
Proverbs 18:12

May 15

Father,
Today I'm going through Proverbs trying to gain some of Solomon's wisdom. I'll probably work in Mark later. I thank you Lord for all the blessings you have given me. Right now I'm a little angry because I'm bored and shouldn't be here in the first place. One of the things that I noticed is that there is no discrimination here every type of person is in here. There is a blind man, a deaf man, an old man who should be infirmed but he's not, and every race is represented in this house. The D.O.C. doesn't care who gets put with whom. There are murderers with drug addicts, lifers with shortimers', and violent offenders with non-violent offenders. I'm glad my cell-mate is only in here for armed robbery and aggravated assault with intent to kill. I can honestly say that it makes thing interesting I've had some great conversations with my cellie. Lord as I work in your word today fill my mind with the knowledge and wisdom of Solomon. I pray Lord that I might have greater understand of you. I thirst for you so much. I love you Father.

G.
Proverbs 18:15

May 16

Father,
I had an opportunity to talk to one of the guards while waiting go to the health department he said that the D.O.C. is trying to shut Stateville down. The state thinks that it's in such bad shape that it needs to be shut. The guard said that with the completion of Thompson that the state doesn't feel the need for Stateville. That would be OK with me but I only have 32 more days left and I'm out of here. I don't think it would be closed before I go. This prison is really in bad shape though, in the hallway between this unit and the others is a holding cell, one which I was placed in for 5 hrs. after L.J. and I got busted for having hooch. The temperature outside was about 20 degrees and a strong wind and ¼ of all the window blocks were missing. L.J. was blue because of the extreme cold. I really am thankful

that you protected us from any serious issues due to the extreme cold. The cells have extra inmate called cockroaches and other little crawling insects, and that is no joke. Lord I'm just so fortune that you have kept me from all possible harm here at Stateville. There is one type of inmate that none of the other inmates can stand and these inmates are also called (bugs). These are the inmates who leech off other inmates even if they don't need to, just to be mean. Lord I know that someday you will even the score and they will get what's coming to them. I do hope though that these pests come to you before it's too late. Time to go Lord, always in you.

G.
Proverbs 17:20

May 17

Father,
I took most of the day off yesterday after I got done writing you. I was very tired and didn't feel that great. Lord heal me, help me to feel better. I actually got a letter from my younger sister K.. She didn't say too much but at least she cared enough to write and for that I'm thankful. My daughter K. sent me a whole lot of books to read and that will keep me busy for the next couple of weeks. My cellmate was talking with the inmate in the next cell and that gab session lasted all night. It was extremely hard to get any sleep especially since I wasn't feeling very good. I don't have a clue as to why these men can't be respectful Lord and I pray that they realize that it's rough sleep here on here on any normal day and stop with the bologna so people can get to sleep. Muffle their voices and give me peace. I pray Lord that the next 30 days are easier for me then the past 5 months were. I love you Lord will write you soon.

G.
Romans 1:21

May 18

Father,
Today was a disappointment I didn't get my commissary which means I have only a pencil to write with and have to use what I have left of the paper I got last time, hopefully the paper will last for two more weeks. I can't mail out a letter because I didn't get my stamped envelopes. I'll survive though besides I have less than a month to go in this hellhole. Lord I want to thank you for getting through this ordeal thus far. With only 29 more days I'm going to make it. Nothing special today for food, then again there has only been a couple of times were the food was better than normal. I think I've had fried chicken only 5 times and that's the only meal that I would classify as special. Lord how I long for some great Chinese food, Chicken egg foo young, chicken fried rice, and two egg rolls from "Jimmy Lee's" in Freeport Il. Most everything he makes is from scratch the food there is out of sight. I'm so longing to eat some high calorie, greasy, and fat soaked food when I get out. I have probably lost about 60 lbs. in the last five months I look like my father Lord and he's in his 80's. I want to ask you Lord for peace, and order in here theses last 29 days. I need your love and arms to be wrapped around me. Thank you Lord Jesus for your gift.

G.
1 Corinthians 15:50

May 19

Father,
Lord, men are taught to be strong and suck it up when facing harsh times and the men here face the worst of these harsh times every day. Lord it's hard to imagine that men are treated this way, and maybe a few might deserve something harsh but not this many men there is no excuse. I thought we were in the 21st century now, I guess not because the treatment here at Stateville is almost medieval. I understand now how so many men come away from prison with a dislike for authorities and people who don't give them the time of day once they find out you're an ex-offender. I pray

Lord for just those things I need to make it through the rough time I'll face in 15 months. I know Lord that I shouldn't complain about the food, at least it keeps me alive. I wished that everybody knew how bad the food really was. I also can't understand how any man would want to offend repeatedly so he could come back. I guess some of these men feel like they can't leave their mother's womb. Lord again I pray for forgiveness for feeling sorry for myself when I should be counting my blessing of having you in my corner. I love you Father and thanks.

G.
Philippians 1:9

May 20

Father,
Lord I love you with all my heart, mind, body, soul and strength. I know there is a progression in loving you Lord and coming to you is priority. When I came to you, you captured my heart with your loving words. When I came to you, you filled my mind with wonders. When my body was weak, you strengthened me. I know there are many elements of self that ignore your truth and just serve ones' person. Self preservation, self worth, self interest, and self absorption are just some of those characteristics. When I do something I shouldn't and lie I'm protecting myself against consequences. When I am prideful I think of myself only. When I'm pre-occupied with unimportant things I'm trying to serve my own interests forgetting to come to you first. When I am so busy at what I do and forget you Lord I'm self absorbed. I know that your love changed my way of thinking so I could gain. I could love without thinking of myself. I know that putting you first I will be able to accomplish all that you have in store for me. I am willing to serve you without complaint leaving my old ways in the dust. With love and admiration I have come to you. May I love you always.

G.
Micah 7:18

May 21

Father,
Lord, not counting today which is almost over I only have 26 day left in this hellhole. Lord I'm just so filled with love towards you. I have been studying in the book of Romans and it states in Romans 6:14 that sin must not be you master and not to live under the law but under God's grace. That we have a right under you grace to be happy. I know that man made laws are sometimes wrong or even unfair but I still have to obey these laws. Lord, I think what you are telling me is that I should put your laws above man made laws, if the laws of man go against your laws that as long as I have your grace I'm under a greater authority than man. I think that's what I'm getting out of this scripture or is this saying that there may not be a law against some sins but if I want you grace I should avoid breaking the laws you want us to keep. I adore you Lord and appreciate your getting me through these tough times, as always,

G.
Romans 6:14

May 22

Father,
Lord I know that it is only through faith that we come to know Jesus and I am thankful for that faith. I have faith that Jesus lived and was sent by you Lord to take away all sins. I have no doubt he was crucified on the cross for those sins. I know that with his resurrection Jesus conquered death and guaranteed me eternal life. Thank you Jesus! I was reading in 1st John 5:12 that whosoever has the Son has life. That whosoever doesn't have the Son doesn't have life. I pray Lord that all people come to know and accept you, because it is through faith in you everyone can be saved no matter what they've done. Your blood for me. I love that you love me that much to sacrifice your Son for me. Lord you have to do something about the mystery meat I still haven't figured what type of meat this is if it is meat at all, with all my heart.

G.
1 John 5:12

May 23

Father,
Lord I know that there is an old saying "confession is good for the soul" and there is a lot of truth in this saying. I know that the truth will set you free and when I acknowledge my sins and confess you have forgotten them instantly. Lord I have broken your laws and sinned, I ask you to forgive me of these sins. Lord give me the strength to sin no more. Lord I know you want everyone on this earth to enter the Kingdom. I hope that I can bring people to your Kingdom Father I would hate to see anyone parish to the pits of hell. I know that hell is real because I have had a little taste of it here in this prison. I love you Lord.

G.
2 Timothy 3:16

May 24

Father,
Lord, I am thankful I have survived this ordeal over the last 5 months and only have 22 days left. Then I'm outta here! I kind of wonder what prison I'll be transferred too. I hope it's not all the way down at the southern most part of Illinois. I have had one visit from my daughter and one visit from my brother in the five months I've been here. I know that everyone is busy and going on with their lives but it sure would be nice to see them a little more. I know that this is the closest prison to where they all live so that should make it easier to visit. I know that when they came to visit they saw me sitting on a stool, with a chain attached the manacles I had on and secured to the stool. There is a Plexiglas window about 1 inch thick with a 4 inch round hole, covered with a metal plate with slits through it, so you can speak to your guest. When you are called for a visit you line up with all the other inmates that are going on visits or going to the health facility. We have manacles around our ankles with a chain linking the manacles to the handcuffs which are strapped around your waist with your hands crossed over one another so your hands are in a totally fixed position. The C.O. walks the whole group out of the unit and takes us to where we are going.

I should also say that all the prisoners are linked on one chain together while we are walking. We are dropped off in order of where we are going. The visiting area for segregation inmates is the first stop so I didn't have to be on the line for any length of time. The building that the visitors come into looks like as bunker that might protect you if a there was a tornado. I know that I'm complaining again and I'm sorry, I was just venting. Lord I just need to calm down and control my anger. I ask for your peace and comfort in these thoughts I'm having. I love you Lord.

G.
Psalm 116:8

May 25

Father,
Lord as I write this prayer; I first give you the glory for all things past, present and future you knew me before I was born. May I always praise and worship you. I know that you love me and I'm forgiven of all my sin I have confessed to and those that I can't remember. I need your spiritual guidance , I need you to help me find my gift and who I am and where I am on the path of life you have chosen for me. Lord I want to forever be in your Kingdom. Lord I still have doubts, doubt about the future, where I'm going, how do I get there and is there a place for me to advance the Kingdom? I know Father that everything is in your time I'm just impatient. Lord I've come to you in bad times and may I also come to you when things are good. I do not want to forget you Lord you are my first love. I know that every day that I spend with you draws me closer to heaven and that's one place I want to be. I love you so much I'll write later.

G.
Philippians 2:13

May 26

Father,
I was thinking back to County Jail back in Stephenson County and remember all the anger I had some at you but most of the anger was aimed at myself. I didn't know the right way to come to you and got very upset that you weren't answering my prayers. I know that as I grew in my faith and understanding, you were there I just wasn't patient enough. I was upset with the way I was being treated and wanted something done. I was so arrogant about my situation, I felt that everyone else in here were beneath me. I am so ashamed that I thought that way Lord I would like to think that I was a better man than that. I know that my time in county started the process of breaking down my spirit, to be stripped away of the garbage in my life so I could come to you with a clean mind and spirit of my own. It was last year at this time that I saw my Christian brother R. for the last time. R. is a super human and has been a blessing to myself and many others. I know that there is no finer boss a live than R. I never came across a man who was so humble and gentle. I know that when I made mistakes he always admonished me with a gentle spirit instead of get upset and blowing his top. I know that when he needed capitol for the franchise that he owned he sold the part of his business that I was involved in. I know that before he sold this part of the business R. had asked them to hire me to do this work for them and to give them a leg up in the area they would now be responsible for. R. said that they were happy to do this. I know that made me feel ten feet tall. I felt very sad about leaving R. but I know Lord that if you wish it I'll see him some day. I just want to pray and give thanks to you Lord for bringing R. into my life, I am so blessed to have known him. I love you and give you thanks.

G.
John 1:12

May 27

Father,
I'm getting closer to the day I get out of this place and head to a new facility that I know will be a lot nicer then here. Lord Just 20 days. Hallelujah!! I was thinking about what I was doing in County Jail a year ago. There was a lot of hurt in a lot of people. I know I hurt my wife, family and one of my friends that I thought I could depend on. I called him up from jail and got his answering machine I left a message to come and bail me out and bring $5,000 dollars. I never heard a word from him. I know that the money wasn't the problem he has enough to help, it was my being arrested and his support for my wife A. I lived in the house next to his so it would be rough for him to help me and explain to A. why he posted my bond, so I sat there until I was sent to prison. Lord I just pray for J. that you heal his heart and he is able to forgive me for what I did. I miss my friends and it hurt me when they abandoned me. I guess that is the human condition. I want to praise and honor you today, you have given me so much and I'm thankful. Love you Lord.

G.
Romans 14:10

May 28

Father,
Lord it's been a long time coming but I think I can let go of my wife, Lord I surrender her to your care. I know I sinned against her and I know that she no longer wants me in her life. I know we had some good times but it seemed that we were never alone there was always one of her kids or my kids around so we always had a full house or apartment. I now am free to spend time with you Father for you are my true love and you will never leave me. I know that with you there is hope and without you there is only darkness. I had two aches in my heart, one for a former love and now for my true love. Thank Father for being there for me. When I come to you my time goes by a lot quicker. I know your love has pulled me from the road to hell and placed me on the road to heaven and I praise you for

that. Father thank you for taking this burden away from me and just let me focus on you.

G.
Hebrews 12:7-9

May 29

Father,
Lord! Glory and honor on this day I feel clean and refreshed and ready to take on the world. I know that the world will have to wait a little while longer I still have some time to go. I am reading your word and getting ready to run the race of my life. I know Lord that if I can bring one soul to you my life on earth will be a success. I know Father that I was prideful most of my life and a lot less humble than I am today and I thank you for your intervention. I know that when I said I needed help I wasn't expecting prison I was hoping for a slap on the wrist. I think I know that I needed this time to get myself right and in a better place in my mind. I thank you Lord for every day that I'm given and I will remember to take my time and do everything with love and compassion. Lord my you shine in my heart forever, love you Father,

G.
1 Peter 3:12

May 30

Father,
Lord my soul is yours and you'll find it wanting. What I want, only you can give. I want Jesus and the grace that he gave me when he died on the cross. Lord I need you in my heart and mind all the time. Lord I have asked to be made new, to be transformed into the man you want me to become. Lord I know that right now I live for today because we are not given tomorrow. Lord if tomorrow never comes I'm still yours for all eternity. Hallelujah! Praise you Lord! I know when I'm presented to you, Jesus will vouch for

me and you will have me as one of your children forever. Lord, open my eyes so that I might see; that I might see what's ahead of me as I work for the Kingdom. Take my hand Lord, and guide my path so I can walk in your ways. Create in me a new heart Lord. Let it be a heart of service, service to you and to those in needed, for I am yours forever Lord. Thank you Lord,

G.
Colossians 2:6,7

May 31

Father,
Lord counting today I have 17 days left here in F. House Stateville, Illinois, Cell 213. I find it hard to believe that this nightmare is finally coming to an end. Lord you have been with me every step of the way and I praise and honor your name. The sun is shining and the weather is getting better all the time. I know that the window in our cell can now be opened without freezing to death. D seems to be in a good mood today he beat me in rummy twice. I know he's good in chess but he only learned rummy from me a few weeks ago. I know I've done a lot of complaining, but I feel I have the right to complain about the treatment of prisons here in segregation. I hope when I'm out I'll be able to help further the rights of prisoners here at Stateville. I love you Lord I'll write next month.

G.
John 14:26

June 1

Father,

Lord I've turned the page on my calendar to June, this is my getting out of Stateville month. I only have 16 more days in here and that feels wonderful. Lord I believe Jesus died for my sins and he was raised from the dead. Lord I do not want to be apart from you anymore, forgive my sins. Lord come and rule in my heart, I surrender control of my life to you. Lord only you can satisfy the emptiness I have. Lord never let me out of your sight and keep me in your arms when needed. If you see me walking down the path without you, draw me close and deliver me from all possible evil and temptation. Lord I love you above all others let me ever stay in your grace, always and forever,

G.

1 John 3:7

June 2

Father,

Lord, I want you to know that I'm thinking about all the unfair things that happen when someone is incarcerated. Last year at this time when I went to jail after my arrest I got a rude awakening. I was amazed by the cold heartedness of the guards. I had only been charged with a crime I was not guilty yet but was treated as if I killed someone. You're not treated like an innocent person, you are assumed guilty by the guards and you have no rights. Lord, when I first came to jail I lost any dignity or pride that I once might have had. I felt as low as a person could go. I know that the only one at this time that cares about you is yourself. I know that the living arrangements aren't like home and that they are barely manageable. I know that the food has to be rated 1 star, edible yet indescribable. I know that if you must use the Public Defender you almost have a guaranteed trip to prison, that a Public Defender usually plea bargains for a lighter sentence then the State has asked for, thus avoiding a trial. The things that are the same weather in jail awaiting your trip to prison and being in prison are these: Your food is almost always served cold, even when eating at the chow hall or the meal is brought in from an outside company. I know that being bored is always on your mind. I know that communication with your family and friends gets less and less as the days and years go on, sort of like being taken for granted that you'll survive and they need to get on with their lives. I know that lights are on in your cell 24/7 no darkness. I know I messed up and that's why I'm here, so I have to accept what is. I know that with you Lord I'm never alone and that which I hunger for you will feed me. Praise you Lord I thank you for your mercy, as always,

G.

Hebrews 10:17

June 3

Father,
Lord I only have 13 more days and I can hardly wait. I am excited with anticipation about getting out of here. I also feel sad somewhat for a lot of the inmate here who will be spending a lot of time in this place. Some of the inmate will be in segregation anywhere from 1 year to 15 years, now that I couldn't do. Lord the time that I've spent here has been a great learning experience. I have learned how to survive duress and undue hardship. I've been able to see all the negative things that go along with be an inmate. Lord the most important thing that I've learned is that you are always with me and will never leave. I know that you have made my stay here bearable and better than I could have hoped for. Thank you Lord. Lord I have seen a lot of evil in this place and very little good. I know that the control of this place is in the hands of Satan, and very few in here are aware of this. I know that men close down inside and do not express their feeling with anyone else so they get caught up in their surroundings and go with the flow. I pray for them Father, that they come to find Jesus and are able to have a relationship with you. Lord you are everybody's God it's too bad that not all the inmates in here accept that fact. I give all my love to you my Lord.

G.
Hebrews 10:22

June 4

Father,
I just thought of something, I have a make shift calendar and have been counting the days until I'm out of here (12) but I have the days at the top of the calendar wrong so what is today I think it's Tuesday but it might be Monday, oh well it makes no difference in here one day is the same as the other. I'm looking out on to the gallery and it looks like someone started another fire in the dumpster. I do not understand how after the last time the dumpster caught on fire the corrections officers could allow the dumpster close enough to the cells that someone could throw a match.

The fire is starting to pick up in intensity and smoke is filling the gallery, got to open our window for some fresh air. I'm back, sorry I had to take a break it was very hard to breathe for a while. I now know what a Chinese Fire Drill is. Its 3 correction officers using 7 fire extinguishers' to try and put out a dumpster fire, it's still smoldering. The investigation unit has been brought in and they are questioning the inmate in the cells close to the area where the fire started. Lord I know it's wrong but it's also very funny how unprepared the C.O.s are. Lord I pray thank you that the C.O.s are OK and didn't get hurt by the smoke fumes. I pray thank you that none of the inmates were overcome by the smoke and we are all right. May I always thank you for your blessings, love you.

G.
1 John 4:12

June 5

Father,
My dearest friend, I come to you with only 11 more days. Hallelujah! I'm getting excited. I know that it's been almost 6 months in here and I know Lord that without you I probably wouldn't have made it. Thank you Lord. I want to thank you for protecting me from all danger and harm, I want to thank you for comforting me when I needed you, and most of all I thank you for Jesus and the sacrifice that he made so that I can have a direct line to you Father. Praise Jesus! Lord they are still investigating the fire from last night and they must have questioned 20 inmates in the area where the fire started. I wonder if they checked the video tape, and if they found anything? I am so glad that this happened on the other side of the gallery. I just want the last few days to go peacefully. I am still thinking about the hooch incident earlier this year and I still haven't heard a word. I just hope that what some of the inmates said that after 2 week if you haven't gone before a board they can't charge you. I hope this is true. I don't want to spend any more time in prison then I have too. I love you Jesus and thank you, as always Lord.

G.
Psalm 17:8,9

June 6

Father,
Lord only 10 more days, almost down to single digits. I got to thinking about Christmas and as I look back I think of all the many Christmas' I've had. Most of the Christmas' were with family except when I was in the service. I would always think of peace and charity to others. Most of all Lord I tried not to get wrapped up in all the gift giving instead I chose to focus on the true meaning, that a Savior came into this world to take away all our sins. This to me is the greatest gift that anyone could be given. Lord I know that everyone falls short of coming to you and yet when Christ was born he started a chain of events that brought hope into the world. I thank you Lord for this blessing for myself and all mankind. I know that when your freedom has been taken away by circumstances I appreciate the things I miss more, Christmas being one of them. I'm looking forward to my first Christmas out of prison in 2006; I know it will be a glorious day, a reunion of sorts with family and friends. The bells jingle, the snow falls, the lights shine bright, the trees are trimmed, the presents under the tree and the feast of Christmas is being prepared. With all these things the one thing that could get lost is the most important thing. Jesus Christ the Savior of the world was born, the greatest gift of all. I love Lord Jesus, thank you Lord. Only 200 days until I celebrate your birth. Hallelujah!!!!

G.
John 1:4

June 7

Father,
Lord only 9 more days until I get out of this terrible place, and I again thank you for your grace and protection. I got a letter from the bank where I had the mortgage on my house stating that the house had been foreclosed on and sold to a speculator for $5,000. I guess my wife didn't keep up the payments, Lord I just wish that thing had been different. I sometimes think that this is a bad dream and I'll wake up and all would be right in my little world. I know that this is not a dream and the reality is

I caused this with the mistakes I made. I will miss that house. I still have not heard anything about my charges, so I guess they were not filed, that's fine by me I couldn't do another year in here. Lord I pray that the next 9 days go by quietly and there is no disturbance in this cellblock. I love you gracious Lord will write tomorrow.

G.
Obadiah 1:34

June 8

Father,
Lord only 8 days left until I'm out of here and on my way, I am starting to get excited. Lord I want to talk about my mother. I ask that you tell her that I love her so much and that I miss her very much, that I know she was taken so she could help you out. Lord let her know that the reason I don't visit her grave site, is that I know her soul is with you and she's in a better place. I think about all the new procedures there are today that might have detected and cured her cancer and I think what if. Lord I think back on how mom always held the family together and how happy we all were. I look at my family now and we are all so busy that we have little time to see or talk to one another. I know that when I get out of prison I will try to change that. Lord I pray that all people everywhere take time from their busy lives and spend time getting to know their family, the world would be a better place I know it. Lord I'll write tomorrow, Love you.

G.
Proverbs 12:28

June 9

Father,
Lord, 7 more days and its hallelujah time I really am starting to feel that I will be OK I wrote yesterday about mom, today I want to talk about pop. Lord I know that you have watched over and protected him so that he could continue to do his work that you gave him to do. Lord I am thankful for the job you did bringing him back to you so many years ago. I was a little child and didn't understand then what problem my dad had. Lord thank you for walking him through the 12 step program. Dad has always been there for me and my sibs and I know we are all thankful. I have seen over the course of my life many people that my dad helped and that they had come to the realization that there is someone to turn to for help in overcoming addiction, if only I had paid attention. Lord my dad is so wonderful and I now fully appreciate him. Lord he gave me the life skills to survive in this world, and the fortitude to survive anything that was thrown at me. Lord I am thankful I have a father when I see so many of the men in here were abandoned by their fathers. I bless the mothers for trying to keep their kids out of trouble. I know that these moms were up against a stacked deck. Society seems very indifferent towards these women. Lord I pray that all fathers everywhere come back to their families and their children so that their kids can have a better life. I love you Father.

G.
Revelation 2:4-7

June 10

Father,
Lord, I'm reporting in with 6 days left here in F-house and it feels good. I haven't talked much about D lately, because he's in his own world. I can't figure him out except to say that he seems to just exist. I think that he feels me inferior because I'm not a repeat offender and only here for a short time. I really don't think he wants to get to know anyone to well because he is always moving from one joint to another. I also think that he's disappointed that I can't play chess the something that he studies and

is very good at. Checkmate in 8 moves. I find it hard to comprehend spending another 13 years in segregation and I'm sure that has to affect his mental state a lot. Lord I just pray that D's heart is changed and he finds the love you have for him. I pray that someday the outer shell is broken and he may come to you and ask for forgiveness. I pray Lord that you keep him safe for the next 13 years. Lord I pray that D. finds a permanent friend it you. Lord I know that D. has no one that he can call friend or family on the outside and that is why it is so important that you are there for him when he is ready, let him find the love that I found in your embrace. I love you Lord, talk then.

G.
Hebrews 9:28

June 11

Father,
Lord only 5 more days until I'm gone, praise you Lord and thank you. I'm feeling kind of sad Father for a lot of these inmates. What chance have they got in their lives? I would probably say that most of these men come from broken homes, absent of a father. The sad part is there is no responsibility taken by the father all he does is have his needs met and leave when his women becomes pregnant he'll leave to find another women to be with and when he gets bored with that one he's gone, with no commitment whatsoever. I know Lord that this is a sad comment on where our society is heading but this is what happens when you are left out. These men are just passing through life without taking responsibility for their actions. I think this type of life gets passed on from father to son and then the cycle continues over and over again. I pray for the mothers who try their best to raise their sons and daughters the best why they know how. I pray Lord that their burdens are lightened in their lives and they are able to have a relationship with you to give them strength. I pray that there are people placed around them to help. Lord I pray that both these men and women come to know you. I love you Lord and thanks.

G.
Jeremiah 31:16

June 12

Father,
Good afternoon Lord. Well only 4 more days, I'm getting really "Jacked" I can hardly wait, I guess I'll have to I haven't got much choice. Lord I know it's been 4 days short of 6 months and a lot of the time things have gotten a little crazy. I have to thank you for keeping my head on straight and giving me the wisdom to know what to do to overcome this horrid situation. I look back on this experience and think if I had been able to perform on the drug test I wouldn't have been here and I might have delayed calling upon you Lord to take control of my life and the hellish things that surrounded me. Thank You Lord. I am on my knees in spirit before you. Lord you are everything I could ever want from this life. Lord may I always walk down your path. Love you Lord.

G.
2 Timothy 4:5

June 13

Father,
Lord only 3 days left in here; can you tell I'm excited about it? You are just so wonderful! I know it's just about time to leave because I'm getting goofy. I wonder Lord what the next prison will be like. I know it will be better than this place. We even had chicken and macaroni and cheese, good but still not very warm. I've been studying in Psalms and I want to thank you for showing me Psalm 139; Lord you are all-seeing, all-knowing, all powerful, and always present. You know me Lord and your gift to me is that I can love you forever. Psalm 139:23-24, Search me, Oh God and know my heart; test me and know my thought. Point out anything in me that offends you, and lead me along the path of everlasting life. I think I'm beginning to understand how much you needed me to focus on you and you only. I know that in this place there are fewer distractions then in other prison. Lord you have given my heart all I was lacking to do the work you want me to do. I will wait on your time for you are a perfect God. I love you Lord can't wait until tomorrow.

G.
Psalm 139:23

June 14

Father,
Precious Lord! Wonderful Savior! I am totally blessed. I'm on such a high and I have you to thank. I never knew how fantastic Psalms is to read and contemplate. I cannot believe I haven't read them before. Wait I know why, I wasn't walking on your road, we were walking in different directions yours was right mine was wrong. I thank you Lord for showing and leading the way. I know Lord that sometimes I struggle with the human side of my nature wanting control and Satan leads me into tempting situations. I fight him Lord and remember that I don't fight alone; I have thousands of unseen angels fighting the battle with me. Lord I may lose some battles but with your help I'll win your war and have eternal victory. I love you Lord and pray that you continue to bless me. Oh! I totally forgot 2 more days, as always yours.

G.
1 Corinthians 15:56, 57

June 15

Father,
Tomorrow Lord, I get out of here tomorrow, Amen!!!! I have conflicting thoughts. I am certainly happy that tomorrow I'm done in here but I also should not have been here. I've learned so much about how strong a man can be with you by his side, I survived only by your grace. I know that at my age it is not easy, but I made it. I only have a hand full of things to pack-up and what doesn't fit in the box D. can have. I hope he likes to read James Patterson, Tom Clancy and John Sandford. I have being reading a lot so my eyes get tired and I'll be able to sleep tonight. I hope there is no disturbance on the gallery this night. I am unable to give you as much praise as you deserve, however you know my heart and I truly love you, I'm a little teary eyed right now so I'll write you sometime tomorrow from my new digs. Good night Lord, one more to go.

G.
James 4:6

June 16

Father,

Dear Lord I don't have a clue about what's going on. I started out leaving cell 213 at about 8 A.M. this morning. I left out of the unit without wearing handcuffs and ankle bracelets for the first time in six months, this was a great feeling. Then I went down towards the property department to retrieve my property box. On the way down I was talking to R.M. about being in segregation, R.M. is a porter in the unit and had been schedule for death, but Gov. Ryan commuted all death sentences to life without parole R.M. fell into that category. Anyway walking down to property I was talking with him about all the crazy stuff that happened when I was there including the Hooch fiasco. I told him that up until today I was worried about getting more time for it, R.M. started to smile and told me that the night the incident took place he was given the tickets that were written up by the Lieutenant for L.J. and me. R.M. was told to take all the tickets down to internal affairs on his way down to affairs he dumped our tickets in the trash, how awesome is that. Lord you did have my back, Thank You! Thank You! So I went and got my box and held inventory. I found that most of my food stuff was stale or melted so I tossed it into the garbage. I was ready to go, that was not the case however I was told to put my box on a cart and follow the C.O. I was lead back towards F-house as I approached the unit the C.O. opened the side door and I went out and headed for an eerie looking building. We came to the door and upon entering I thought this can't be good. I came to a large doorway and as I entered I saw a group of 16 cells. The cells were a lot larger than the one I just came from. 12 ft. high, 8 ft wide and 12 ft long. This is where I'll spend the next few days until I get my assignment. This unit was at one time the holding cells for death row inmates. The unit is called X-house. Lord I guess I'll have to wait for a few more days. I Love you father and I know your here with me. I'll have more tomorrow. Lord keep me save and keep a close watch over me.

G.

Isaiah 40:31

June 17

Father,

Good morning Lord, well today is my first full day in this transition unit. I feel a little weird in this cell. I wonder who was in this cell that was scheduled to die and weather he was executed. This cell is a little chilling. My cell-mate is a devout Muslim and he has his routine that he goes through every day. He has a Koran, a cap and prayer rug. M. prays 6 times a day and goes through a cleansing ritual every time he gets ready to pray. So far we respect each others' religious beliefs. I will have the opportunity to become more familiar with his Islamic beliefs. Lord this brings up a question. Since both of us pray to you Lord how can the Muslims be so confused? I know that they believe that Jesus was just a great man and not the Savior according to their belief why did they turn to the Prophet Mohammad? This is the question I would like to find out. I hope M. can help me understand his beliefs more completely; there is so much I need to know. Lord give me the wisdom of discernment to discover what I need to know. Lord I know that we both love you and pray that M. sees there is more to understand about who you are. I love you Lord.

G.
James 1:5

June 18

Father,

Lord I had the opportunity to ask M. if it would be proper for me to take a look at his Koran. M. seemed a little hesitant, he was afraid I might not have enough respect for this book. I assured him that I would have total respect for the Koran. I pray Lord that I can understand what the Koran has going for it. Lord I go totally lost reading this book, for me its 114 chapters of speculation and acceptance of the Prophet Mohammad's visions that were given to him by the Angel Gabriel as M. put it. What I read seemed generic and not from you Lord, everything I've read can be interrupted anyway and for whatever suits the readers' needs for fulfillment. The Koran talks about a Holy War and that all believers should try to overcome all non believers of Allah by whatever means possible, this Jihad as it is called is troubling to me because Lord you are of love not hate. I thanked M. for allowing me to take a look at his Koran. There might be sometime in the future I'll want to look at the Koran again but I highly doubt it. Lord you are the true God, a God of mercy and love for all and I thank you for that Lord. I love you Father and I will always walk in your ways. I love you Lord.

G.
Hebrews 4:16

June 19

Father,
Good morning Lord, I'm in a new cell, with a new cellmate and I'm going to have an opportunity to go to the exercise yard. I can't really tell you how excited that makes me. Lord I need out of this place I really have had enough. I found out that M. has 25 more years to go for aggravated battery. I'm glad he found his God, Allah that would make him peaceful I hope. M. seems like a nice guy. I got the opportunity to watch a Cubs game on M.s' T.V. I haven't seen any T.V. since Dec. 16th of last year. Lord I just ask for your protection and keep me safe while I'm in this cellblock. I know that with you I can feel relaxed and give everything I have difficulty dealing with and I thank you for this. I don't like to complain but there comes a time when you are unsure. I love you Jesus and pray for the safety of all the men in here. I'll talk tomorrow. Oh, by the way have a happy Father's Day. Thank you for all your blessings

G.
1 Samuel 22:2

June 20

Father,
Lord I went to yard yesterday and my body is telling me that I have muscle that need some exercise; it's been a long time since I've used them. It was great though spending time in the fresh air and the sun shining down. When I got outside to the yard it was the first time I had the chance to see how tall the walls are around this prison. Let me tell you Lord these walls have got to be 30' high. I could not believe anyone would try to escape from here. I don't think they want anyone to go anywhere. It's nice to see the inmates playing soccer and basketball it reminds me that there still is life outside these walls. I figure that I'll be here for a couple of days yet so I'll try to make the best of circumstances on this hot 90 degree day. Well Lord at least one thing hasn't changed the Cubs lost, and to the Yankees, how totally Cubs! I like them anyway as far back as I can remember. I love you Lord will write tomorrow. Always with you Lord.

G.
Isaiah 38:8

June 21

Father,
Oh! Lord my sins are many; my ways have not been your ways. Let me remember the words of your Prophets, and the words of you son Jesus; let me be a beacon for your Kingdom Lord. Lord give me the wisdom to do right in your eyes. Let me be there for you Lord. I look for that eternal peace, to worship you and have supper at the bridal table. Glory to you Father, glory to your Son Jesus, and the Holy Spirit. Forgive my sins in the name of your Son Jesus. Lord cleanse me, robe me and let me serve for the poor, the hungry, the weak and those unable to take care of themselves. I am less than perfect; my failings have brought me down. You have humbled me before men and it is only your judgment that saved my soul has brought me back to you. Praise you Lord, I know that you have used less than perfect people to do your will let me be one of those people. Take and hone me with a sharp edge so I may have a bountiful

harvest for you. Let me see and understand what your plans for me are. I wait and pray, I study and think, I watch and I learn so when the time comes I'll be ready Lord. I surrender to your will Lord, there is no greater glory than to put on my armor for you. Oh Lord I thank you for listening to my prayer, your will is my will Lord, thank you Father.

G.
Psalm 32:1, 2

June 22

Father,
Lord my thoughts yesterday were about my future and what's in store for me. Lord it's scary but that's just Satan attacking, playing tricks with my mind. I have to remember that you are right here with me and that you know my future. Lord I'll let you guide my steps one day at a time. I will not give into Satan, I can feel the forces of darkness often and then I feel your loving arms wrapped around me. Lord I will always be tempted and I am so glad of your watchful eyes over me, thank you Lord. I am so blessed. Lord let me pray for D. and the hope that he is doing well, work on his heart Lord. The Cubs lost three straight to the Yankee that is so sad. I love you Jesus, you blood for me. What is real truth? The truth has been distorted by so many for so long that people find it difficult to believe in the one truth that is there, you Jesus are the answer. I pray that you work on all the hearts of men that call upon you.

G.
Ephesians 5:6

June 23

Father,
Good afternoon Lord, I am now at Hill Correctional Center in Galesburg. I arrived about an hour ago. I left Stateville behind at about 9 this morning. I got here after a stop at Graham for a transfer to a bus going to Hill. I just hope that this is the last time I'll be shackled and chained while being transported; the wrists get very sore from the weight that is distributed unequally. Hill Correctional is almost identical to Western at Mt. Sterling both are level 2 facilities; they are medium-maximum prisons. I just hope and pray that I will be able to finish my time in this prison and not have to go anywhere else. Lord give me a better outcome than I had at Western. Lord you are my strength and rock that I stand on, glory and praise to you name. Lord guide my steps and prepare me for the work you have for me. I love you Jesus you are paramount in my life. Thank you for all my blessings, I'll write tomorrow.

G.
Romans 8:9

June 24

Father,
Lord, I am going to have plenty of time to talk to you and study in the word. There is about a week waiting period before I can get into a permanent unit so I'll spend some time with you. I was thinking Lord that I can make a wonderful life for myself with you leading the way. I know that there is no going back only forward, one step at a time. I know that I can try and apologize to the people that I hurt and only they can forgive or not. I know that everything happens for a reason and if you want certain people from the past in my life when I get out all the better. Lord if I could take back all the wrong things I did in the past I would, I can only take them back in my heart and mind. My work at staying on the right path will be on going, I know that I have to walk the walk and talk the talk, by my actions people will come to know a new me. I shake a little over what the next few years have to offer and I know that you have them planned out for me.

Let me do your will Lord this I pray. I know that those who really love me will stand-by me and those who don't will be out of my life. I really want people to see me with a Christ like attitude. I know that I will be facing the demons that attack me with you at the forefront of the battle, I will succeed, God to you be the glory. I have sometimes had trouble relaying my feelings to other people because I was afraid to let them see the weaker and sadder side that I had, not anymore you have set me free. Lord I pray to be able to listen to what you are telling me and surrender to your will, and I will turn all the garbage in my life for you to cast aside. Lord be my guide and my strength. I will write later, always,

G.
Romans 8:16

June 25

Father,
Good day Father, I just got finished reading, "The Weather Man" it was a very good read, the book gives an inside look at Stillwater Prison in Minnesota. Most of the description is of their death row unit, the author show the interaction between prisoners and it's basically the same here, a lot of lost souls hoping for the best. I see now why a lot of men turn to you Lord when things can't get much worse and yet when things do get better and they are no longer tied down to their chains they forget you and go back to their old life. Lord you know my heart and I will always remember that you brought me to where I am today, tomorrow and beyond. I take pleasure in the fact that you comfort me all the time. I know Lord that when my time here is over that you have something planned for me, let me listen and take everything in. I need you to guide me. I love you Lord, it's almost time to go to chow so I'll write later. Hallelujah! I actually go to chow. To you goes all the glory.

G.
Colossians 3:13

June 26

Father,
Lord I have a good feeling today because I know with you, with Jesus and the Holy Spirit my life will be a blessed and as long as I remember to call upon you I'll be OK I know that everyday might be a challenge for me but with you in my corner I will overcome. I need to stay in the word so I can obtain wisdom, knowledge and strength. Lord I'm just on a godly high, Praise You! Help me to become worthy of your Kingdom and give me the time to work on the hearts of those who either forgot you or never have known you, let me be a pipeline to you Lord. I pray this with all my heart that I may have that honor. Love you, I'll write tomorrow.

G.

1 Peter 1:6

June 27

Father, I'm still in orientation unit and will be getting my housing assignment next week. I would like to report Lord that the food is much better here than at either Western or Stateville, much better. This could also be because I go to the chow hall instead of getting Styrofoam containers. I'm still reading everyday Lord and studying your word. I am reading in Romans and Revelations. Paul and John are my favorite followers of Jesus. I know that both of them spent time in prison and I can empathize with their struggle, and never did they lose faith. My cellmate is learning about you Lord through reading you word, I'm trying to help out where I can especially when he gets confused. I'm hoping that I don't confuse the both of us. B. is 19 yrs. old and got here by being stupid; he got caught breaking and entering. Well I hope this experience is a lesson learned and he doesn't come back. I don't think either of us will, he's too young and I'm too old. Lord, please guide both B. and myself down the right path; keep us from falling into the same garbage that got us here. I will get the opportunity to call home as soon as my call list is approved and that should be tomorrow. I'll write latter Lord it's time to go to chow. For being here with us Lord I thank you. Let us glorify you name forever.

G.

2 Corinthians 4:8-10

June 28

Father,
Lord today is sizzling hot, up in the 90's, and of course the air isn't working very well, I pray Lord that you help in bringing me and my cellmate some relief we really could use a break. I've been studying in the book of Ezekiel with a lot of interest. I'm sad to think that I and so many others did the same thing that the chosen people of Israel did falling into great sin and putting you Lord as an afterthought. To follow you Lord is the only way for all of us. Lord I will commit myself to you to do whatever you want, wherever you want me to go, and whenever you ask. I had been indifferent to you and the word all my life. My God was not you but all the things I thought necessary to live the good life. I never put you first and you weren't even a close second, forgive me Lord. Lord it is so hot in here I could fry an egg on the window cell; I need some relief I call upon you Lord for some help. Lord I want to thank you for a good day. I got my call list today and had the opportunity to talk to my daughter H. and my grandson before my time ran out it was wonderful I hadn't talked to her for over 6 months, praise you Lord. I will be able to sleep in peace tonight. I love you Lord.

G.
Ezekiel 33:7

June 29

Father,
Lord I just want to thank you for the time I got to spend with B. We had the opportunity and time to work in your word, and I am grateful. I pray that B. continues to work in the word I wish him well in his life. I want to thank you for relief from the heat after I prayed yesterday the heat started to dissipate, we had rain and a nice cool down. Today I moved from orientation to general population so hopefully I can have a settling and start my new journey with peace. I can feel you with me Lord and I must remember to stay humble and not be proud or arrogant. When I was on the phone yesterday I found out that my best friend was having a hard

time dealing with the fact that I went to prison, and his brother is trying to sell the house he lives in. I forgot to pray that he gets a blessing and his brother changes his mind and let D.H. stay in the house, so I pray now for this blessing. D.H. is my most important project; he has issues with his belief in your existence. I know he can't understand why all the bad stuff that happens in the world isn't taken care of with the wave of your hand. Lord how can I get D.H. to understand that the problem isn't you but the free will given to man? I hope when I get out I can present you to him so he will come into the fold. Lord help and protect him, cradle him in your loving arms while I'm gone. I'll write you tomorrow, thank you Lord.

G.
Ezekiel 33.9

June 30

Father,
Today is the last day of the month and there is relief from the heat. I went to yard this morning did a little bit of walking to get the kinks out and got some well deserved fresh air. Lord thank you for providing me with extra envelopes so I could give one to my cellmate so he could mail a birthday card to his kid. I was glad to help, as you give so can I. Lord it feels good to put someone else's need before mine. Lord I was such a fool when it came to what was good for me. Thank you Lord for being there for me, I would have been damned without you. I'm eternally grateful for all that you have given me. I have a Hispanic cellmate who likes to rap and is constantly using the cell bars as drums. I guess that I'm too old to appreciate this rap music nor do I like what it is saying about hate and anger. Oh well this is still better than where I came from. I love you Father, talk to you next month.

G.
Romans 12:8

July 1

Father,
Good morning Lord, today was a quiet day, very laid back and relaxing. I went to chow for breakfast at 3:30 A.M. I know it's hard to believe when they say that chow comes early they weren't kidding. There is actually a menu posted on the gallery door and it gives you some idea of the wonderful food that is being dished out. Today's early bird breakfast was powdered eggs, turkey sausage, grits, 1 milk carton, 1 juice carton and the only natural thing on the menu, a banana. I spent time reading a novel by Nora Roberts, don't say it, yes it's a romance novel but they are light reads and I get a whole new prospective of women. These types of books are actually fun at least I think so. I do not have very many commissary items left, a few envelopes, about 5 Ramon noodles, and a box of saltines. I'll have to do some trading so I can get some smokes. I know Lord smoking is bad for my health, so is prison. I have to hang on until next week when we go to store. The corrections officer brings an item sheet around for us to fill out and later in the day they collect them and send to store for approval, I've got my T.V. on there and I may finally get the T.V. I was supposed to have last Dec. Lord I just want to pray thank you for a relaxing and uneventful day, it's been a while since I have been able to relax, and I thank you. Lord may I ever praise your name, forever yours.

G.
Philippians 4:7

July 2

Father,

I come to you today with thanksgiving, to just thank you for your protection when I was in Stateville. I know that many things could have gone badly and yet you were there to watch-over me and keep me out of danger. I know that is was you Lord that had R.M. get rid of the ticket that was written up about the "Hooch" fiasco and I thank you for that. I thank you for protecting me from L.J. who was shown to be very dangerous; I could have easily been attacked if I had said the wrong thing. I thank you for teaching me your ways and giving me the knowledge I will need when it's my time to work for the Kingdom. I thank you for guiding me through your word, and giving me the understanding that there will be an end to this insane world and you will be the victor. I thank you for making the Word come alive and placing the right words in my mouth. I am so glad I gave everything up to you Lord; there is great freedom in that. Most of all Lord I thank you so very much for Jesus sacrifice for me, if not for him you and I would probably not have this talk. I know Lord that I will make mistakes in the future and that's OK, because I have the Blood of Jesus giving me the right to bring my mistakes too you. I know that you forgive and forget what I've done and I thank you for that. I love you Father God!!!! I will write tomorrow, as always,

G.

Psalm 104:4

July 3

Father,
Lord I was working in Revelations last night and this morning and realized that when John address the seven churches in his writings that each one could reflect the way churches are today. The church in Ephesus to me is an example of a church that accepts the lifestyles of people who go against the laws that you have set down long ago. To ignore your laws Lord is as big a sin as the people doing those things that are forbidden by your law to do. I listen on the news about churches accepting people who continue to go against the law because they are afraid of conflict. Lord I care about all the people who have a different lifestyle than I do, but I also know that these are sins against your teaching and for a church to accept these alternative lifestyle is totally wrong, I'm thankful that you will deal with these churches when the time comes. I know Lord that this is not the popular opinion in today's society but I think it's the correct one. I know as I see the new world order slowly coming about I shudder to think what will happen. I love you Jesus, praise you Lord. I will write tomorrow, need to talk about the second church, as always,

G.
Jeremiah 17:14

July 4

Father,
Happy Independence Day! Good afternoon Lord, today is our freedom day celebrating the signing of this country's Declaration of Independence. I like this day a whole lot the one day where a small contingent of men from 13 colonies stood up to King George of England and told him to put a sock in it. I couldn't help myself. I know you really aren't that interested but you are all I have to communicate with. I hope you understand why I come to you with these silly things that aren't important; however I just need to express myself. You said I can come to you with anything so here I am. I just like the 4th because I like those who fought in the Revolutionary War, as I did in the Viet Nam War. I know that you are not a great proponent

of War unless it's to your gain and benefit but I kind of think that it was time to give the people of this country a chance to mess things up like so many other countries have done. As I look at our country it seems we have done a fairly good job. Lord I am thankful that when men fought many took you with them into battle as I did when I went to Nam. I know you were looking out for me and I could feel your presents when I took a glimpse of the sky while on guard duty. Your sunset, your stars, and your wonderful world, how could we all be so stupid as to put our own interests first and not check in with you first, stupid, stupid, stupid! Lord you are ever present and with us always and we are blessed because of this.

G.
Psalm 33:12

July 5

Father,
Had the opportunity of watching the fireworks in the town of Galesburg last night and what I saw of them was enjoyable. I can remember when my dad who at the time was a Fireman would go out to the high school and get the fireworks set in the ground and ready for that evenings celebration. When the skies were dark enough the firemen would light a flare and start sending up the fireworks, it was an awesome display, it was fun to be young. I now enjoy watching other young people as awe-struck as I was when I was young. I thank the Chinese's for the creation of fireworks. Lord speaking of fireworks, I truly don't want to be around when you call a halt to the things that go on in your world. I know you left us with a great world and as men we have messed this world up, I pray Lord for all of us who damaged this world with our selfish actions that we might be given another chance to set things right. I pray Lord for a godly leader to take a stand and put your armor on to fight your war. Lord the glory is all yours I will always love you,

G.
Daniel 9:4

July 6

Father,
Lord yesterday I had the opportunity to meet an inmate who was in need of some advice. B.A. was suffering and unable to release these burdens and free himself from the attack of Satan making him feel guilty. B.A. finds it hard to let go off the hurt he caused his family and friends. We talked about You Lord, and B.A. ability to forgive himself if he just asks for it. I hope that B.A. will be able to come to you Lord; he seemed relieved and able to understand that you are always there. I hope I'll see him tomorrow at yard so we can talk further. It felt good being able to give someone help, at least this is a starting point for me. I hope to get a handle on who I am and in doing so I should be able to help other people. I'm not a doctor but with my life lessons and many years of observation, I know what I know and can help. I would like to stop the suffering that these inmates have and the only way is to talk about forgiveness. Let them know that all can be forgiven if they want it. I know you have a plan for each one of us and I hope that as these inmates realize that they will have positive thoughts again. All they need do is to open themselves up to you. I pray Lord that B.A will start taking control of his life through you, love always,

G.
Psalm 55:22

July 7

Father,
Praise you Lord, you are the Almighty one given to me so that I might live in Eternal Glory forever. I Father shall not forsake you, without you I am like a speck of sand that blows in the wind, never having a firm foundation. I have been reborn and made new upon your rock, you are my rock and my salvation; my everlasting love. Lord as your child I've rebelled against your word and teachings. I've taken short cuts in life and tried to hide from you like Adam did in your garden. Father God let me always remember and never forget that you are my first love and to always put you first. I know

that the Holy Spirit is with me at all times and came to me after the death of my Lord and Savior Jesus Christ. God you are the only one; three-in-one, Father, Son, and Spirit. I cry Father for my weaknesses and pray for your love and strength. Give me a blessing Lord, that I may have wisdom and understanding, make things clear to me so I can further the Kingdom. Let my heart be open to receive that understanding, wisdom, strength and love. Teach me Father do not let me be puffed up or prideful make me whole again and let me humble myself before you. Praise you Lord God! Praise you Lord Jesus! Praise your Holy Spirit! Ever your servant.

G.
Psalm 31:3

July 8

Father,
Lord how far have I come? I've come far enough to know that I finally like myself for who I really am. I know that my issues in the past have been dealt with and issues in the future will also be dealt with through forgiveness. That you have forgotten my sins Lord and given me a new day, to be taken one at a time like a recovering addict. Lord you have saved my Soul and given me your grace, I'll be OK Am I scared? Yes I'm scared because I do not know what tomorrow has in store, or what the days after will be like. I know Father I need not worry because I'm in your most capable hands, hands that are greater than mine. Lord it sometimes feels like I've been abandoned by a lot of people that at one time were called friends and I just hope that it's because they don't know what to write or questions' to ask. First I felt hurt and then realized that all of us deal with pain in different ways. I know I can't worry about anyone who has chosen to forget me. I've learned and observed that there is no one in prison that does not carry pain around with them. I know that surrendering to the demons that cause the pain is not acceptable; these demons must be dealt with to eliminate the pain. I know Lord that you can remove all pain and give instant relief for anyone who asks. Lord you are love and the light for all. I love you Lord.

G.

Daniel 9:9

July 9

Father,
Lord I got to thinking about what Paul said in Galatians 5:22, 23 Paul writes: 22. But the Holy Spirit controls our lives', he will produce this kind of fruit in us: love, joy, peace, patience, kindness, goodness, faithfulness, 23, gentleness, and self-control. Here there is no conflict with the law. When I break it down I look at how you love me is how I should love others. Lord that you have joy over me following Jesus and that I should have joy in myself because Jesus set me free. Lord that you are at peace with my acceptance of Jesus and that I should have peace knowing that I am forgiven. Lord that the kindness you have shown me is the same kindness I should show others. That the goodness you've shown for my forgiveness is how I should forgive others. Lord that you have been faithful to your word and I can be faithful in knowing that Jesus is love. Lord that you have been gentle with me in your correction that I should be gentle with others who are in need of your grace. Lord that your self-control gave me the chance to come to you through Jesus, and I should use self-control to understand that all people are not on the same path and may need time for correction. I know Lord that this is just my opinion and I hope I'm on the right track. Lord I need your guidance and love. I'll write tomorrow.

G.
Romans 8:2

July 10

Father,
Good morning Lord I started thinking about darkness and light as I was reading in the word and I would like to tell you my experience with darkness and light. When I began my journey back in April of 2004 I was placed in a cell at the County Jail. When it came time for lights out I was not expecting the light in my cell to just dim from bright white to a low amber color, there was no darkness in the cell. I found out as the days passed in County and was sent to prison that like minds must think the

same, because it's the same thing in prison. When you are incarcerated regardless of where you are in the system there is no darkness. So I find myself accepting the light of Jesus and rejecting the darkness of Satan, but in terms of incarcerated life I would like the darkness and no light when it's time for lights out. I think that would be considered irony. I know that this is done so the guards can observe the prisoners in the cell and I can understand that. I just will be thankful for that day when I'm free and be able to have darkness and no light. I Love you Lord and I'm not asking for you to turn out the lights just that you've listened to me is enough, always in your grace,

G.
Psalm 27:1

July 11

Father,
Dear Lord I'm a little upset, my commissary list was disapproved and I won't be shopping this week. The money that I had on the books when I was in Stateville has not arrived here at Hill. This means no supplies what so ever and no T.V. I really was hoping to get the T.V. so I could have more to keep me busy. I will have to wait at least two more weeks. I guess we are still bound together Lord. Lord I would hope that my having a T.V. would not take away from the time that we spend together. I like to talk and I know that you like to listen at least I hope you do. I love my Lord and I desire to gain and gather all that I can from my prayers and studies in the word. I am so on fire for you Lord and it's hard to get enough when I love this journey so much. Lord I will build my life on your rock. I will seek all that I can to make me into the person that you want me to be. I ask only to follow you and keep your way the best that I can. Lord you delivered from the pits of Hell and I owe you all of me. Thank you Lord for always being with me whether I knew it or not. I'll write tomorrow with something new I'm sure of that.

G.
2 Peter 2:9

July 12

Father,
Lord, I think of all the wonderful things that you blessed me with and I ask myself why. Why did I rebuke you Lord and go my own way. I think the word stupid would fit. I only wish that I had stopped to consider all the people I hurt by my addiction. The shame was hard to get over, and yet when I asked you to forgive me you did. I had only to ask and you gave. I thank you Lord for you generous love. I know that I could never have come to you without the blood of Jesus, your Son for me. I know now that of all the people that my actions hurt some will never forgive me and that's OK Lord. This is something that I must accept. I can only hope that these people may come to know you as I have. Lord I give these people over to your care. I will always love them as friends and family. I know that my dad, daughters and son still care about me and that's a blessing in itself. I glorify your name Lord above all others. I know Lord that I may come up short sometimes but I can always count on you to pay the bill. The greatest love I've ever know is you my precious Father. I look forward to that day when I can worship you on high. I love you dearly,

G.
John 12:28

July 13

Father,
I just want to say thanks for giving me a nice day. I had the opportunity to go to yard today and spend time making some good contacts, men who have a heart for your grace. One of the exercise yards has a huge track and I spent almost all of the time walking around this track talking to these men who have a heart of you. While walking around the track another inmate came up and asked if he could walk with us and we said no problem. When we continued our walk this inmate said that he had written some thoughts about you Lord and he would like to share these thoughts with us. I made the suggestion that tomorrow when we go out to yard to bring what he had written and we would be more than happy

to listen. So Lord we now are 4 and I hope that our little group grows. I also got the opportunity to join an empathy group where I can dialogue with other inmates who face the same problems that I had and hopefully learn from each other. I am so grateful that you are giving men all these positive things in my life I need them right now. Praise you Lord! I was down and you lifted me up, there is nothing better than that. Hallelujah. I'll write tomorrow.

G.
2 Corinthians 12:9

July 14

Father,
I had some time and I got to thinking about all the different names the men in here use, it seems they would rather be called by their handle. I know that almost all the men who I associate with call me Pops, I think that's because I'm the oldest man in the cell block. I also think that one of the reasons is that our Id's are never worn when we are in the gallery; if you lose your id they take 5 dollars out of your bank. That's not the only time they charge you for an id, you are also charged if they have to update your id because your appearance changes. For example when I shaved my head that was a new look, so when the C.O. saw that my id showed hair I was ordered to go down to I.A. and have a new id made. That cost 5 bucks, what a rip-off. Well I was talking about names; K-town, this handle lets everyone know that he lives on the upper west side of Chicago. GD that indicates that this guy is a member of the Gangster Disciples a notorious gang out of Chicago. Black this handle indicates the color of skin. One of the men is called Hip-Hop an indicator of the type of music he likes. There are countless nicknames and these are a few. Lord on a more serious note I would like to pray for the men here in the cell block that instead of playing games that they come to know you, I will do my best to help in any way I can, one inmate at a time. I love you Lord I'll write tomorrow.

G.
Matthew 11:28

July 15

Father,
WHAT IS LOVE? I think of your love; Lord you love me, John 3:16. I am to love you, Matthew 22:37. Because of your love for me I am cared for, Matthew 6:25-34. Lord you want everyone to know how much you love us, John 17:23. Lord you love everybody who hates you we must do the same, Matthew 5:43-47, Luke 6:35. Lord you seek out those who are away from you, Luke 15:4-7. We love you Lord when we obey, John 14:21, 15:10. Lord we must put you first in our hearts. Matthew 6:24. Lord you love your son Jesus, John 5:20, 10:17. Jesus Love you so shall we, John 14:21. Those who refuse Jesus are not loved by you Lord, John 5:41-44. Jesus loves us as you love us Lord, John 15:9. Jesus proved he loved us by his death on the cross, giving us eternal life. John 3:14, 15, 15:14-15. The love between you and your son gives us a blueprint in how to love others, John 17:21-26. We are to love one another, John 13:34-35. We must demonstrate love for others, Matthew 5:40-42, Matthew 10:42. We are not to love the praise of people, John 12:43. We are not to love self recognition, Matthew 23:6. We are not to love earthly belongings, Luke 6:19-31. We are to only love you, Luke 16:13. Jesus love is for everyone, Mark 10:21, John 10:11-15. Jesus wants us to love him through the good times and bad, Matthew 26:31-35. Jesus wants our love to be genuine, John 21:15-17. This is what I think is love.

G.
John 3:16

July 16

Father,
Lord I went to yard today and met up with the other guys in the little group that we have formed. The one inmate that I talked about the other day joined us and read us what he wrote. What he wrote was very inspiring, and it was exciting to know that this inmate has a heart for you. I feel that even though he is doing the work he doesn't believe what he's working through. I get the feeling that he is still having issues. It appears to me that

he can't forgive himself for what he did. He has not told us what he did but I pray someday he can. He said he told the Corrections Officer that he needs to talk to the Psychologist and that the guards are just laughing at his request. I worry for him and the problem he is having difficulty with. I hope I'll find out so that I (we) can help him through it Lord. Lord help us to help him. I love you Father with all that's within me.

G.
Psalm 46:1

July 17

Father,
Lord I would like to understand why people take their own lives. When I talked to you the last time I was talking about this one inmate who brought his writings that he had done and our group really got a lot out of them. I found out by way of the grapevine that this particular inmate committed suicide between last night and this morning. I am totally blown away. He had come to you Lord with his problem, didn't he understand that you would help him with his problem or was Satan's hold on him to great. I pray Father that this wasn't the case. Is there something that our group could have done to better make him understand that his guilt could be removed just by praying to you for forgiveness and help in relieving his pain? Lord I know that takings one's life is a sin but I still am not sure that there wouldn't be some of these poor souls with you in heaven that is a question for the ages. A question that I'm unable to answer nor even attempt to try. Lord I love you so much and I could not stand the separation from you. I know Lord that I wrestle with demons constantly and I fight the good fight I just know that someday I will overcome until that day. I have your love, until tomorrow Lord.

G.
Romans 8:35

July 18

Father,
I am angry and upset; the agony of this inmate who committed suicide could have been averted if the Correction Officer had listened to this man's plea for help. I know all he asked for was to see the psychiatrist and the C.O. dropped the ball. I found out that at some point during the night he broke his disposable razor and took the blade and slashed his wrists. He drained the blood into his property box and in the morning when his cellie woke up he saw this inmate lying on his bunk dead. The C.O. was called and then his body was removed, an investigation took place and it was ruled a suicide, case closed. I guess there is no value on a human life in here. I just think that the indifference in this place smells. Lord I pray for this young man's soul. I hope you heard his plea and saw his pain and agony. I love you Lord and I'll write tomorrow.

G.
Hebrews 10:39

July 19

Father,
I'm still getting over the last couple of days they have been rough for me. I got to thinking how important a life is and am still mad. Lord take this anger from me and give me peace with this man's death. I think about my own mortality and I must try to remain health and not get sick. There is no telling when an inmate might get aid and at my age I do not need this type of drama. Lord I am entrusting my health and welfare to you, keep me healthy and well for the rest of my time in prison. I only have one year and change left, keep a watchful eye. Lord I want to pray for the family of this inmate who died a few days ago. Please Lord ease their pain and grief. This is all for tonight I will write tomorrow, love you Father,

G.
Philippians 4:7

July 20

Father,

I prayed to you Lord and my mind is at ease today, thank you Father. I know now that everything that happens for a reason and it's not my job to understand why, so I'll let this incident go. I will be starting my empathy group tomorrow and I'm sure that I'll get an opportunity to take with the psychotherapist at group. I'm curious to see how many others are in this group, and whether it will be helpful in my recovery. I hope you don't have a problem with playing cards with some of the other inmates, they asked I accepted and there is no gambling just fun. I am hoping to stay a little involved while I'm here, this will give me another outlet to pass the time. My cellmate is rapping his so called songs out the chuck hole and it's driving me nuts. I can't stand all the hate and anger that these songs have. I pray that someday he comes to understand that this world is better off with love then with hate. It was a good afternoon and lunch was not bad today. We had fried chicken and cold French fries. I'm going to rest up before the card game later. I hope I can remember how to play spades and not embarrasses myself. I feel a little more accepted in here and things are running a lot smoother. Lord may I ever put you first in my life and not forget you when the good times take place. I will let you know how things went.

G.
Proverbs 15:1

July 21

Father,

I had my first session with the psychotherapist today and I had the opportunity to meet others who have the need to deal with their addictions and crimes that they committed. We all introduced ourselves and told the others what we did and then started to discuss how the group would be run. Dr. P seems like an understanding man and it appears that this group might be a lot of help for all of us. There are seven in the group and it will be interesting to see how many will show up next week. One of the benefits of the group is that I get the opportunity to be out of my cell more and extra hour each week thank you Lord. One of the men in the group said that he was drunk and attacked his wife and raped her, and that he fled the scene and jumped off a bridge into the Chicago River. He said he was trying to commit suicide, but the cops fished him out before that could happen. I just will never understand about suicide. I don't know the minds of these men who try to kill themselves but I do know Lord that there is a great need to come to you. I hope that I'm able to interject my thoughts on how important it is to have you in their lives. Dr. P wants us to decide what type of format we want to use in these sessions. Lord this gives me something to pray for. I pray that we decide to use the most helpful format he has so that we can have a greater understanding of our problems and the ones we will face on the outside. I'll write tomorrow.

G.
Psalm 71:5

July 22

Father,
Today is Friday I know we will have Mac & Cheese along with our fish, thank you Lord for the Catholics. Well it's time to get ready for the weekend, got to see if someone on the gallery has a good book that I can read, taking a break from your word Lord, I hope you don't mind. Except for chow and dayrooms there is literally no movement. All other facilities are shutdown. So this makes for a very slow time. I am hoping to get my T.V. next week; that would be a great help. I heard that the terrorist stuck the U.K. or at least tried to. I pray that these terrorist weren't successful. I could really enjoy watching the Cubs play if I had a stupid T.V. I'm hoping that I'll be able to get it at commissary next week, my money is on the books and I'm good too go. I've been playing cards with a group of guys when we have dayroom privileges and that's been a lot of fun, my skills are coming back. I should also know if my school request has been approved if so then I get to move to the school unit and there you get even more movement. Well it's almost time to go to the yard. I think that we have the yard with the baseball field in it, if so then there are some picnic tables and benches to

sit down on. I had thought about playing ball but I felt to avoid injury I'd let the young men enjoy the game, better safe than sorry. So far you have protected me from any sickness or injuries and I thank you Lord for that blessing. Time to go Father, I'll write later.

G.
Ezekiel 34:26

July 23

Father,
Good afternoon Lord well I got a good book to read for this weekend it's a book by James Patterson call "Roses are Red" I enjoy James Patterson a lot especially the series of books with Alex Cross. I figure that I will have this book done before Monday. Lord I have not forgotten your word Lord and I'm still working in Revelations and Romans. Before I was sent to prison I read a series of books by Jerry Jenkins & Tim Lahaye; called "Left behind," the series had 12 books and it gave an account of what might happen if the Lord called his people home and those who were nonbelievers were left behind and given the opportunity to chose Christ or the new world order. The books were mesmerizing and I read all of them. When I started to study Revelation I realized how well these books pretty much mirrored Revelation, very chilling. I am just thankful Lord that I won't be left behind if this happens in my life time and by all indications we seem to be living close to the end times. I know that a while back I was asking about the seven churches that John talks about in Revelation and it is so fantastic how these seven churches in Revelation mirrors all of the different church and denominations that we have today. Lord may I always take the words that you have placed upon my heart and come to a greater understanding each day. I know that you love is so great that there is really no need for anything else. Tomorrow's Sunday and I'll talk to you.

G.
Proverbs 10:12

July 24

Father,
I thought I'd give you a rundown on today events. Got up for dayroom, played cards with the guys won most of the spade games we played. Went to chow and had soy meat and noodle casserole total crap so I gave it away for a Ramon noodle later. Came back from chow and have spent the next 6 hours reading in your word and reading the novel I started yesterday. I found out that the Cubs have taken 2 in a row from St. Louis and that's always a good thing. I think that still leaves them behind the Cards by about 11 games, not a very good year for Dusty Baker and company, I say get rid of Baker and find a new manager for next year. I'm hoping that this week I'll get my T.V. so I'll be able to watch a lot of the Cubs games on Superstation WGN. I went to chow for dinner and we had baked chicken and cold scalloped potatoes at least it was better than lunch. Had dayroom from 7:30 until 9:00 and just played cards, had a good time winning. It's now 10 P.M. and about time to hit the hay. Today was quiet and uneventful, thank you for this day, I'll write tomorrow Father.

G.
Ephesians 2:14

July 25

Father,
Good evening Lord, I just want to say I'm very disappointed right now. The gallery is on lockdown and this will probably be about a week. I guess from what the porter told me there was a fight between two inmates walking to chow and the tower guard fired warning shots to stop the fighting. The two inmates were taken to segregation, and then the prison was placed on lockdown. With this unfortunate event I can't go to my empathy group, I miss commissary on Thursday and there is no telling when we will be off lockdown. I know that the routine is for the C.O. to search every cell in the prison and strip search all the prisoners, I am sure glad I lost my shyness a year ago. I am totally OK with this as long as I have your work to keep me busy and my novels. One of the other disappointing parts of this

lockdown is the food get a little lousy. This will bring a lot of cold cuts and I am not fond of that. I guess I have no choice in the matter I'm just thankful that I have some Ramen noodles for back-up. I am sure glad that the fight didn't happen in the chow group that I was in. I think that the rifle being fired would have shaken me up a lot. I am also glad that I took a shower earlier I was going to take one tonight, thank you Jesus! This is so familiar, and so unnecessary to have lockdowns like this. I know this means that the C.O. have to deliver the food to the inmates and that means they have to earn their pay for a change. Lord I just pray that things go smoothly and there isn't too much destruction when our cell is searched later this week. I have to listen to my cellmate and his rap lyrics for the next week and I don't have my ear plugs yet. Lord I know that I'm complaining and again I'm sorry this is just the human nature side of me coming out. I get tired of the injustice that is very prevalent here in prison. I get tired of seeing the whole prison population punished by the mistakes of two inmates. I love you Father I will write tomorrow.

G.
Psalm 63:3

July 26

Father,
Today is the first full day of lockdown and the kite lines are flying around the gallery and everyone is getting their supplies of cigs from the guys that have. I am fortunate that I have a good enough supply and I won't have to run a line to anyone for cigs. I know that you can get a ticket and loose privileges like no yard for a couple of weeks or worse yet lose of commissary privileges.I think that privilege is not worth risking something illegal in the rules. On to another topic, I figured out the A.B.C.'s of forgiveness. A. Admit you sins, B. Believe in Jesus, and C. Confess our sins to you Lord. Lord it says in Luke 18:1 that we must pray constantly, I would ask you this: does this mean when we are praying for something that we need done or does this mean all the time? In looking at the passages in Luke 18 it seems that Jesus is saying that when we are praying for something to continue is to invite you Lord to answer? I have heard people say that we need to pray all the time even when we don't have a need or want something from you. I know that there are times when I see a

sunset that I give thanks for your great universe, and when I'm nearly in an accident I give thanks for your protection. I feel that there are prayers of thanks to be said all the time. I guess this is one of those questions that will keep me thinking all the time. Well enough talk and now Lord as I pray, I ask that you protect me from any harm or danger that might come my way here in prison. I love you Lord.

G.
Luke 18:1

July 27

Father,
Good morning Lord its day two of this lockdown and all is going just the way I thought. The meals are much worse than at the chow hall. There is less to eat and the meals are icy cold. I guess I shouldn't complain these meals are still better than Stateville. I was thinking about my animals that I had when I was at home. I had two beautiful German Shepherd Mix dogs, Caesar and Marco. Caesar was big and proud, Marco was small and dumb and I cared a lot about them. I have not heard what happen to them since I last saw them on April 29th of 2004. I also had two cats Misty and Taz. Misty was my soon to be ex-wife's cat and Taz was wacko and so much fun. My question is where are they now? I might never know. Lord I hope these pets are being taken care of and are in good health. I think it's amazing the things that you think about at any time. I wonder why I thought of them at this moment when I haven't thought about them for over a year. I guess my mind just has a lot of extra time to use while in prison. Lord I haven't got much to write about today so I'll write tomorrow. I pray for my animal and their care that you provided for them.

G.
Luke 2:4

July 28

Father,

Good day to you Lord it's day three and no news yet as to when the lockdown will be over. My cellmate is driving me nuts with all the rap music he is creating, if I can call it that. He says he's going to start up a studio when he gets out in a little while. I have a feeling that the C.O. get bored when there is a lockdown they literally only have to feed the animals three times a day, and check the cells once an hour if that. This has to give the C.O. a rest also from the daily routine and garbage that goes on daily when the prison isn't on lockdown. Today would have been commissary day if we weren't on lockdown. There is disappointment in knowing I've had money on the books since Dec. of 2004 and my plans to get a T.V. have been delayed for over 7 months, this is getting old, so am I. I'll have to wait until Aug. 11th to try again. I just wonder Father if you might be the one telling me to wait you still have things for me to know. I accept your will Lord and wait upon your timing. From what the C.O. says we will probably be off lockdown this coming Monday the 1st of Aug. I can only hope. One of the things that I really appreciate is taking a shower; birdbaths just don't do the trick. Lord I want to pray that we get off lockdown soon to ease the tension that is building up because of the confinement to our cells. I pray that I can stand the annoyances of my cellmates rap crap for a little while longer. I'm going to try and get moved to one of the other cells if possible so I don't have to listen to the ugliness of this so called music he is writing; help me Lord with a positive solution. Father I love you so much and I thank you for holding things together for me, as always.

G.

Psalm 46:1, 2

July 29

Father,
Day four and what am I looking for, relief, relief, and relief. The weather is getting hotter and you can tell by the warmth in the cells. There is no air moving at all and what air conditioning there is doesn't bring much relief. I heard from the C.O. that the cell searches have started in 1 house and I'm in 4 house so it looks like Monday. I give you all the glory Father for keeping me in a positive frame of mind. I think having spent 6 months is segregation at Stateville makes this transition a lot easier than never having been isolated before. My cellmate is still driving me crazy with his rap music, and I can't wait to get away from this stuff. I find it hard to remember what day it is so I made up a make shift calendar so I'll at least know the day. Today is fish Friday so at least I'll have one descent meal. It's been almost a year that I've been in prison and I wish no one would ever have to be imprisoned ever; this is not the place for anyone to be. The prison system is one of protection for the people and punishment for the offender. When I was on the outside some people said that the prisons seemed to be like a country club well I can relate to them that it is not and there is no fun here at all. I pray Father that no one ever has to suffer the humility of being in a cage for any length of time. I know now how important freedom is and have come to the conclusion that I'm not coming back. Lord please work with me and mold me into the right person you want me to be. I want to serve you in any way possible. Lord please help me to start a new life in Christ and give me your peace and understanding. I love you Lord.

G.
1 Peter 2:20

July 30

Father,
Today is day five and everyone is looking towards Monday, I hope the rumors are true. I looked at myself in our stainless steel mirror and either the mirror is distorted or I am looking real old. I can see why I'm called Pops, I look like one. I think one of the things I need to do when we have movement again is schedule a hair cut I look like Charles Manson my hair is long and straggly and very messed up. I also have lost some more weight and I must be down in the 170's if so that would mean I've lost 60 lbs. in a year's time. I never thought that this would be the diet I needed to lose weight. I understand from the C.O. that the search of 2 house is almost complete and that would mean that we would get our shakedown on Sunday. I just pray that all goes well on Sunday and nothing stupid occurs. I really am not very fond of strip-searches. Lord I just am so caught up in your Word; I think that Paul was the most effective minister you have in the word. I know that you turned an accuser of Christians into an aggressive follow of Christ and I just pray that you work in me so I may live for you and the Kingdom. Father you know my heart and love for you. I would love your blessing to do your work from this day forward, as always tomorrow.

G.
1 Thessalonians 3:1

July 31

Father,
Lord its day 6 and I understand that 3 house is finished and that today is our day to be shaken down. I pray Lord that everything goes OK in the house and that there are no problems and then maybe tomorrow we will be off lockdown. I know that it's coming because we were fed lunch already and its only 10 A.M. I am assuming that the C.O.'s will be here soon. I know that today is your given day and I realize that a prison is on their time not yours so let the shakedown begin. Things are still pretty warm in here and there seems to be no relief from the heat, Lord I pray for a break in

the weather and a cool down will come. Guess what, here comes the C.O.'s to shake us down. I see that there are about 20 C.O.'s and this shouldn't take too long, at least I hope this is the case. Lord I'll let you know how things went in about 1 hour. I'm back and the shakedown is over. I think it went OK Our cell is a mess but then that's the way it always is with a shakedown. This was a complete shakedown including a strip search and being removed from the cell in cuffs and cuffed to the railings outside the cell until the inspection is finished. I know that nothing was found out of order in our cell and it looks like the gallery came out OK at least no one was taken away to segregation, and that is always a good sign. Lord thank you for an uneventful search this should mean that we will get off lockdown tomorrow. I love you Lord and will write tomorrow, as always,

G.
Psalm 145:18

August 1

Father,

Good afternoon Lord we came off lockdown just in time to go for lunch. I am so glad I needed a break from my cellmate, thank you Jesus! Went to lunch and we were served a breakfast type meal. Scrambled eggs, hash browns, biscuits and soy sausage gravy, and I can't forget the only thing that can't get messed up a banana. This was one of the better meals I've had while being here. Here again Lord I have learned a lot about the human condition. It is very difficult to keep two seemingly strangers together especially from entirely different backgrounds and the adjustment period could get tense. I know for my part I stayed quiet a lot and read. Thank you for the Bible I have used this lockdown to get further into who you are and all that you did and who I am and all I will do for you for the rest of my life and I thank you for that. I know one thing I'm going to do is request to transfer to another cell I just hope that will happen I need a break from all this rap crap he's been spouting while on lockdown. We are back on a dayroom schedule and I've got dayroom this evening. I'll get a chance to catch up on all the news and play some cards. Lord I pray that you give me some help in getting moved to another cell with someone who isn't as abrasive in his actions and talk, I need this Father, I need this bad. I love you Lord and pray that you are here for me. I'll write tomorrow.

G.

Colossians 3:8

August 2

Father,
Good afternoon, well things have gotten settled down now and this is a good thing. I got my pass to go to empathy group tomorrow so everything is coming together. I am still waiting for an answer on getting into school and I hope I get a response soon; this would be a great blessing. I know if I can get into school and take some courses I can reduce my time and get out sooner than October of next year. Lord I pray for a positive resolution and that I'm able to go to school, and I wait on your timing. Lord I was blown away by what Isaiah 40:6-8. A voice said "shout!" I asked, "What should I shout?" "Shout that people are like the grass that dies away. Their beauty fades as quickly as the beauty of flowers in the field. The grass withers and the flowers fade beneath the breath of the Lord. And so it is with people. The grass withers and the flowers fade, but the word of God lives forever." I feel so great knowing that your Word is forever and true. That you gave your instructions for me to follow and insight though you word that gives me this eternal life. I thank you Lord for this encouraging passage of scripture. I also enjoy the facts in Isaiah that tells of a future King, a King for the ages bringing life to those that choose to follow this precious King. Isaiah predicted Jesus close to 700 years before his birth. Wow! Lord I know that many times I have fallen short, that your ways were not my ways and now I realize that I've been doing things the wrong way, I thank you for the correction. I praise you Father! Well it's a good day and I'll take it, will write tomorrow.

G.
Isaiah 40:6

August 3

Father,
There is something to be said about getting together with other men that are in the same situation that I was in. The empathy group seems to be very positive 8 out of the group of 9 participated and in this first real session I was able to come to the realization that what I did was wrong but others have done worse. I have the freedom in are group to talk openly

and freely about what I did and what happened in my life that may have contributed to my offending. I know that this is the first time I ever told anyone that I was molested when I was 13, and being able to tell someone has been a huge relief a load off my shoulder, besides you Lord my secret was unknown, I am so relieved that this sad part of my life that had been suppressed for over 40 years is out in the open. Thank you Lord for teaching me not to be afraid and that you are with me always and I need not be afraid, for nothing can hurt me ever again with you standing by my side. I wish that the group was a little longer than an hour. I'll take what I can get and be happy for with what I can get. The weather is not as bad as it has been and there is a nice breeze coming in the window of the cell and I thank you for this relief. From what I'm hearing we might go to store next Monday instead of next Thursday this would be a huge blessing, I pray Lord that this is the case. Lord you are my Savior and I owe my life to you, praise you Jesus. I'll write tomorrow Father.

G.
2 Peter 1:12

August 4

Father,
Blessing and honor to you Lord Praise your Holy name. I was working in Isaiah again today and got to thinking. I know that you Love Israel so much and that these people became hardened to your will, why was that? Why did they turn away from your mercy and love? I know Lord that you know everything from the beginning that you have known us before we were born, what was it that change the way people of Israel thought? Did the people of Israel turn to sin because they got tired of you Lord? I know that you promised these people that you would always be with them but they forgot you Lord, you were their first love and they turned away. I look at the world today and it is less religious then in the days of Isaiah and yet you still give us grace and mercy. Lord you gave us a Savior in your Son Jesus which even made it easier for us to come closer to you and yet there is a mentality that you only exist when you are needed. I know that you are aware of everything and I know that we can't hide, yet we still feel that we can get away with our immoral acts without being accountable. Lord when

did we become so arrogant that you were left out of any of our decisions? I know that you gave us free will to decide our lives and give us the chance to turn to you Lord and that is a blessing, I just don't understand why so many turn away. Who can we blame Lord? Lord you promise comfort, deliverance and restoration. Comfort in knowing that we can always turn to you. Deliverance from our sins so we can have a direct line to you and restoration of our lives to live for your Eternal Kingdom all in the name of Jesus how wonderful is that. I just thank you Lord for you mercy and kindness. Jesus died so I and all people who believe can live with you forever; that's so great, I thank you Father. I will write tomorrow Father.

G.

Isaiah 5:25

August 5

Father,

Glory and honor and blessings to you Son Jesus. Lord for all that you are or ever will be I thank you. Forgive me Lord for any sins I've committed since my last confession forgive me for my wrong thoughts and words that I've used. Lord if I offended you I'm sorry. Humble me Lord that if I have the opportunity to introduce you to someone in need that you give me the right words to say. Let what comes out of my mouth be from you Lord and to give you the glory. Lord let "The Spirit" work in me to help further the Kingdom. Lord thank you for being my guide in the wilderness as I journey towards your Kingdom, you are the light beacon in the storms of my life. I know that I am wanting and I still have much to learn, I also know that you are there for me and it's a warm and wonderful feeling knowing that. I pray for the other men on the gallery that you ease their hearts and minds and make them strong as they go through these tough times here in prison that they might come to you Lord for comfort. I know Lord that although we are still prisoners of the system we have our freedom in your blessed Son Jesus. Clean us up Lord and make use of us as we ever walk down your path to eternity. Father I love you and always want to serve you. Lord I will write tomorrow, love you.

G.

Galatians 3:2

August 6

Father,

I had a good meal last night it was fried Catfish fillets and Macaroni & Cheese so all in all it was pretty good. I was up for breakfast this morning and got up at 4:30 am I crazy or what. We had scrambled powder eggs, turkey sausage, and a banana so at least I won't feel hungry today. I hope I get some mail today it's been awhile so Lord I pray for mail. I've been studying in Isaiah and I still am in awe of the prediction of Jesus being born over 600 years later, totally awesome. Lord I would ask you to guide me in what is planned for my life. I want to serve you the best way I can. I know Lord that I will soon be 57 and I've messed around most of my life I'm through running I'm too old for that; so I'm yours Lord do with me what you will. I know that you have a track record of using people to do your work. Moses was in his 70's when he lead the people out of Egypt. Noah was around 460's old and he sailed an ark. Sarah was in her 90's when she gave birth to Isaac so you used them now please use me Lord I want so much to spend my life serving you. Father tomorrow is your day and may I rest in the peace and knowledge that you are always there for me. I thank you Lord.

G.

Psalm 92:14

August 7

Father,
I am using Sunday to read and enjoy Psalms, they are so beautiful and very magical I just love them so much. I feel peace and calm, and a can relate to David in the suffering he went through and the questioning of his faith. I know that when we are weak we start to waffle in our faith. I know that David overcame his fear and just trusted in you. I have a kinship with David. Lord I just thank you for rescuing me from my downward spiral. I left your ways and all I got was a lot of trouble. In the course of my life I've been married three times and each time I thought that the grass was greener on the other side of the mountain. I have lost everything that I owned and had gained nothing. There was temporary gain but nothing permanent. I know Lord that in losing everything I gain you Father and your Son my brother Jesus! I played the game of life extremely well and my pride and haughtiness became my undoing. I have nothing if I don't have you Lord. I know that with you no army can defeat me that the battle for my soul has been won and I thank you Lord. Lord you are my strength, my rock and my fortress, I find comfort in your presents and am not afraid of today, tomorrow or any day after. I just totally love you. Lord again I say thank you. Lord I'll write tomorrow. I pray for all the lost souls here in prison, that they might seek you out and know there is hope, as always,

G.
Psalm 96:1-3

August 8

Father,
Lord I'm a little down today our shopping day has been moved back to Thursday so I will have to wait a few days longer. I am so looking forward to getting my T.V. especially to help break up the humdrum of my day. It would be nice to take a break from reading. I have to laugh when I think of the glasses I'm wearing they are huge and weigh a ton, they serve the purpose and for that I'm thankful. I heard that the College that's been doing the classes here has decided to pull out and go in a different direction, so I'll have to wait for the new College to get on board, one more delay, oh well everything in your

time. I also put in a request for a switch in cells because of the friction that has developed between me and my cellmate. I hope that my beliefs give me a leg up on getting a different cellie. Tomorrow would have been my mom and dads' 58th wedding anniversary had my mom lived that long, but that was not to be. I think about her often and you took her so young, I was angry Lord but I know she's in a better place. You are a wonderful God and I won't know why she came to you earlier than a person normally lives but I know you have your reasons. Lord I pray that your brightness shines over my mom and her gaiety keeps you smiling. I will write tomorrow.

G.
Psalm 16:11

August 9

Father,
I got some mail Lord and my daughter says that everyone is doing fine, she wants me to call and talk to her mother, and she says that my youngest daughter H. is going to get married next month and that she and J. are finally going to do it, good for them. I can only guess what her mother wants to talk to me about and I don't think I could talk my daughter out of marrying J. nor would I want to. She's over 21 and has two boys who need a father and J. has always been kind to them and they might be able to make it work. I know this is one phone call where I will just have to listen to their mothers ranting and raving oh well life goes on. Lord I ask that you stand in the middle and intercede in the discussion that will take place when I call the girls' mother tonight. I know Lord that their mother is a caring person but she also is always sticking her nose into where it doesn't belong. I guess she has nothing better to do. I think that's one of the big reasons I left their mother I couldn't deal with her being such a busybody. I just stopped caring about what she did and gave up. Lord I pray that there is peace in our conversation. I'll write you tomorrow and give you my report. Love you Lord.

G.
Proverbs 24:5

August 10

Father,
Good afternoon Lord it was an interesting night yesterday. I called my ex-wife last night to see what she wanted to talk to me about and as expected it was about my daughter getting married next month. I have no idea what I can do from in here nor would I do anything to derail my daughters' marriage to J. I will talk to my daughter and congratulate her and I will not take sides with her mother. I know that there comes a point when I as a parent must let go of control over my children and let them go their own way. I think that this is the time; in fact I know it is Father. I think it is much easier doing this when I'm in prison because my circumstances don't give me much choice. Father tomorrow is the day; and I'm looking forward to getting my T.V. One promise I will make Lord is that I'll give you the first hour of my day. I will remember to put you first. Lord I'm not a perfect person and I try to live everyday for you, continue to feed me your Word. Lord give me the things I need to serve your Kingdom. Father I pray for H. & J. that their union be blessed by you and that it last for all eternity. I give them over to you Lord to watch over and protect them. I know that H.'s kids did a father influence and that J. will be a good father to my grandsons so I thank you Lord for you love and caring. I will talk tomorrow after I get to commissary. I love you Father.

G.
Colossians 1:11

August 11

Father,
Hallelujah Lord I got my T.V. and at a discount. I went to commissary today and stocked up on supplies and if I had known that my T.V. was going to be $40.00 cheaper I would have been able to get more food stuff. I'll just have extra to spend the next time I go to commissary. I got the set all hooked up and it's working fine. I guess I didn't realize how small these sets would be. This T.V. is only 12" and takes up very little space. I am glad I have decent eye sight or I would be in big trouble. Lord it has been

an adventure trying to get this T.V. And it's only taken 8 months, in prison that seems like an eternity. Lord I give a prayer of thanks to not only you but the family who all contributed to this purchase. I will remember my promise to give you the first hour of my day. I love you Lord and you are first in my life. I went to my empathy group and got to know the men in our group a little better. One of the group members talked about being drunk and going home and forcing himself on his wife and after he was done he was so remorseful he tried to commit suicide by jumping off a bridge. He says that he was rescued by the police and fire dept. and then his wife filed rape charges against him. T. is doing 10 years and he seems to be doing it OK I'm glad Lord that he didn't succeed; no one should surrender their life by suicide. I know that as our group grows in trust that greater understanding will come of what we did and how to succeed in our life outside the box we're in now. Lord I thank you for this group and may I gather more information to help me when I get out. Lord I'll write tomorrow.

G.
2 Corinthians 4:12

August 12

Father,
Blessings, love and adoration to you my Lord. Great is your glory, praise you Jesus for the love you showed to me from the cross. Forgive me Father for the sins I have committed over the course of my life. I adore you Lord. I thank you for all that you have given me over the years, I surely wasn't worthy and yet you gave me all sorts of blessing. It was I who abused what I was given, forgive me for my evil ways; forgive me for the illegal things I did to land me in prison. I was lead into despair and you raised me up out of the ashes and I thank you Father. Create in me a new person dedicated to your glory Jesus. I want to win souls for you my Lord so let it happen. I pray Father for the prisoners that they see the error of their ways and repent. I pray that they be given a new life one filled and dedicated to you Lord. I pray that the Corrections Officers are kept save in the performance of their duties. Let me have a greater understanding of

the men here and what their needs are. I am but a humble servant doing the Masters work. I thank you again Jesus for your sacrifice at Calvary. The greatest gift is love and you gave that to me. I love you Father and will write tomorrow.

G.
Romans 12:2

August 13

Father,
Good afternoon Lord. Today has been very quiet there has been absolutely nothing going on. Played some pinochle this morning and that was a lot of fun. The last time I played pinochle was in 2004. It was a lot of fun. It brought back memories of a happier time, sitting around the table with my wife and neighbors J. & M. I remember that I never played with my wife and usually J. would play with her just to keep peace in the family. I know that if I played as her teammate we would have arguments later and I don't like hassles. I know that she's good but it's better to keep harmony in the family. Well I'm getting off the subject, I have made some acquaintances and D.J. knows how to play so it was a fun time. Since I got back to my cell my cellie has been rapping at the chuckhole. I am so tired of this, I get disgusted with the foul language and hate that he spits out. I had a break though went to chow and spent time eating a soy burger and cold soggy fries. I hope that my request to get moved is approved and hope that I get a new and decent cellie. I will get an opportunity to watch the Cubs play St. Louis this afternoon. I hope they can pull out a win against the Cards. I hope the game is played they said on the pregame that is a little overcast. I thank you Lord for getting the T.V., it helped that it was $40.00 cheaper. I am glad I have an outlet when I get bored. Lord I love you and will write tomorrow, as always,

G.
Psalm 147:6

August 14

Father,

Good afternoon Father I just had an interesting conversation with one of the inmates about all the gang members here at Hill. There are several gang members here but there are only a few that make a difference. The biggest group is the G.D. with is the Gangster Disciples. This is the largest gang in the City of Chicago. This gang is mostly black and their activities are basically drugs and prostitution with a little arms dealing thrown in for good measure. Most of the members have a G.D. tattoo on their neck or torso to let others know that they are a member. There are a lot of Latin Kings here also this is another large gang from Chicago consisting mainly of Latino and Hispanics. Lord the only reason I'm talking about this is the fact that these gangs use "Almighty" in front of their gang names. I find this ironic slandering your name especially since you are about love and these gangs are about hate, why they do this I don't know I think it's about power. Talking about power brings me to the third gang. The Aryan Brotherhood and this is the gang that scares me the most. The gang was formed to protect white prisoners from blacks and has evolved into a white-supremacy group with the sole intent of eliminate the black race. Lord this is the type of hate that can destroy nations. When I see these guys walking around with a Swastika tattoo is makes me cringe. I know that our country allows freedoms that no other country does and I think that this was good at one time but this freedom has led to so many power hungry, and hate groups and that's scary. I am so ashamed that these white-supremacy groups feel they represent a majority of whites who hate blacks. Lord I'm just rambling now and I don't know if I'm even making sense, I think I'll drop this subject. Lord the Cubs lost yesterday and maybe they'll win today. Let me praise you Lord and thank you for my life. I'll write tomorrow.

G.

Proverbs 4:14

August 15

Father,

Good evening Lord, well the Cubs beat the Cards yesterday and that's a good thing. Went to yard today and walked around the track with my Christian brothers. This is the first time I've been out since the lockdown. I needed a break from the gallery, things seem to be getting a little tense and there could be something going down in here. Lord I just hope and pray that there is peace I don't want to be locked down again. Lord I just want to thank you for Psalms. I was reading in 139: 1-6 and there is so much love in these Psalms. Lord you examine my heart and know everything about me. You know when I sit down or stand-up, you know my every thought when far away. You chart the path ahead of me and tell me were to stop and rest, every moment you know where I am. You know what I'm going to say even before I say it, Lord. You both precede and follow me. You place your hand of blessing upon my head. Such knowledge is too wonderful for me, too great for me to know. These words are so beautiful, that even if I'm not doing the right thing you still are with me, even when I forget you; you still love me and always have. I am so blessed in your love it makes me want to cry, not out of sadness but out of love. I thank you Father for your compassion. I will write tomorrow,

G.

Psalm 139:1-6

August 16

Father,

I am so enjoying Psalms Lord and in studying them I find a wonderful blueprint for my life. Psalms 27:4-12. The one thing I ask of the Lord, the thing I seek the most is to live in the house of the Lord all the days of my life delighting in your perfection and meditating in your Holy temple. For he will conceal me there when trouble comes; he will hide me in his sanctuary. He will place me out of reach on a hard rock. Then I will hold my head high, above my enemies that surround me. Listen to my plea Oh! Lord be merciful and answer me. My heart has heard you say "come and talk with me." And my heart responds. "Lord I'm coming." Do not hide yourself from me. Do not reject your servant in anger. You have always been my helper don't leave me now; don't abandon me. Oh God of my salvation! Even if my father and mother abandon me the Lord will hold me close. Teach me how to live Oh Lord! Lead me along the path of honesty, for my enemy is waiting for me to fall. Do not let me fall into their hands for they accuse me of things I've never done and breathe out violence against me. Yet I am confident that I will see the Lord's goodness while I'm here in the land of the living. Lord I know that when I go through trials and tribulation that you will always be there for me as you have all my life, when others attack or abandon me you will not. I thank you Lord through David's struggles showing me how to appreciate your blessings and love. I'll write tomorrow, as always.

G.

Psalm 27:4-12

August 17

Father,
I wrote down after my studies what is a Christian life. A Christian life is not a paved road to wealth and ease, being a Christian is work. In my life I may suffer, be ridiculed and persecuted for my belief. I must focus on the good Lord that you bring out of my failings. I know it will take work for me to follow you and at times that work will be hard for me to do, yet you will be with me. I know that there may be a time where I may have to surrender my life for my belief. I'm ready! I know that when I fail I can come to you and all will be forgiven and forgotten and I will have to let go of my failing. I know Lord that my position on being a Christian is not a popular choice in today's society; that it's not politically correct yet it is the correct view. I can obtain victory over sin and temptation through faith in Jesus and not by any of my own efforts. I know that faith is a gift from God given to me by Jesus sacrifice at Calvary. I know that growing in faith is a daily process, and a constant renewal of faith keeps me on the right path. I know that through prayer I can gain a greater understanding of you Lord and the things that take place around me. All I can say is thank you Lord, I will right tomorrow.

G.

Matthew 21:21

August 18

Father,
Lord I must turn away from sin and turn towards you. I must choose to live a moral life. I need to have a personal relationship with you. I need to remove all sin and trust that you'll guide me. In preparing for Jesus return I must focus on him. I need to always find time to read your word. I have to let you lead me in the right direction. I have a yearning for a new life, through that new life help me avoid disaster and overcome the weaknesses I have. I am committed to follow your ways not mine. I will follow and trust in Christ turning from sin and act on what was presented me through the Gospel. I need to share with those who don't know about your love and let you give me the words to say. Lord let me ever stay connected with you give me the strength to change my life. Lord you have put me through the fire and I came out a little singed but not burnt. Lord I ask for your blessing in whatever I do to further your kingdom. Lord you are my first love ever since that blessed day in February and I thank you for saving me, as always.

G.
Romans 7:4

August 19

Father,
Good morning Lord, as the old expression goes "Thank God it's Friday" and I truly mean that. One of the few meals that the facility doesn't mess up to much is the fish meal, and I thank you for that. Today seems like a good day to go to yard. The Cubs game isn't on until later. This could turn out to be a pretty descent day. Lord I am so happy that I have you in my corner. I just worry that along the way I might fail you; and that would break my heart. I have feelings inside that are deep rooted and demons attack me all the time help me to become an over comer, and keep me on the path towards your Kingdom. I still haven't heard who will be coming in to offer college courses I hope it's soon though I need to get some good time so I will be able to get out sooner than October of next year. I year

ago around this time I got my first experiences of prison life. Wow I've been in prison just over a year; I hope that if I can get some school good-time I'll get out this time next year. Lord I pray that the school opens up again and I will be able to take class to get good-time. Lord I know that everything is in your time and I'm not even mad about the 121 days I lost when I was taken from Mt. Sterling and sent to Stateville. I just pray for a little help Lord I think I'm ready. Lord you are my Alpha and Omega; the first and last. I'm looking forward to Monday it's my 57th birthday and maybe I'll get some mail. Lord I'll talk tomorrow.

G.
Proverbs 4:1-3

August 20

Father,
Good afternoon Lord, good news from the baseball world the Cubs beat Colorado, in Colorado. Yesterday was a pretty good day everything I said would happen came to pass. I had some good food, had a good time at yard and spent time working in Psalms. Lord as I looked at the trees by the banks of the river that passes by this prison. I longed for the day when I might be able to see your beauty without the fence and razor wire staring back at me; a chilling reminder that I am not free. I have been in prison for over a year and in that time there I have seen the horror of human beings being turned into animals. I doubt that any of the prisoners started out with a need to be in prison. I know that Satan grabbed hold of them and even me. I know that the only way back is to put my faith in you, in the grace that you've given me through your Son Jesus. I thank you so much. In Psalms 24 your blueprint was clear that to stand in your Kingdom the hands and hearts must be pure, truly a difficult task for anyone; even a King as exalted as David. You gave all of us a better plan through Jesus, praise you Lord I have a chance to be in the Kingdom. I long for your blessing and to be in your presents sing to your glory. I know that my day will eventually come when I can breathe fresh air and see you beauty unobstructed by fences and wire and that there is a brighter day or days to come. Lord you have a perfect plan and I want to be included in this plan.

Lord all I need is the opportunity to show you. You knew me before I was born and you know my future. Please let that future include me. Well I'll write tomorrow, as always,

G.
Psalm 24

August 21

Father,
Good afternoon Lord this is the day that you made I will rejoice in it. I was contemplating time this morning and found it interesting that although I or my cellie don't have a watch we can still tell the approximate time of the day it is. I know that when the door clicks open in the morning for chow it's between 4 and 5:30 A.M. It makes sense to have breakfast this early especially since there is so much to do. I personally think 7-9:30 would be a better time for breakfast that's just me. The next indicator of time is when the door clicks for the second time this is when we are given time out of our cell for dayroom this means its 9:30 and we have an hour and ½ to spend outside our cell. I could go on but you know how things work and I'm just rambling again. I pray Lord that peace continues to abound here on the gallery. There are some factions that would like nothing better than to create problems for themselves and others here in this cell block. I will have the opportunity to see my fellow Christian brothers at yard this afternoon and spend time with you. I am not a big fan of walking but its good exercise and I need to keep my figure in good shape besides its healthy for me. I think that when I get out I might write a book, I don't know if it would be a best seller but it might be of interest to some people about life in prison. I will write tomorrow it's almost time for yard. Thank you for listening Lord.

G.
2 Corinthians 6:8

August 22

Father,

Good evening Father, today was a great day I turned 57, I feel like 70. I shouldn't complain on my birthday however this isn't where I thought I'd be spending this or any other birthdays. The day wasn't so bad though I received several birthday cards and I got some novels to read, and money put on my account. I know that there are still family who love and care about me. I thank you Lord for touching their hearts. I saw the menu for today and I was happy to see chicken on the menu, and biscuits and gravy two of the best meals that are served here so that was a blessing in itself. I look at the calendar and October of 2006 isn't that far away so one more birthday in this joint. The only disappointment of the day was that Chipper Jones hit 2 HRs and the Cubs lost 4-2 to the Atlanta Braves. I guess it's not the Cubs year I'll do the same I do every year wait. Lord I pray that at some point in my lifetime the Cubs are in the World Series. Lord I thank you for the blessing that my family sent for my birthday with the extra money I'll be able to go to commissary this Thursday and I can treat myself to some extra snacks I see Honey Buns in this equation. Lord on this day 57 years ago I was first brought into the light. I'm sure that you had a plan for me set-up and a path to follow. I didn't choose that path I chose my own, I'm sorry I let you down. In this the twilight of my life I still have a chance to follow your path, your ways I'm truly blessed. Lord I'm looking forward to many birthdays. Lord in knowing that I'm serving you with my whole heart and all that's within me I have a glorious feeling about today. I love you Lord and I thank you for my birth and rebirth, praise you Father.

G.
John 3:8

August 23

Father,
Good afternoon Lord and I hope I'm correct about it being a good afternoon. My request for a change of cells has been granted. My new cellie is Hispanic and seems to be a really easy going guy. Tr. Is about 35 and has got about 12 more years to go on a 2nd degree murder charge. I know from the way he acts we will have no problems. We both have T.V.s and that's a plus. Tr. seems to have his head on his shoulders I will see as we get to know each other better. I thank you dear Lord for delivering again on a prayer. I feel so blessed and honored to call you Father. I just got my selection list for commissary so I've been spending time with my selections. I promise Lord I'll be faithful with the fruits that you've provide, Honey Buns being the exception. Had a nice time at yard and was able to get a mile walk in 17 times around the track. I felt pretty good as I walked spending time praising you. The guys that I was talking with about our faith haven't been to yard for about a week. I am spending time with other inmates from the gallery trying to get a handle on them and their faith. Lord you gave me and everyone else a gift for free I accept it I hope that all men will eventually do the same. I pray for all people to accept your free gift. Jesus is the only answer. I love you Father.

G.
Acts 16:31

August 24

Father,
Good afternoon Lord, I was thinking back to this time last year, I arrived at Mt. Sterling (Western C.C.) after we had our restraints removed we were herded into the gymnasium. When we were all inside we were told to strip and stand-by for inspection. We were searched and cleared to put on our prison uniforms. From there we went to I.A. where we were given new I.D.s, than we were given a net bag with the rest of our gear that we would be responsible for while we stayed at Western. From there we were issue a property box which I still have today. This box has everything I have collected over the past year. Everything that you have needs to

be in the box at all times. We were issued a legal box for all our books and papers we have. From there we were ushered to 4-house and there I would stay for the next two months while we went through phase; a two month program that kept us in our cells for 21 hours a day, only going to chow three times a day. I think it was just their way of saying there wasn't a cell in population available. This was very rough at the time but had I know about Stateville Segregation I would have said thank you when going through phase. Looking back where I'm at now is pretty good, thank you Lord. Lord you know my heart and how much I cry out to you I'm so thankful that you listen. I will write tomorrow.

G.
Romans 12:12

August 25

Father,
Morning Lord, as I write this in the early morning I listen and hear nothing but silence and this is very welcome. I know you answer my prayers Lord and always have. I know there have been times when I needed to seek forgiveness and you gave it. I know there have been times when I asked for things that were unimportant and you gave them to me. I know you are the only God and my needs have always been meet through you. I am a sinner Lord asking for direction. You know my future; you know my thoughts, my deeds and needs. Lord help make and mold me with love into a strongly convicted man for Christ. Lord give me the honor of following you all the days of my life. Lord help me to know right from wrong, remove my weaknesses. I know my sins are forgiven, my short comings and pitfalls noted. Help me Father to do your bidding. Lord show me the way, the truth and light. Lord give me your peace, comfort and love. I ask for the wisdom to know when to act and when not to act. Lord the knowledge to know when to run and when to fight. I ask and pray this in your Heavenly name as always.

G.
Romans 1:17

August 26

Father,
Good evening Father, got to go to commissary yesterday and stock up on supplies, I should be good for the next couple of weeks. I'm happy; I wish I could say that for the Cubs they have lost two in a row. I know that the fans can't be happy with Dusty Baker. I went to yard this morning and had a nice relaxing day. I sat on the grass and watched the younger guys play baseball; how I wish I was a few years younger I'd be right there. I am reading James Patterson's "London Bridges". And I enjoy his books tremendously. The nice part is I can escape the boredom that comes from sitting in the cell for long periods of time. One of the odd things I've found being here in prison is that most of the inmates like anything that involves murder and mayhem. I guess that I'm in this group because I enjoy these things also, for me it's an escape from reality I'm not so sure about the others. My cellie Tr. has been working on his appeal to the appellate court trying to get a new trail. The way he sees it he was railroaded by the police and wasn't anywhere near the scene of the killing that took place. The police had nothing but the testimony of a known drug addict and circumstantial evidence. Lord if there is justice and he's telling the true let justice prevail and get him the appeal he deserves. Lord thank you for a good fish dinner. Lord the doors are opening for day room and I need a shower so I'll talk later as always,

G.
Psalm 100

August 27

Father,
Judgment. Father what a word, if you had told me that I would be thinking about that word prior to April 2004 I would not have comprehended it and all it meant. Why am I talking about judgment because now I know a lot more about it having been judged, convicted, and sent to prison for what I did. I know that before I was convicted everyone prejudged me without knowing the fact that led to my conviction all the things that went on in my life before I was arrest. I know that I could have fought the judgment if I felt myself innocent but I wasn't so I copped a plea. I took the best deal I could and I just wanted to get my time in prison over. This world judges through the law of the land and that's human nature. Paul teaches that only God has the right to judge and his judgment is all that counts. I'm guilty Lord of sin, I know that my sin is no different in your eyes than a person who might lie or steal. I know that a sin is a sin no matter how big or how small. I stand on the sentence the court gave me and I stand before you a sinner and claim the blood of my Lord and Savior Jesus Christ. The world may find it difficult to forgive but you've already forgotten and I pray thank you. Lord may I ever be faithful as always.

G.
Psalm 69:13

August 28

Father,
Lord I so want to thank you when I accepted Jesus as my Lord and Savior I was given a gift. I was at 12 years old unable to totally understand that there was work involved in understanding what that meant other than I had a place in the Kingdom. The knowledge that I would be spending all eternity with Jesus was exciting, exhilarating, and extra special. The gift was free and the benefit was being able to walk in Heaven with Jesus. I know that I am not alone in accepting this gift many have come before me and many came after. Lord from the time I gained this gift and the time I needed to understand was 46 years. I ask the questions; why did it take so long? Will you take into account all the negative things that happened to me? Lord at what point did my life become altered? I think if I had

done my homework I could have avoided most of the pitfall that I had throughout my life and been walking with you sooner. I should have learned to lean on you when darkness came and led me in a different direction. I think that if I stopped feeling scared and let someone know what happened I would have been with you sooner. I can't dwell on what was all I can do is take another step forward on the path to your glory. I have chosen this path as you have chosen me with love; and the greatest of these is Love. I love you and you love me what a happy union that will be. This is your day and I thank you for opening my heart and guiding me down this narrow path I praise you Lord.

G.

1 Peter 5:6, 7

August 29

Father,

Good morning Lord, well yesterday was a great day for the Cubs they blew out Florida 14-3 and D. Lee had 2 HR it sure is nice to be able to watch the Cubbies play. I know that I got a little melancholy yesterday and I know that it's OK with you. I just feel awkward complaining about my life. I know you gave me a great life and I've been blessed with three wonderful children and you protected me even when I did things that were stupid and thinks that you did not approve of. I know that you have forgotten my yesterday and I have a fresh start today and this is a terrific feeling. Praise you Lord! Praise you! I feel your presence Lord all the time and that's a great feeling. I know that as I walk with you there are many tears in the past and there will be many in the future and that's OK because you are the light that lead me out of the darkness. I know that being a new person means that I died in my sins and yet was given new life through the blood of Jesus and I thank you Father. I know that my sins were laid bare at the foot of the Cross. I know Lord that I was prideful, conceded, selfish, opinionated, and wrong in my thoughts but you corrected me and I thank you so much. I know that I'm on fire for you Lord and that you are what I want and all I need. I love being a follower teach me your ways, until tomorrow.

G.

Hebrews 4:12, 13

August 30

Father,
Good evening Father, I had a good day today. I read in Psalms today and got such hope. I know that David even with his love for you failed in many areas of his life just like me; I glad I'm not the only one. The one thing I know is that he could come to you and ask for forgiveness and it was granted. I look back on my life and I want to apologize to my two ex-wives N. & D. and soon to be ex. A., they did nothing but try to love me and I let them down. I didn't know how to have a solid relationship with any of them; I was in it for me and my own satisfaction. My relationships were always founded on sand I never allowed them into my life the way I should have. I always chased after a new relationship, a bigger high if you will. I know now that without a relationship with you I will never be able to have a solid relationship with women. I have always gone searching on my own; from now on I will let you do the selecting when the time is right. I know that my choices have been for the wrong reasons. Lord you are my refuge and strength ready to help me in times of trouble I will not fear anything as long as you are with me. Lord I love you so much. I want you with me every step of the way, I will talk tomorrow.

G.
Philippians 2:3, 4

August 31

Father,
Good evening Father another month down and only 14 more to go. This is the halfway point in my imprisonment tomorrow I'm on the downhill towards a new life. I have ideas Lord of what's going to happen but only you know what they are and that's a good thing. I'm happy that the Cubs beat the Dodgers yesterday 6-3 it's been an up and down season to say the least. Father as I closeout August I want to thank you for listening and always being here for me. I am nothing without you in my life. I pray Father for all the other inmates here on the gallery regardless of what they have done we are still your creation. We all have sinned and fall short of

your glory and yet when we turn to you Lord all our faults are forgiven. Lord you truly are a loving God. I close out the month with hope for the future and ask for your help in securing that hope. I love you Father for never deserting me. I will meet you in September.

G
Deuteronomy 6:3

September 1

Father,
Lord I just want to say thank you. The prayers I write are exciting to me because I I'm able to communicate with you on a daily basis and maybe someday I can use my prayers as a ministry for you Lord. Maybe some inmates might someday read my prayers wouldn't that be neat. I know that time on this earth could be very short I feel like all the signs are coming together. I know that through the free will that you gave us we have made a mess of things that you gave us out of love. I know to be given Eden and have it taken away wasn't your plan and it started us on a downward spiral. We as a people have put everything else we've done before, and abandoned you as our first love. Lord what will it take for us as a people to come back to you? To Satan I say: I know I will always be tested, that I may at some point fall into your traps. I also know that you do not have the power of the Lord and that neither you, nor your demons can conquer the Father, Son and Holy Spirit. The power you have will not claim victory over me know matter how many stumbling blocks you put in my path. I know you will fail Prince of Darkness; the Lord will win in the end Satan you're not as powerful as the Lord and the bottomless pit is waiting for you. Lord all who stand by the river waiting to cross over to the promise land pray to you for deliverance. We wait for the time to be called home. I know that one day I will be called home and I hope that I have fought the good fight and won the race. Lord with love and joy I say thank you Lord.

G.

2 Corinthians 6:4

September 2

Father,
Lord you are my help for today and in the future. I've been studying in Psalms 27:4-13, David was seeking you out and letting you know that he wanted to be with you forever, in your house. David knew that you were his sanctuary when trouble came. I also cry out for you Lord I too want to live in your house forever. You are perfect Lord and will always protect me. I know also Lord that you call me to come; to come and talk with you and I answer: I am coming Father. Lord you have been merciful to me and have not rejected me like so many others. Lord you have helped me on my journey; in times of gladness, in times of sadness and in times of trouble. I ask you Lord as David did to teach me how to live so I may teach others the same. Help me lead Lord and set a good example as a true servant of yours Lord. I know I will have enemies when I'm free of these chains and know that you won't let me fall into the arms of my enemies. I have been accused of things I've never done and been threatened with violence from people I don't even know. My crime has been distorted and false accusations made. I fell away from you in a time of weakness and yet your goodness and mercy prevailed you have helped me in the past and how to release the past so now help me in the future. Lord as David prayed so do I for you infinite love and kindness. I thank you for presenting the Psalms to me I can relate 100% to David's agony and pain. I can also relate to his comfort and joy to be with you all the time and forever. I'll write tomorrow as always.

G.
Psalm 136:1

September 3

Father,
Good day to you Lord and it looks like I'll be going out to yard later this morning. The Cubs beat Pittsburgh last night and I hope they can win today. The weather outside is about 80 degrees and that's good enough for me. I know that with the Bears opening up the football season a week

from tomorrow that fall is in the air. I know that the autumn will lead into my last winter in prison. I have always enjoyed looking at the turning of the leaves; like life the leaves will fall and the tree will grow new leaves next spring. I see my own life in the seasons of change. I see a renewing and refreshing of my spirit. I see hope for me in the future and am looking forward to my season of change, I know longer feel as young as I did and time has caught up to my body. I am 60 lbs. lighter than when I started my journey in the system, the strength I had before is gone and the aches in my body are getting worse. I need not complain though you have another area for me to work in and I'm sure I won't have to physically work as hard. Lord I ask that whatever I'm to do I do it with gusto and enjoyment knowing that I'm serving you. I like the leaves am turning and growing anew I thank you Lord for where you are leading me I know that I will be ready to serve. I praise you Lord and will write tomorrow after the game.

G.
Ephesians 4:23

September 4

Father,
Lord I want to pray tonight for all the people in New Orleans. Hurricane Katrina was so devastating and not only killed, and injured a lot of people thousands were left homeless. Lord I am in disbelief over how this government of mine is handling the disaster. I'm sure when everything is said and done the insurance companies will find a loop hole so as not to pay the claims of the people who have insurance and that a lot of the poorer areas won't be rebuilt. So Lord I just ask that you put your arms around all the people of New Orleans. I pray Lord that the community stands shoulder to shoulder to rebuild their city. I see by the news that the Federal Government is saying a lot about help but I'm sure this is more Government hogwash. I know that my situation is not the greatest however it pales in comparison with what happen down south in the gulf. Clothe them Lord, feed them Lord, and give them rest from their struggles I ask this in the name of Jesus. Today was an uneventful day I just stayed in and played cards this morning and this evening. I ate a

couple of indescribable meals that I will soon forget. I had my own chili noodle dinner with squeeze cheese and crackers it was better than most of the food served today at chow. The Cubs won again so that's three in a row against the Pirates, I don't think we'll make the playoffs this year. If I didn't like the Cubs so much and was afraid of getting bored I wouldn't watch them. I'd choose something else on T.V.; even a cooking show. Lord I again pray for the people in New Orleans let them lean on you. Praise you Lord with all the love I have in me.

G.
Proverbs 19:17

September 5

Father,
Lord I pray thank you for your love and faithfulness to me a poor servant. I do not deserve your love for all the sinful things I did over the course of my life and yet good sacrificed your Son so that all mm sins were erased and I am washed clean. Praise you Jesus! I trust you Lord and I know that your word will be our bond for the rest of my life. Lord you are too beautiful to describe and I want to glow in your beauty on that day that I am called home. Your justice is correct and my punishment was right, I accept your judgment completely. You are merciful to me because I have repented. I know what awaits me when my life is finished and that is a wonderful feeling. I love you Father and will write tomorrow.

G.
Hebrews 12:15

September 6

Father,
Good afternoon Father, I was reading again in Revelations and was fascinated about the Seven Churches again and I was looking at the second church that Christ told John to write to. The church at Smyrna was told that they would suffer for their belief and to be strong that there would be a crown even in death that this life was not as important as the next. I think that the toughest part of what was said is that they would not have an easy time in this life and that their prize awaited them after their suffering and although they might have a physical death that they would be alive for all eternity. I know that there was a time when I might have not remained faithful to you and chose life but now that I've seen your magnificent glory and what you gave me I am ready, willing and able to face whatever Satan will throw at me. I love you Lord and there is no other. I think knowing that when we all pass away there is going to be a second death for those who don't believe is scary. Lord as I pray today I pray that when my times up I'm with you the instant I die. You are my God and there is no other, love always,

G.
Luke 2:14

September 7

Father,
Lord as I talk to you this evening I think about all the hate in this world and as I study 1 John 4:11-17, I look at all the hate here and on the outside and I know that you love us and we all should love one another. I just thought about the perfection of your plan and feel sorry that this world doesn't seem to feel the same. I will try to do my best to love all your children weather they are Christian or not. I think back to a time when it was the community at large that raised all of us. The home was a sanctuary where children felt safe. The neighbors kept watch when the parents were busy. The nucleus of family, friends and neighbors was always a safe environment where door didn't need to be locked and you could feel

safe. I know that when I got out of line the neighborhood would always go directly to my parents. This safety net has eroded so much that people now days don't want to be troubled with the problems of other people let alone their children. I remember a time when churches were filled, people actually resting on your Sabbath. I remember Sunday being a day of rest. I see a world today fighting to forget their first love Father and that make me very sad. I know that people needed you Father and I will try to bring all those I can to you so you can do your work. Lord I pray that people come back to you Lord as I did. I know putting you first was the best thing that ever happened to me. Lord I will write tomorrow,

G.
1 Corinthians 1:10

September 8

Father,
Good evening Father today was a good day. I went to yard, had a decent lunch and was able to go to commissary for supplies. I didn't get any Honey Buns this time; just got essentials. One of my old cellies got in trouble with some of the hustlers here on the gallery and has no way of paying back on the food stuff that he borrowed and that's going to be a problem with some of the guys he borrowed from. I pray Lord that he doesn't get hurt and he can work something out. I would venture to say some of his clothing might be traded for what he owes but I'll have to get back to you on that. I think I can help a little with some food stuff and maybe the combo will ease the tension. Jesus you are my Savior and I know that the time will come where we will meet face to face and I will weep for you selfless act for me. I thank you Lord and pray that I will walk in your footsteps as best I can. Lord teach me and nurture me so I will be ready to do your will whatever that may be. I pray also Lord that my former cellie can get out of his sticky situation. I love you Lord, thank you from your son,

G.
1 Timothy 4:10

September 9

Father,
Good morning Lord I thank you for my brother in Christ R. and his wife C. I've had them on my mind for a while now as I just want to pray that they are doing well. I am very fond of them and hope they are doing well. I know their love for you Lord and their heart is true you are blessed to call them your own. I hope that one day I will feel as worthy as they are. I've come a long way and you have been there every step, praise you Lord. I know that when I was in deep trouble and was deserted by many others R. was there for me. I know it was very comforting for me to have a friend who did not judge and affirmed that it is you who will judge what a blessing he was in my darkest time of need. R. was someone I could go to and I never took much advantage of that for that I'm calling myself stupid. I've done a lot of stupid things in my life but I always tried to do things alone and I thought that my way was the right way. I think the word humble comes to mine. I humble myself before and seek your wisdom. I love you Lord and am glad you're with me, as always,

G.
Isaiah 51:3

September 10

Father,
Good evening, today is what I would call a real great day and for me also a sad day. This day gave birth to my Mom and my Son. I was blessed to have such a wonderful and loving Mom and am blessed to have a wonderful Son who is working on his own identity which all children should do and I love him dearly happy birthday E. I lost my mother when she was 52 years old, too young for her to die. I know Lord that she's in heaven with you and you had your reasons for calling her home. I know when she left us everybody said she was with you Lord and at the time I would rather have heard that she was going to beat the cancer that took her. I know that a more vibrant and happy women has never existed in my eyes like my mother. I only wished I could have had her around for her grandchildren to see the

beauty of this wonderful woman, a woman who could have taught them about unconditional love the way she taught my brother, sisters and me. Lord we had so much fun with her and I can only imagine that you are having a blast with her there with you. I know it took my whole family a long time to get over her passing but I know you were there with us. The sad part about this day was it was on this day she got sick and shortly found out she had cancer, so like I said a good day and a sad day. Lord I pray that I will always remember all the great things about my Mom and never take for granted the Son that gave me. I'll write tomorrow. Lord a little side note Cubs won today only two wins away from .500.

G.
Colossians 1:5

September 11

Father,
Dear Lord I pray for all family members and loved ones that lost their relative or friends in the 9/11 bombing of the World Trade Center. I remember what I was doing that day and that hour of the morning. I was listening to the news while I was driving to a town south of where I worked to do some cleaning. I was about 10 miles away so I got all the info from WGN out of Chicago. I found it hard to believe and felt like it was an Orson Wells prank like his famous "War of the Worlds" radio broadcast. I was stunned. I listen to WBBM out of Chicago which had greater coverage. I know as the Jets kept hitting their targets I was angry at the people who did this horrific thing. When I finally drove in to town I stopped at the local Dept. Store and went to the T.V. section and turned on the set. I started viewing scenes of carnage like I'd never seen before it was like something out of a movie. I know that as it was sinking in I was choked up over what I knew would be a loss of life in the thousands. I normally liked to get my work done right away and head back to the shop however this took total control of my mind. I remember watching when the first tower collapsed and the smoke and ash came billowing down the streets out from where the first trade center building was it was unbelievable. Then the second tower crumbled with the same end result

it was just horrible. In between the buildings collapsing; the focus was on the Pentagon and it having been attacked by another jet. My thoughts went; to who, why and how. I thought that we had a safe country and was just blown away. Lord I take comfort in the fact that you have a grand design and no one knows it but you so I need to trust and be faithful to that no matter what takes place in this world of ours. Lord I pray for peace to come to all people in this mixed up world. Father I love you and accept your perfect plan, as always.

G.
Psalm 37:4, 5

September 12

Father,
Good evening, I had another eventful day. I got up for breakfast at 4:30 a.m. I came back at 5:05 a.m. I than went back to sleep until the doors opened for dayroom at 9:30 a.m., my dayroom was over at 11:00 a.m., and I went back in my cell and I waited for 15 minutes. I went to lunch at 11:15 and had the chefs' special, soy-burger on a bun and dried out fries. I came back to my cell by 12:00 p.m., and waited for yard at 1:30 p.m. I went to yard and got back in my cell at 2:45 p.m. I waited until 3:30 p.m., then I went to dinner; a mixture of ground turkey and noodles. I came back to the cell at 4:15 p.m. I then waited until 6:30 p.m., and got out for dayroom. I then got back in my cell at 8:00 p.m., and this is where I'm at until breakfast in the morning. Lord this is why it's so boring in prison the activities are limited, the food is lousy and not much to do. I am thankful Lord that I have you to worship and study. I thank you for listening to my prayers about my old cellie, with a little creativity he was able to pay back most of what he owed to the sharks. I helped with the noodle he owed. Father God I pray thank you for giving me my soul; that yearns to serve you. I will write tomorrow.

G.
John 4:24

September 13

Father,
I just got some good news today I will be going to school starting in a week or two, I hope it's sooner than later. I signed up for an English composition class and Political Science (Illinois Constitution) class. Why I signed up for these class is they will give me a refresher on my English and familiarize me with our states laws, more important I will get good time and that reduces my sentence and I get out earlier. If everything works out Lord I can be out of here by Aug. 2006. Father I pray to you today for the blessing of going through these classes and getting good-time so I might get out sooner. I know Lord that I have to do the work and pass the classes and that should be no problem still I need your help so that the courses aren't halted for some stupid reason; like lack of funding. I really would like to get out of here earlier than October, 2006. Lord I put my faith in you to give me the knowledge to pass these classes, let me study and understand the subjects I am taking. I also will be moving over to three-house which is the school wing and I'm looking forward to that. I will miss TR. he has been a great cellmate and I learned a lot and he was always watching my back. Lord this is a happy day for me and it would not have happened without your intervention. I know from what the guards told me the facility couldn't afford having a college program in here so I know you were able to work it out. I thank you Lord for all you do for me especially your Son my brother Jesus. Love you Father will write tomorrow.

G.
Hebrews 11:6

September 14

Father,
Good evening Lord, I went to my empathy group today and we came up with a game plan in how we will run the group. I know that some of the guys aren't excited about doing homework but I think it will be good to learn about the thing that will help us from offending again. I know Lord that there are not any lessons on one's beliefs and there should be, but I know that I will get the facts that believing in you is important into the

class discussion. I kind of like the fact that the guys in the group like to take I know it's better than staring at each other for an hour. I am happy that I'll be out of my cell for a good portion of the week to attend school and my empathy group sessions. Hallelujah! I just pray Lord that what happened at Mt. Sterling doesn't happen here. Lord protect me from any adversities that may come my way, let me be a good student and positive example for others to see when I go about your work. You are my God, you are my Father and your Spirit lives within me, Thank you Lord, thank you! I know Lord that whoever believes in you will be saved and I so want everybody will comes to realize how great you are. I will write tomorrow.

G.
2 Corinthians 3:6

September 15

Father,
Lord I was watching some religious shows this past weekend and got to thinking about false teachings and so called evangelists. These so-called Christians seem to seduce the crowds of people who want to believe in something; into a frenzy. I see this as being so against you teaching and I hope my thoughts in this matter are right. I know a lot of people only have T.V. religion and what they are presented with is sometimes wrong. I see a lot of these T.V. programs out only for the money. Send money and you'll be healed, send money and you'll be helping the only true believers and send money and every dime will pay for the jet that they travel around in. I get so tired of seeing this garbage on T.V. Lord you have a simple plan of faith, faith in the blood of Jesus and no other why oh why doesn't it work. I know the answer Satan has control of this world and he's been at it for a long time. I think the T.V. Christians may have started out with good intentions however they have been seduced by their desire of pride and great financial benefits. I know Lord that I could be wrong but I don't think I am. I need some fresh input on this subject. Lord give me the right thoughts and understanding to know the good from the misled. I love you Father and I will write tomorrow as always.

G.
Proverbs 16:18

September 16

Father,
I come to you today Lord with a humble heart and I thank you for the amazing grace you have showed me in my walk. In the last part of the 18th Century a former slave trader named John Newton wrote a song that today is a standard hymn in almost every church and it all parts of this world: "Amazing Grace" this song was written in repentance for what Newton had participated in for a good part of his life. Lord you touched his heart and he asked for forgiveness and you gave it. I see in here that there are still those who would like nothing better than to keep the men of color; slaves to their stereo-type. There is a great division between the races here and I would venture to say its' worse in here than on the outside of the fences I see every day. When Newton penned the words to this song I'm sure that he would have never dreamed the effect it would have on all believers. Lord! Amazing grace! How sweet the sound that saved a wretch like me I once was lost and now I'm found was blind and now I see. I know that whenever I think about this song now I have an open heart for all men and women who are slaves to their addiction, their circumstance, and emptiness in their souls. Grace is not about color it's about your love, given to us for all eternity on the cross of Calvary in the sacrifice of your son, Jesus. I know Lord that when I am called home that it is by this grace, and I with all my heart thank you Lord. Lord you are Amazing! You are Love! Hallelujah!

G.
James 3:6

September 17

Father,
Good day to you Lord on this wonderful Saturday. I'm happy today for my sister K. It's her birthday and I can see her smile and the happiness in that smile. I know that her smile is infectious and it reminds me of mom, her glass being half full and never half empty. I can't wait to talk with her when I get out it will be a glad reunion. I wish you a Happy Birthday K. where ever you are. I love you sis so very much and miss you. Lord I'm

getting ready for tomorrows football game and I'm hoping that the Bears have a better outcome this week against the Lions than last week. I want to be nearer to you Lord so keep me working in your word and studying those things I need to study to be a servant in your army. I want nothing more than to put your armor on and fight for your Kingdom and all people everywhere. Oh Lord! I love you so much and with all I have in me. Lord I thank you for a good dinner last night fried catfish and macaroni & cheese. I was able to swap a couple of Ramen noodles for one of the other guys' dinner, I got pretty full but it was well worth it for one of the few edible meals here. I still haven't heard when I'll be transferred to the school wing but I know it will come; all in your good time. Lord you are my everything and I enjoy spending this time with you along with my quiet time studying your word. Lord you gave me hope when I thought there wasn't any and for that I pray thanks. I will write tomorrow after the game as always.

G.
John 7:6

September 18

Father,
Good afternoon Lord victory in your grace and victory for the Bears against the Lions. I know that this doesn't interest you that much but I thought I'd mention it anyway, so that in the distant future I might remember I was in a good place with you in my heart. Lord I just want to pray for my soon to be ex-wife A. I hope that someday she will bring her issues with me to you and then forgive me. I know she is yours now Lord and for that I'm thankful. Please change her heart Lord this is what I pray. Maybe someday I'll be able to at least talk to her and get that forgiveness. I am still waiting to start classes and I hope it's soon I'm getting excited. I will wait with patients knowing that it's all in your time. I pray Father for all my friends and family, that they all be kept save until I return from this prison. I thank you again Lord for my life and will thank you over and over again I pray that you don't mind. Lord I'll write tomorrow; thanks.

G.
John 20:23

September 19

Father,
Lord I know that you answer prayers in your own way and in your time. I know that you take the impossible and make it possible. I know that I must listen to you for what I'm to do. I need to allow you to work in me. I know you saved me and are gracious to me. I know that you are for anyone that comes to you. Lord I know that you have no human limitations and your power is without measure. That anyone who has a heart and humbles themselves before Jesus he will be accepted by him. I know that there is no gray area it's either accept Jesus and eternal life or reject him and receive eternal death. Lord I confess to you I am a sinner and ask for that forgiveness in the name of my Lord and Savior, Jesus. I will be with you in your house forever. I will write tomorrow.

G.
Exodus 9:16

September 20

Father,
Good morning Lord I know Father that through you all things are possible and I thank you for that gift. I was studying in Mark 6:37-52 and it's a warm and comfortable feeling that we can believe in miracles. I'm sure in my life there have been many. I know when my children were born and I held them for the first time that was I miracle, the miracle of life given to them by your breath. I know that after my brother G. and his wife V. had their Daughter D. that was a miracle especially after the doctor said it would almost be impossible. Lord you are always there and have control. I don't think that a lot of people see the miracles that go on around them every day. Lord please correct me if I'm wrong but doesn't the earth rotate on a perfect axis and spins so fast that this force holds us in place? Lord don't we have an atmosphere made up of different gases that allow us to breath? Lord aren't we the only creature that is able to use our intelligence to comprehend and communicate through speech and writing? Lord do we not have a body perfectly constructed to withstand everything that might

destroy other creatures quite easily? Lord your healing power is already built in to the body what a blessing. Lord don't you give us the ability to learn and take that knowledge and do wonderful things that make our lives easier and give us a longer lifespan now? I know there are things that we totally take for granted and that we lose sight of Jesus forgetting that it was his miracle that defeated death so that we may live for all eternity. I know that when things seem impossible we can through prayer ask and see the miracles you can perform as Jesus did with the multitudes. I know that if I had greater faith in you I could walk on water, as Peter failed we all fail. I know Lord that in my own life there are times when I fall short in my belief that things can come to pass and yet you have always protected me as I've walked on dangerous ground. I know that when I could have died you were there watching out for me. I know that your angels keep us protected. I know that a lot of us strive to be perfect and we will never be because of the first fall but the greatest miracle came in to this world and gave us the only protection we will ever need and that's a direct line to you Lord. Lord I've had a good day so far and I pray that it continues. Love to you Father.

G.
Isaiah 9:6

September 21

Father,
I honor you Lord today for the blessing of your word. I have gotten so excited by what you have passed down to me through your word. I know that Jesus is the answer for this world today and anyone who doesn't accept that is a total idiot. I hope I'm not being too harsh that's just the way I feel. I know Lord that when I present Jesus to someone and do it right and with love I just get so frustrated I could scream to the heaven for their lack of understanding. I feel like a failure and yet I know that they have to come to you and if I planted the seed I did my job. I know that I've tried to raise my children to love you Lord and I know that they know you I just hope they have accepted Christ, I think they have but that's a personal decision and I'll just pray that it's true. In Mark 7:8-11 and Mark

7:18-23 it lets us know that Christ is the standard for guidance in all that we do, to live as Christ lived is our ultimate goal. I know that I try and lots of times I fail and fall short. I also know that I can come to you time and time again until I succeed and that is such a blessing. I will honor you Lord by helping other people as you helped others. I will strive Lord not to do evil and work towards a reflection of Christ in me. I know that as I think about you I'll think about truth, honor, rightness, purity, love and admire your handy work. I know that in my walk, the closer I get to you the better man I become, thank you Lord. I pray Lord that I have a clean heart in my love for you, blessed be your name. Father you are everything and I am blessed, will write later,

G.
1 Timothy 5:17, 18

September 22

Father,
I started my new journey with you Lord when I was first was incarcerated. This journey has been paved with good intentions. As I sit here writing you those good intentions have grown by leaps and bounds. Lord to say I had a Godly experience is an understatement. My mind is working all the time to understand what I need to be a warrior in your army. I've been in the Book of Mark for a few days and I just read Mark 8:32-38 and it looks like I'm on the right track. I know that the path I travel is not easy and this path is not paved with gold. I know that this path requires work, hard work. I know that I might be persecuted, deprived of things, and suffer. I know that I must focus on good not evil. I know that I need you from moment to moment. I know it will take great effort on my part to do your work but I will do your bidding even when things get rough. I know that the future is bleak and for my beliefs I may even lose my life for the sake of the Good News. In all that I am I would rather follow you than have sin in my life. Lord you are in control and you know what's best for me. Lord I submit to your loving ways and if I do I will life and a good life in this world and in your world forever. Lord I have no excuses they ran out a

long time ago I am a sinner and you have forgiven me time and time again. I ask for your grace and mercy as I walk down your path on my journey through this life. I love you Father.

G.
Luke 15:7

September 23

Father,
Good day my Lord, I'm reporting to you on the good day I had yesterday. I went to store and got my supplies so that was good. I got my confirmation that I will have two classes to take in school, English (composition) and Political Science (Illinois Constitution) these will be accredited college courses and there free unless I decide to have them on my College transcript. I get good time for the classes and it will reduce my time by about 18 days so this is a good start. I still am waiting for a transfer to the school unit and I hope this will happen soon. I thank you Lord for each step that I've taken and I know they are one at a time and I'll gladly take them. I know I have to stop thinking about what if and focus on today and for me this is a great start. The food last night was good and you can't go wrong with chicken which is what I ate along with dehydrated mash potatoes, if only they were warm instead of cold. I was just looking at some pictures TR drew and they are really good, very detailed and thought provoking. I sometimes wish that I could draw but that's not my talent. I'm a pretty good singer when I'm in the shower so I'll just accept that. TR has been a wonderful cellie and I'm going to miss him but I'm ready to move on. Lord I pray that TR has a safe time in here until he gets out and that life outside of here is good for him. I will take tomorrow.

G.
Luke 18:1

September 24

Father,
Lord, Jesus loves me this I know for the Bible tells me so. Little ones to him below they are weak but he is strong. Yes Jesus loves me, yes Jesus loves me, yes Jesus loves me for the Bible tells me so. Lord I just had to sing that children's son it was in my mind. I was thinking of all the times I would sing lullabyes and songs to my kid's as they were growing up and I wonder where they are at and what they are doing right now. Sometimes it seems like they were just born and were listening to this song. I guess that they will always be my babies as I'm sure I'm still my dad's. There was never enough time to spend with them the way I would have liked to and I can't go back. Lord I pray that all people everywhere take the time to renew their relationship with their children and spend more time with them so they have no regrets in the future, I recall a song called "Cat's in the Cradle" by Harry Chapin and it spoke to this subject. I think of time and think of my mother on her deathbed. The Pastor said that she was ready and was thinking about time. I wonder what time she was thinking about, may the same thing I'm thinking about right now. When I get home I'll have to ask her or maybe you will relay it to me in a dream or thought? I guess all I know is that she loved me and was ready to come to you. I thank you Lord for cradling her in you warm and loving embrace. I can't wait for my time so I also can embrace you and know the love you have for me. I will take tomorrow and we can continue in Mark.

G.
1 John 4:8

September 25

Father,
Lord I just want to tell you how much I like peanut butter. When I went to commissary on Thursday I picked up some squeeze packets of peanut butter and my usual box of crackers. This is the first time that I've had peanut butter in 17 months and Lord is it good on crackers. I went to chow today and found the meal to be pretty bad so I traded my meal for a couple of noodles. I came back and had a meal of chili noodles and peanut butter and crackers. This to my way of thinking is a much better meal then trying to figure out what they are serving at chow. I'm sorry I know this isn't important but it's nice to appreciate something you like and haven't had for a long time. I guess that sometimes you need to not have something for a long time to realize how much you've missed something. Lord I missed spending time with you for so many years that now I thirst for a drink of that living water. I need to be fed what I need; to continue to do your work here and forever. Lord help me claim victory over sin and temptation through my faith in your Son Lord, Jesus. I know that my faith is tested every day and that every day I grow in that faith and I just seem to love it. Lord I pray to you and tell you my stories because I depend upon you Lord I am nothing without you. Lord may I ever walk and work in your steps helping and caring for others giving them the opportunity to come to you Lord. I will talk after the game tomorrow.

G.
1 John 5:4

September 26

Father,
I got some poems from my daughter and I want to present them to you. The first one is called While You Were Sleeping: "While you were sleeping I snuck away; to a far place beyond the bay. It is beautiful there you see; there are glorious flowers that grow beneath the tree. I go to be alone and have some peace; for society itself is such a tease. In my secret place there's a special glow; it comes from the stream that continues to flow. This glow means so much but little is shown; its Gods love given and grown." I love the poem very much because it shows her love for you this is from my Little Butterfly. The next one is called I Had Been Lost: "I had been lost for so very long; yet you searched for me non-stop all the day long. I had not followed your rules; yet you forgave me no matter what. I had wallowed in hatred and despair; yet your love you were willing to share. I have strayed away many times; not a care or thought on my mind. When the path ends and there's no place to go; your compassion and guidance leads me to the right road. It is now time to thank you for all the work you have done; and I thank Jesus who died for us your one true Son." I think my daughter K. has a lot of love for you Lord and I thank you for giving her the heart to write these poems. I love you Lord and I'll write tomorrow.

G.
Proverbs 3:17

September 27

Father,

Good evening Lord, I'm getting ready for tomorrow I'm going to move over to the school unit. I am looking forward to going over there. Lord I just pray thank you for all my relatives that have been sending money to me to help with the commissary costs bless them all and store their treasures in heaven for them, thank you. Lord I find that being in the word in the morning is less of a strain then in the evening, in the morning I'm refreshed and ready to go. I love praying and writing you in the evening because things have quieted down and it's a little more peaceful for private time. Lord I want to thank you for the changes in me. I am so proud that I now put others in front of me and am no longer selfish with my time. I know that I can be a help to anyone in need and a comfort for those who are seeking a relationship with you Lord and I thank you for that. I thank you Lord for giving me a humble servants' heart. Lord I know that I could not save myself from total destruction without the precious blood of Jesus and I thank you for that. I know that I'm a work in progress and I don't mind besides I have a lot to catch up on and plenty of time to do it I'm not going anywhere for awhile. Lord I'm sad the Cubs lost to the Pirates this day and I know that they will be in fourth place for the year so I guess it's; wait until next year. I'm kind of tired right now so I'll write tomorrow.

G.

1 Peter 1:19

September 28

Father.
Good evening Lord it's been a wonderfully beautiful day. The weather was balmy; my hours today were filled with lots of movement. I said good-by to TR this morning around 9:30 A.M., and started my move over to 3-house which is the school unit. I'm on the upper floor in a cell all the way to the end of the gallery. I have mild traffic by my cell and it will be a much quieter cell than any I've had before. Lord I'm not talking discrimination here but most of this unit is Caucasian which right now works for me my cellie seems nice and we haven't had time to get to know each other yet. I thank you Lord for helping me get to this point where I'm doing something productive. I have always been a man on the go and being here in prison and locked up most of the time I haven't been able to do much so now I'm able to be constructive. Lord I pray that my class go well and I'm able to complete them without incident and gain the good time so I might get out sooner.

Let me see is there anything I forgot, oh yeah the empathy group was held today and one of the inmates started ranting and raving about his treatment and the possibility that he might be transferred to a Psychological control unit at another facility and it's not a good place to be. I guess from what I could understand if he gets placed in the unit be will only be allowed out when the doctors say he's fit and would feel sure that he wasn't a menace to society. Lord I pray for T. that he's able to make his out date and not have to go to this unit where his chances of getting out are a lot slimmer by going to this place than remaining here. Lord I pray that T. is able to rehabilitate his thoughts and thinking so he'll be well enough to function in society. Lord I'll write tomorrow.

G.
Matthew 19:26

September 29

Father,
Oh what a Savior you are. You have given your life's blood for me on that tree a long time ago. I am guaranteed eternal life thanks to this sacrifice. Lord you took all the pain, sorrow and sins and carried them on your back for all of us who need your loving embrace; what a wonderful blessing. Lord I know that you have been a great friend to me while I've been writing my thoughts and prayers and you know my true heart and that's all the blessing I need. Lord you know that I pray for the men in here, my family and friends (the ones who are left) out in the world and also that world in general. I just pray that my ministry is one of positive service in your Kingdom. I know that in February I had that life changing experience and always want to remember that you save me a poor humble man not worthy and yet you made me worthy. Lord people will say that this is all a ruse and that I'll never change but you my Lord know different. I cannot worry about others I need worry only that I'll be able to make you happy. Lord I will say this many times; I love you, I love you, and I love you! I'll talk tomorrow.

G.
Genesis 32:8

September 30

Father,

Lord it's the last day of the month and hopefully I won't see another September here in prison. I know that if my schooling goes good I won't and I thank you for the chance to do the work. I like being about your business showing the other inmates that there is a better way than the one that they chose. I see by my own eyes why things are so difficult for people to realize that you are all that matters in this mixed up world. People are afraid to let go of the control of their lives to someone or something they cannot see. I know Lord that you are there because I can feel your presents all the time and that is so comforting especially being in prison. I don't have to be force to go to a church service to spend time one day a week. I do not forget you Lord you are with me constantly. I know that as I grow stronger, and stronger things will become easier for me and I'll feel that I'm less of a failure. I won't get down on myself for all of the things I've done in this world because they are gone and you have forgotten, I need only to remember that and I'll be OK Lord you are my first love and always will be. I'll talk to you next month. In the name of your Son Jesus I say thank you so very much for all the blessing you have bestowed on me.

G.

Psalm 23:4

October 1

Father,

Father I go to my first classes on Monday and I'm looking forward to starting them up. I enjoy school and it also keeps my mind off of being in my cage. Well only two days of baseball season left after tomorrow the Cubbies are finished until next year. The Cubs are the same year after year I guess that is why I can stand disappointments. One of these years Lord I would like to see the Cubs win the World Series. That's enough of the small talk it's time to get down to the nitty-gritty. In Luke 6:45 it says that a good person produces good deeds from a good heart and an evil person produces evil deeds from an evil heart. Lord it also says what comes out of your heart is reflected in our speech and behavior. I think this means that the truth will always win out over our behavior because of what's in our heart. In Luke 6:48-49 states that if we obey you Lord it's like building a house on a strong foundation. I know that I must build on the strong foundation of Jesus Christ and that without him as our strong foundation, our building will crumble. In Luke Chapter 7, I see a Roman officer calling upon Jesus to heal his slave but he felt unworthy of having Jesus in his home but this soldier also knew that Jesus could heal this man's slave right from where Jesus was because he truly knew that Jesus was the Son of God. I hope I got this prospective right. I will write tomorrow after the season is over. I Love you Lord!

G.

John 14:16

October 2

Father.
Praise honor and blessings to you Father for you gave me eternal life through you Son Jesus, Hallelujah! Today is my day of rest and I'm spending my church time with you as I contemplate what the Bible is telling me and where you are leading me. I know that when I started my journey in the Word, Romans was the starting point and from Romans the Psalms. This was my starting point and the Spirit is selecting the books for me to study and this is fantastic. I've been in Mark and am now in Luke. I was thinking that in some of the churches I've been in would think that I desecrated the Bible with all the underlining that I do. I just like to think that you don't have a problem with me marking up the word in fact I think that you would encourage this practice. I also study a little bit here and there about Revelations. I can't worry too much about it, I need to learn more important thing that will help me understand me and bring others to you Lord. I think Lord that the Word is perfect and abiding in the word will make my life a lot safer and easier. I love you Father and I'll write tomorrow after school. Blessed am I to be able to bask in you sunshine.

G.
Psalm 119:105

October 3

Father,
Good evening Lord, day is done gone is the sun and I had a really good day too. I got up early and went to breakfast, spent time working in the Word and then got ready for my classes. We left to go to classes at about 8:30 a.m. and got searched before going into the school building. There is no contraband allowed and the C.O.s make sure that there won't be any problems. The Political Science class is held on Mon. and Wed. the English class is held on Tues. & Thurs. We will spend about 1 ½ hrs. in the morning and afternoon for class. This gives me and extra 12 hrs a week out of my cell, and that works for me. I felt good going to class like a young college student on his first day. Our professor is from the local

college and he's of Indian descent and has a wonderful accent when he talks. We started right in with a lecture on the Government and its role here in Illinois. I know it will be fun to see how it's supposed to run and the way it really works. So tomorrow is my English class and then back to P.S. on Wed. I even have some homework for my class due on Wed., how about that. I got to talk with TR. today he's in the P.S. with me and it was good to see him. He said that he just got approved for the class and it's nice to see him. I asked if he was going to get transferred over to the school unit and he said that because he is only taking one class they won't transfer him. I also get about ½ hr for lunch because we have to wait for the instructors to have their lunch and they don't have to rush like we have to. So anyway I've done my homework for Wed. and watched the Cubs loose the last game of the season, I said good-by to Dusty Baker and I'll wait to see who they hire for the next manager. Lord I just thank you for the opportunity that I have to get some of my good time back. This prison could have gotten rid of the school all together if they wanted to and no one would have said anything, so I thank you for placing it in their hearts to find another college to take up the cause of educating prisoners. I firmly believe that the more educated a person receives the fewer problems they will have on the street. Well it's time to rest got class tomorrow, love you,

G.
Isaiah 40:31

October 4

Father,
Good evening Father, well I got to go to my English class today and instead of eating breakfast I opted out of it this morning for some more sleep, I felt I needed the extra sleep so I can be fresh for class. Had a good class, learned that I'll be doing a lot of writing and breaking down compositions that I write, so this should be a fun class. I hope that this class will give me the opportunity to write my story maybe, to let people know what it's like being in prison. I might become an author. I get to write a little story about my life and where I've been. I was thinking Viet Nam and what my thoughts were on that subject from my first hand experience. I could

write about my various jobs or even about my many wives. Lord I'm just trying to lighten up the situation; I want this class to be both a learning experience and an opportunity to get some time knocked off my sentence. I should have fun with the class no matter what the outcome. I know that at the end of the day if I gave this my all than that's good enough. Lord I pray for the intelligence to pass this class and learn some positive stuff I can use when I get out next year. Lord I just want to glorify your name above all others and thank you for your saving grace. I love you and will write tomorrow, as always,

G.
John 12:28

October 5

Father,
Grace and peace to you Lord this evening. I just got done watching the White Sox in the playoff with Boston to try and advance to the World Series. I know I'm a Cubs fan but Chicago is still my home town. So go White Sox they have won the first two games and one more and they will advance a step closer to the World Series. I had my second class of Political Sci. and I had forgotten how much I'd forgotten about the State government and all that goes on. I know that the only info I can get comes from the State Constitution handbook we have for class so that will have to do. I see that this class is both a G.E.D. and college class. I don't know how that is but it is. I do not question what takes place here at Hill. I just know that it's great being able to spend time out of my cell and doing something creative. I had thought about trying to sign up for some work around the facility but there are 800 men waiting for 3 positions. I went to my empathy group today and we are still trying to figure out which way to go to give us greater meaning to the group. I guess T. has decided to drop out of the group, so that will only leave 5. This group is not mandatory so he can. I wish him well in whatever happens in his life. I hope and pray that he find his strength in you Lord to help him on his road to recovery. Lord I will write tomorrow; and as always will write with love in my heart for you.

G.
Isaiah 26:3

October 6

Father,
Lord I figured that I would get back in the Word and give school a break until this weekend. I decided to write my composition on Viet Nam, I think I know a little something about it. Lord as I go back over Luke 6:20-26, I have chills going up and down my spine. God bless you who are poor for the Kingdom of God is given to you. God bless you who are hungry now, for you will be satisfied. God bless you who are weeping for the time will come when you laugh with joy. God bless you who are hated, excluded, mocked and cursed because you identify with the Son of Man. When that happens rejoice! Yes leap for joy! For a great reward awaits you in Heaven and remember that ancient prophets were also treated that way by your ancestors. What sorrow awaits you who are rich for you only have happiness now, what sorrow you who are satisfied and prosperous now, for the time of awful hunger is before you. What sorrow awaits you who are laughing carelessly, for your laughter will turn to mourning and sorrow. What sorrow awaits you who are praised by the crowd, for their ancestors praised false prophets. I see the positive blessing in the beatitudes and the negative result from people who try to fill their life with riches; only to have sorrow and temporary happiness. Jesus was love and that's all anyone needs. Put your mind on him and all will be right in this world we live in. I love you Lord and a will surely write tomorrow.

G.
Genesis 12:3

October 7

Father,
Well Lord the White Sox are moving on to the next round with the Angels and I hope they are as successful as they were in the first go- round. Lord again I bring my study of Luke to you for greater understanding and awareness. Luke 6:27-35 talks about loving our enemies about doing good to those who hate you. That we should pray for the happiness of those who curse you. Pray for those that hurt you. I think that here in prison that's a tough sell. I know that most of the guys here would love to hurt

a lot of people when they get out and payback what they received as a sentence to the ones who put them here. I would have a hard time if I didn't realize that someone else's life is not my responsibility. I find it easier now to wish someone well and wish them happiness. My life is not of this world even though I'm in this world. I hope I got that right, my place is in your Kingdom not in the kingdoms of the earth. Lord I know that I have to take the higher road when dealing with anyone from my past whom at this time hate and despise me but that's OK for I can't change the way they feel. I would hope that their attitude might eventually change by seeing the person who I am now and not the one I was. I hope that living a life in Christ their attitude towards me will be different and they can get on with their lives and not worry about the life I'm living. Lord you are my God and there is no other, I praise you and worship you. Lord I give my life in serving the Kingdom. I will write tomorrow.

G.
Genesis 12:3

October 8

Father,
Good evening Lord, had a nice fish fillet last night with Mac & Cheese, it was a gourmet meal and one I could eat every day. Lord in Luke 6:37-42 it addresses the attitude of judging others. That we need not be critical of them for we will receive criticism ourselves. It says that we need to be compassionate, that we should treat others with generosity and be gracious if we do we will also receive the same compassion, generosity, and grace. I find that loving others is becoming a lot easier when I realize that you love why not me. I just need to remain humble and give better than I get, that is your way Lord and I thank you for your teaching. I know that we are all sinners and that we all fall short of your grace and that is why I know that no one person is better than the other. So Lord I will remain humble and loving the way that you would. Lord I'll write tomorrow, with love.

G.
Psalm 34:2

October 9

Father,
This is the day that you have made let us rejoice in it. Good evening Father. It has been a relaxing day and very uneventful, just the way I like it. The food today at chow was better than average, and serving Chicken helps. The Bears loss to the Browns was disappointing but then again this is Chicago sports and we are use to disappointment. I hope that the White Sox do better on Tuesday against the Angels I'll wait and see. I was just doing some studying on the Ill. Constitution and see where it compares with the U.S. Constitution and they are pretty much the same, basically the state has more infrastructures than the U.S. does. I guess if you see one constitution you have seen them all. I just hope that the quizzes are not too technical. I decided to do my composition on Viet Nam. The story will be about my first day & night in Viet Nam at a B.A.Q. in Saigon. It was February 8th, 1968; I arriving at Tan Son Nhat airport early in the morning. I remember like it was yesterday. I remember that before setting down the country looked peaceful and very beautiful, as the jet approached the run way there were burning drones and small aircraft that had been damaged in an attack by the Viet Cong. I knew at that point I was in a war zone. So I decided to write about that first day. Lord as I remember my time in Viet Nam many years ago I pray for all the men that lost their lives to the senseless violence that took place it that war, for the families of the fallen I pray for their comfort, I guess I'm better late than never in my prayer. Lord I love you and will write tomorrow.

G.

Isaiah 51:3

October 10

Father,
I have been studying Luke, Chapters 8 and 9 and I love that it gives me hope. I know now Lord that I need to always listen and read the teaching of your word. I need to understand what you word is telling me, and I must stay in the word and bring to you those in need. I know that in the truth of your word the light will glow in the hearts of those who want eternity with you. Lord I pray that through your word I grow stronger and am able to impart to others the importance of your grace and love. Lord I know that you control my destiny and I can be assured you will calm the waters when the storms of life approach. I know Lord that I will be attacked constantly by the demons that Satan has under his control and yet these demons are powerless over me because I put my trust in Jesus. Praise you Lord! I know that I must constantly resist Satan and his demons. Lord I claim the blood of Jesus to protect me from all evil. Lord I reach out for your comforting touch to heal my weaknesses and give me the strength to defeat my weaknesses. Lord I know that I need to always hold on to my faith, and reflect the life of Jesus in me. I will try to always obey your instructions. I will always seek what you want to give me. Lord I know that sometimes I can be boring and repeat a lot of the same things but it's just that I love you so much. Lord I am weak and you are strong and I know that your love will always be there for me.

G.
James 5:16

October 11

Father,

Good evening Father, I would just like to praise you Lord you raise me up, I know Lord that I can be all that you want me to be, so lift me up and cradle me in your arms. Lord I know that without you there is no life; not in this world or the next. Lord I want to be faithful, faithful to you Jesus, I am crying out for you Jesus. Lord I've needed you in my life and although I was unaware, you have always been there for me. Never have you abandoned me like I abandoned you. Lord I come back to you a poor sinner saved by your grace. Thank you Lord! Lord I have such a burning to work for you and the Kingdom let me be a faithful warrior in your army. Thank You Jesus! It's about 11 P.M. The White Sox lost the first game of series, same old Chicago. I hope they can get their act together, Chicago deserves a champion. I got the OK to write about Viet Nam for my English class. I now need to figure out what I want to write about. Do I write about the racetrack in Saigon being bombed with Napalm and lighting up the night sky? Do I write about all the rain we got during the monsoon season? Do I write about one of the guys after a shore party jumping out of the boat and drowning in the Basac River on the way back to the Harnett County? Lord do I write about the night I was on deck and a snipers bullet whizzed by my head, you were there with me Lord. Thank you. I will just see where you lead my heart and mind. I got some letters from my daughter today and some more money for my account, I thank you K. I guess that's all for tonight. I know there isn't much to report on but I still shout for joy that I am able to talk to you.

G.

Matthew 6:13

October 12

Father,
Good news to report the White Sox beat the Angels in game two of the series to even it up. I hope they can go out to L.A. and take a couple of games before coming back to Chicago. Lord if anyone had told me I would be rooting for the White Sox I would have told them that they were out of their mind. I guess that's the hunger for a Pennant and World Series in Chicago it's been so long. I think the last time the Sox were in the World Series was 1959 and they lost that one. I know Lord to you this isn't important and I am getting off track, it's just human conditioning once a person begins to like baseball. Lord I pray for greater insight on the power of Jesus so I can present his love to those who are seeking. Lord I know that there is no shortage of people who have a want and need of Jesus in their life so bring them forth so I may give them what they need to make their personal decision to spend eternity with you. I once was afraid that I would be rejected by those people who couldn't or wouldn't come to you Lord and I now realize that I just present you to them and that it is you who change their hearts. I thank you for lifting that weight of my shoulders. Lord I pray that I present you with love and a clear vision of that love. Lord I am not a well educated man so my presentation will be simple and I hope not to confusing, just plain talk. Accept Jesus and live, reject him and die. I know it's that simple but I'll give them a good explanation and how to get to the grace Jesus gives through his sacrifice. Lord I love you and will write tomorrow.

G.
Joel 2:28

October 13

Father,

I just got back from school, and getting ready for commissary so I thought I'd write you until I go. Had a good session with my empathy group yesterday, everyone participated in one way or another. I know that the handouts that we were given were very helpful on what triggers are and how to avoid them so as not to re-offend. I know that some of the group didn't do the homework but still presented their thoughts to the group. I know that my Political Science course is going to be easy but boring. I had this course a long time ago and it's all starting to come back and the tests look like they will be simple. Lord I know that you light my way so I can stay on the path and not lose my way. I know that you give me insight and understanding, I know that I need to remain every focused on you and that the more I stay fixed on you the less sin can enter. Lord I know that you are everything that I ever wanted in my life. I can say without hesitation that without you I was lost and with you I am found. Lord I know that you are love and that love shines in my heart and may that love stay locked in my heart forever. Lord I have to go now and I'll write tomorrow.

G.

Matthew 5:16

October 14

Father,

Good evening Lord, the White Sox beat the Angels and lead the series 2 games to 1. I just hope that the Sox can win the series and claim the American League Pennant. Lord with you; all things are possible. I know that my relationship with you is more important than any other thing in this world. I know that you know what I need and provide for me. I know Lord that you answer my prayers in your way not mine. I just have to remember that our relationship is always on going even when I might forget you never will. Remember to bring me back when I start to drift away. Lord I choose to give you my life and I will try and do the best that I can do for the Kingdom. You guide my every step and I know that I need not worry, that's just the human side of my nature, forgive me. Lord

I must be watchful and diligent, obeying what you commanded us to do. I know that I can use the talents and resources that you provide to aid me in my work advancing the Kingdom. Lord if I must suffer for the Kingdom I will be ready. I know there is no other given to men but your precious Son Jesus to guarantee our eternal life. I love you Lord and am looking forward towards the day I am free from my chains of prison and trade them for the chains of life working for you. I will write tomorrow.

G.

Psalm 119:50

October 15

Father,

Most precious Lord I was trying to figure out about prayer. Lord you say that we should pray without ceasing, I got to thinking: What does this mean to me and I came up with the following. Pray thank you for another day when you wake-up. Pray for a safe day, and pray for your fellow men and their individual problems. Pray a thank you for the food that is offered for your meals, and pray at the meals for his provision. If you are taking a walk pray thank you for the sun, the sky and the beauty of the land that you walk upon. Pray for nothing more than a thank you for creating us. When you are in the world you can pray in your car, while waiting for the phone call you made to be answered. You can pray while watching T.V. Lord I thought that it would be hard to pray constantly and yet as I practice praying all the time I am able to see the fantastic picture of beauty and love that you laid out for me, for all of us. I also realize that the more I pray the closer I stay to you. I know Lord that if you did not exist I would not feel the warmth and tenderness you show me when I call upon you. I know that many of my prayers have been answered when I expected no answer, and yet you came through. I just thought I'd lay theses thoughts before you. That's enough of why pray I just got done watching the Sox beat the Angels again that's three in a row; one more and it's the World Series. Wouldn't that be an answer to lots of people who have been praying for that to happen? I guess they will have to wait until tomorrow night. Lord I love you and will write tomorrow.

G.

Isaiah 52:7

October 16

Father,

Dearest Lord I know you probably aren't really interested in sports but today was a good day for the home teams. The Chicago Bears beat the Minnesota Vikings 28-3 and that's a good thing. The big thing that happened was the White Sox beat the L.A. Angels and are going to the World Series. Hallelujah! The last time was 46 years ago in 1959, amazing, simply amazing. The Sox have only lost one game in both series that they played; that is so awesome. I was also glad for the Bears that they got back on track and won a game. I want to thank you Lord for a good day. I can't forget to thank you for the wonderful breakfast of biscuits and gravy, the soy burger lunch and the fried chicken and mash potatoes for dinner, all in all it was a great day and I will sleep with a smile on my face for the first time in many months. Lord I have not forgotten that today is your day and a day of rest, so I have taken that advice and spent time working in your Holy Word studying some more in Luke and reading some of the Psalms. Lord it is pure joy reading in your word and the real nourishment I got today was not from the food I ate but the food I was fed through my studies this day. Lord I am waiting with patients for the time of my deliverance from this prison and the time afterwards when I'll serve you with all my heart, mind, body and soul. Lord be thou ever near to me. I'll write tomorrow after school. I love you Father.

G.
James 1:4

October 17

Father,
Good evening Lord peace and honor to your name. Lord may your glory be shown to the world. I love you Father and I thank for your grace through Jesus Christ your Son and the Holy Spirit. I was thinking about today and I remembered that it was my best friends' Birthday, so we are now the same age. I always remind him to respect his elders even if it's only 2 months difference. D. has been a great friend and I love him as I do my brother, even closer. I forgot that with my own problems to communicate with D. over my arrest and eventual imprisonment. Lord forgive me for the hurt I caused him to suffer by my mistake. I think that's one of the things I need to work on; to take into account the feelings of others when I do something foolish. Lord I haven't forgotten to come to you first I was just addressing an issue on the human side. My friend D. has always been there for me through everything I've ever done like you Father he has been ever faithful and that's what brothers are for. I only wish that his kindness and love would extend to you Father. I know that his not accepting you will lead him to hell and that scares me. Lord I've tried to get him to come to you and I've done all that I can do the rest is up to you. I will still plant seeds and pray that you make them grow. Lord I pray that I become a living example of your grace proven worthy by the blood of Jesus. I know that my arrest and eventual imprisonment was a surprise to all my family and friends and I just pray that this error of mine brings them closer to you. Lord I know that in Romans 6:23 it says; "For the wages of sin is death, but the free gift of God is eternal life through Christ Jesus our Lord." May all my friends and family repent of their sins and have eternal life with you Lord. I'll write tomorrow.

G.

Isaiah 54:10

October 18

Father,
Dearest Father I pray that you have my mom wrapped in your arms and she is happy with you. I almost forgot that Oct. 11 in 1981 she was called home 24 years ago. It seems like as the years go by my pain over her death is forgotten. I think because it happen so fast no one in the family had time to grieve over her illness. I am so thankful Lord that you took her home within a month of her finding out she had cancer. I am thankful that her suffering was minimal compared to other who have suffer this disease called cancer. I know not why you took her from us but I know you have your reasons and we may know when we get home also. Mom I miss you so much and I hope you are listening to what I am saying; there is nothing that you did to cause me to be in this situation. I was given free will and I chose to do something stupid. I brought dishonor to our family but that's on me and no one else. I know mom that I'm forgiven and will be forgiven again for mistakes I might make in the future and that's the greatest gift he gave to me, so I'll see you when I'm called home. Mom I know that on your death bed you were thinking of time. I want you to know that although it's been 24 years that you've been gone when I get home it will be like only an instant. Mom you have a lot of great grandkids and they would all love you. I love you mom, I love you Lord and I will write you tomorrow.

G.
Romans 6:23

October 19

Father,
I want to thank you Father for your instruction and teachings from the Bible. I have been doing a lot of studying in Romans, and Revelations. I've been spending the first hour of my day in your word and found it to be a great time to study. The time is quiet, peaceful and I'm refreshed from a good night sleep. I can't wait to meet Paul when I get home; I seem to gravitate to him more than any other apostle. I know that we both had flaws and you got us on the right path. I thank you for your mercy and for the removal of the scales from my eyes. I praise and worship you Lord every day. I am so blessed with what I've learned from the Word and from being incarcerated. I'm beginning to understand the human condition without you in it. I know Father that if you were with most of these men here in prison with me corrections would have been made in the lives of these prisoners and there would be less repeat offenders. I know that a lot of the prisons would be empty if only you were in the lives of these prisoners. Lord I pray that all these prisoners turn to you and develop a relationship with you. I want all the prisoners to know that anything they have done can be forgiven, that nothing is too big for you Lord. Lord I know that the destroyer Satan is here all the time and he seems to have a captive audience but I know that you are also here waiting for these prisoners to turn from their evil ways and come to you. Lord I just hope that these prisoners find the love that they never had from the one who created them. Lord before I close tonight I just want to wish the White Sox success over the Houston Astros in the World Series. Go,Go,White Sox! I love you Father and will write tomorrow. Glory and Honor to your name!

G.
Job 1:7

October 20

Father,

Dear Lord I am ARMED, armed with the word to do battle in this world. Lord I know I will be BAPTIZED with fire and sword for my faith. Lord I am CALLED to follow you for the rest of my life. Lord I DEDICATE myself to you Word. I EXALT and glorify you Lord above all others. Lord I will remain FAITHFUL to you for the time I have left here in this world. I come to you with a GENTLE spirit of love. I know my HEART is given to you. I ask Lord to INHERIT my birthright to be with you in eternity. Lord I know that you have been JUST towards me. Lord I thank you for your KINDNESS to me, a poor sinner. My life is one filled with LOVE for you Lord. Lord your MERCY towards me is all I need. Lord your NAME is above all others. Lord there is only ONE and you are that one. Lord you have PIERCED my heart with your sacrifice. Lord please continue to QUENCH my thirst. Lord thank you for my RENEWAL in Christ. Lord you are the SAVIOR of the entire world and there is no other. Lord I THIRST for living water through Jesus. I will have UNFAILING love for you Lord. Lord let my VOICE shout to the world of your love. Let me always WALK down your path. Lord X-RAY my heart to see that it's true for you. Lord let me be YOKED to you with my love. I want to remain ZEALOUS for you. This is my alphabet to you Lord from A-Z. Lord you are the beginning and the end, the Alpha and Omega, you are my God forever. I'll write tomorrow, as always,

G.

2 Corinthians 6:14

October 21

Father,
I was thinking about yesterday when I wrote my alphabet to you. I just felt like putting a different spin on how much I love you, I did it my way. I have been thinking about the things that happened in County Jail over a year ago, and the people you brought into my life. I kind of wonder where they are now especially Bro. B. and Bro. J. they were both very helpful in bringing me back into the fold. Both B. & J. didn't pull any punch, they both told it like it is. The need to get right with you Lord. To repent for my actions and ask for you forgiveness with a sincere heart. I am so thankful that I listened to their advice and brought my situation before the throne. I think about my Christian Bro. R. and how he did not desert the ship when others did, and I thank you for him. I thank you for the protection when one of the inmates was going to come after me and you removed that threat. I also thank you for the men that I counseled while await trial. I may never know what happened in their life but I would like to think that they are working for your Kingdom. Tomorrow is the first game of the World Series and I'm so thankful that a Chicago team is there, even if they don't win the series it's great to see them playing into late October. Lord I pray for a favorable outcome for the White Sox in the World Series. I will write tomorrow after the game. It's time to go get some fish and macaroni and cheese. I talk tomorrow.

G.
Acts 2:38

October 22

Father,
Good evening Lord and it is a good evening to, the White Sox won the first game of the W.S. 5-3 only three more to go and they will be World Champions. Tomorrow is going to be a busy day because the Bears play also, so it will be flip-flopping back and forth. Well Lord enough about sports. I just want to thank you for your servant Paul, I know that before he was an apostle he was like a lot of people in this world today. I see his

conversion and I see mine. I know that like Paul mine was life changing and for that I thank you. I knew you and yet it took so long for me to come to you, I wonder if it's being afraid of losing control or just being stubborn. I do know that it was the wisest decision that I could have made. Lord I know I must be watchful not to get over confident and also to remain humble, that being proud and haughty is wrong. Lord may I ever remain your servant doing what you want me to do. Lord let me work with due diligence and use what you provide me to do your bidding effectively. Let me stand on solid ground and remain faithful to your word. Lord you know my heart and you know that I pray for all the men here to come to you. That they realize that with you Lord al thinks are possible. Lord I love you and will write tomorrow.

G.
1 Timothy 5:8

October 23

Father,
Good evening Father this was a great Sunday. The White Sox took their second game of the series and the Chicago Bears beat the Raven make that two in a row. So in sports it was a great day. Now it's time to get to some serious issues in the Word. Lord teach me to do your will oh Lord! Listen when I cry for help. Lord accept my prayer as an incense offering to you and my upraised hands as an evening offering. Lord take control of what I say oh Lord and keep my lips sealed. Don't let me lust for evil things; don't let me participate in acts of wickedness. Don't let me share in the delicacies of those who do evil. Lord let the godly strike me! It will be a kindness! Lord if they reprove me, it will be soothing medicine. Don't let me refuse it. Lord I'm in constant prayer against the wicked and their deeds. Lord I find that Psalm 141:1-5 David wrote is very insightful. To think that a King would ask for a Godly person to rebuke what he's done is awesome. It shows that David may have made mistakes but was still in love with you Lord. I know Lord that it is very hard for us to go to anyone for help because of our pride and wanting to solve our problems by ourselves. I know that if I had taken the advice of my Christian Brother I wouldn't

be where I am now. I am ready to be reproved. Lord let the people that I will come in contact with when I'm out help keep me straight and give me sound advice when I am doing something that is against your will. Lord you know that I love you and I'm looking forward towards working in the Kingdom. Lord I just hope I'm worthy enough to work for your glory, gain and benefit. I ask again that you teach me your ways. I'll write later.

G.
Luke 22:42

October 24

Father,
Lord as Christians we do battle against the demonic. Satan and his fallen angels are well experienced at fighting against you Lord and your chosen people. Lord although Satan's been at this for a long time you have given us the blueprint to win. Lord in Ephesians 6:10-18 we are provide with all that we need for victory. The Belt of Truth; Body Armor of Righteousness; Shoe of peace of the Good News; Shield of Faith; Helmet of Salvation; Sword of the Word of God. Lord your Spiritual power will defeat Satan at every turn. Lord as long as we are in communion with you through prayer we can withstand Satan's attacks. Lord you are the Champion and you were knocked down but you rose again to claim the crown of victory, let us as your people also claim the victory. Lord you are my God and I will always love you. I know that there will be times that I try to separate myself from you in times of weakness and I have no excuses it's in those times I need you the most and for you to take the lead. Lord I hope that someday I'll be able to come back to what I've written to you and reflect on your love. I pray that my writings are not lost and I'll be able to take them with me when I leave. I will write tomorrow as always.

G.
Ephesians 1:19

October 25

Father,

Good evening Lord well I am so amazed that the White Sox are at this present time up on Houston 3-0 in the World Series. I am so proud of our Chicago team and I never thought I'd say that about the White Sox being a Cubs fan, oh well. Lord you are my King and I will bless your name forever, I will bless you every day and praise you. Lord you are the greatest and worth of praise. Lord you are mightier than anything that exists in this universe. There is goodness and love in all that you do and put us through. Everything that you do for us is for our gain and benefit. You have given us chances time and time again throughout history to follow your teachings. Lord you are still giving out your love for anyone who wants it. I praise you Lord for your great mercy. Lord I know that your Kingdom has no end and I can't even comprehend eternity but it's ours for the asking, and I thank you Lord. I have been stubborn in my life not wanting anyone to have control over me and the life that I lead and that was foolish of me. I am so glad that you have taken my pride and broken me down to be a better person than I was. I pray Lord that I always do your name honor and put it above all others. They say that with knowledge comes wisdom and that about as correct as it could be. For the knowledge of your grace is sufficient for me. Lord your Word has pierced my heart and the Word is true. I know that I get thrilled and excited when I'm being nurtured with the word. I know that if it were to be false my excitement would disappear and that would be the end. With your Word this is not the case. Lord I love you, I love the Word and I want so much to be able to fulfill my obligation as a Christian to glorify you Holy name. I will write tomorrow.

G.

Proverbs 16:18, 19

October 26

Father,
Dear Father I am just elated that the white Sox won the World Series, in 4 games straight what an accomplishment for a Chicago team. I wonder Lord if you might not have helped them win? I know you don't work that way, I was just reflecting. Lord I lift your name on high, Lord I love to sing your praises, you came for heaven to earth to show the way. These are the beginning words to a song I can't remember all the words except to say that your name should be lifted up for all to see and come to, when people search for ways to a better tomorrow it seems to me that you are left out of the plan. So instead of putting you first you end up last. Lord may I always come to you when I am in need. I know that with you Lord all things work for the good and that separated from you things usually turn out wrong. Lord I know that you answer when I call and I am given resolution to my question or problem. Lord you have always been faithful to me but I haven't been faithful with you. I am just so blessed by your forgiveness. Lord let me bask in your glow and feel the warmth of your love. Lord I'll write tomorrow.

G.
Zechariah 13:9

October 27

Father,
Dearest Lord I have some questions and so I bring them to you. Over the last few weeks I've watched a lot of Christian programs and have been utterly disappointed. I watch one where the program was held in a place called the Crystal Cathedral. What I'd like to ask you is why? Why do preachers feel it is necessary to spend untold amounts of money on such a gaudy place? Lord is it going to ensure them a place in heaven? I really don't think so and I'm sure you are not thrilled either. I could see where the money spent on this so called worship center could be used for a more important need and that's to feed the hungry, find homes for the homeless and give work to the needy. I think when non-Christians

see these type of things that have got to laugh, knowing that what true Christians are suppose to believe and what they do are different things. Lord I can't believe you're on board with these types of places. I see other mega churches doing the same and this is where I feel ashamed for all of us Christians that have a different opinion on how our money can be spent. I look at the Catholic Church and see the money that they have and they horrid it like a miser does. Lord I know they can't take it with them, so my question is why? Why don't they do the world a favor and help end poverty? I know that there are preachers out there telling everyone that they are entitled to be rich and powerful and that by praying to you this will happen, but I think that they miss the point; that there needs to be work done to obtain these thing, they are not going to win the lottery. Lord I am searching for the answers and I need your guidance and help to find the true church as Christ would want it. Lord I will search the scriptures and I know you will give me the answer. I love you and will write tomorrow.

G.
Philippians 4:19

October 28

Father,
Lord I want to thank you for all the great things I'm learning about putting you first. I now feel a peace that never was there before. Lord you have taken away the rough path I've been on and given me a less bumpy road and a much smoother ride. Lord you have calmed the sea around me and given me smooth sailing. Lord I've been able to come to you with questions and you've given me answers. I wrote you yesterday about my feelings of the problem with churches today and asked for an answer, you gave it to me when I went to Revelations and went through the churches John gave messages to. Lord I chose a Philadelphian Church; this is the church that you blessed the most. I know that when I get out I need to look for a church that not only exalts your name but preaches that Jesus blood was shed for me and he should be the head of the church. I need a church where the efforts and moneys coming to the church are used for the good of all mankind. I need a church family that feels this same way.

Lord your church is a church with no trimmings and it doesn't look like a Christmas tree. Lord your church has a heart for service; this is the type of church I will look for. I pray Lord that my journey is fruitful, and you will find me a place to land. Lord let me search with understanding and wisdom.

G.
Matthew 16:18

October 29

Father,
Lord in studying John, Chapter 10, I know that Jesus is my shepherd and I am his sheep. I once was lost and yet he found me. Jesus you're the good shepherd. Jesus you are the gate to the Kingdom. Jesus you offer me safety and security. Jesus you are my protector. Jesus you gave me a new life, and made my life full and made me abundantly rich. Jesus you are life eternal. Jesus I live on a greater plain because of your forgiveness, love and guidance. Jesus you protect me from eternal harm. Jesus has my souls even if I might have to suffer for my belief, I am assured eternity with Jesus. Jesus you and the Father are one in the same essence and nature. Jesus you are not merely a teacher you are God. Jesus I accept you as God and accept the truth of the Bible as the Word you gave me passed down from Moses to all mankind. I know Lord that there may come a time when I will need to choose whom I serve and may I be ready to surrender my life for your name, written above all others. Lord I wish to be a cornerstone for all people to see. I wish to be a beacon of light to guide your people home. Let me be a sentinel and stand watch to protect those who are your people. I love you Lord above all others, I know that I have many shortfalls and yet you still have a plan for me and I can feel that. Lord may I ever remain humble.

G.
1 Corinthians 16:13

October 30

Father,

Well Lord another good day for a Chicago team, the Bears beat the Lions to win another game, 3 in a row let's go! Lord I spent time in John again Chapter 11. Lord I need patients and to trust in you. Jesus when I need extraordinary help you give it. Jesus I can ask for assistance and you will help me. Jesus whatever trials I face you will face them with me. Jesus when I face those trials let me bring honor and glory to your name. Jesus you can turn bad into good. Jesus when trouble comes instead of grumbling, complaining, and blaming you, let me honor you instead. Jesus your timing is perfect for me whether it's immediate or I have to wait only you know why. Jesus you will meet my needs and I will wait on your perfect timing. Jesus the day brings forth light, the night brings for dark. Jesus do not let me stumble in the darkness. Jesus you are the resurrection and the life and I will believe in you and live again. Jesus you have the power over life and death. Jesus you have the power to forgive sin. Jesus you are life and can restore life. Jesus as you conquered death so will I. Jesus I have certainty and assurance that trusting in you I am blessed. Jesus as you declared your faithfulness towards me I declare my faithfulness to you. I have your word that you will heal me, that you will listen to me and that believing on you I am forever yours. Jesus you conquered death, you paid the price for my sins and no one can lay claim to a portion of your Kingdom without accepting you as the risen Lord. Hallelujah Lord! Hallelujah! I am so proud to be blessed by you. Lord I thank you for giving me back what I had lost in my past life. Lord today, tomorrow, and forever I can walk in your presence. Lord you gave and I obtained your precious love thank you, thank you, and thank you. Until tomorrow Lord when I write again.

G.

Psalm 51:6

October 31

Father,

Lord in studying Matthew 6, I find myself thinking about the calm I might have when I've gone through the storms here in prison. Lord I thank you for the peace you have given me. I know now that I need not worry. Lord I know I can depend on you and I won't be ignored. Lord I know that if I take care of today you will take care of tomorrow and beyond. I know Lord that with faith in you the worries are lifting and I will in time have learned how to lean on you completely. The freer I become; my relationship with you will grow. Lord faith can move mountains and I do and will have many mountains yet you will remove them for me and I thank you Lord. Lord I put you in my life and always will. Lord in Matt. 8, Jesus calmed the storm and demonstrated to his disciples that if they have faith they can weather the storms that will come upon them. Once the disciples began to realize that Jesus was God, a new day began to break. Lord I love you and will write next month.

G.
2 Corinthians 5:7

November 1

Father,
I want to thank you Lord for everything that you have given me. I'm not talking about material possessions, they fade away, but the real things that are important: Your Son for my sins, your constant love regardless of my faults, your constant forgiveness when I do the things that you disapprove of, and for a life eternal with you. I was weak and sometimes still am and yet you see past my weakness and shine down with your magnificent love. Lord if it wasn't for Jesus we would be separated when I die and now I know that I have a home with you in heaven. Lord I know that I do not have to earn my way to heaven it's already guaranteed. I also know that I want to make a difference in the lives of men who don't stand much of a chance when they get out. I do not know how to do this so Lord I am asking you to help; teach me, and mold me for this purpose. I ask Lord that you place me with the right people, the right church and the best situation to succeed at this task. Lord I feel that you are leading me in this direction and I will listen. Lord let me use the wisdom that you have given me to do this for the advancement of your Kingdom on earth. Lord you are my first love and may I always remember to put you first and to call upon you when I am having difficulties.

G.
Romans 15.20

November 2

Father,
Good evening Lord: well it's late and I thought I would ask some more questions. I was thinking about my past life and I'm feeling foolish and ashamed so I will ask you because I've been asking myself the questions and I need your thoughts. What happened in my life to lead me down the wrong path? Why did I do the things that I did? I know that I was raised by very loving parent. My siblings and I got along pretty well, we didn't have much but you met the family's needs and we were always provided for. I accepted Christ at about 12 years old, so I ask what happened. Lord was the turning point after I accepted Jesus and there was no one to guide me and I started to separate myself from you? Was it when I allowed an acquaintance to molest me when I was 13 years old and too stupid to say no? Was it because I didn't remain focused on many of the good things in life and embraced the sinful things in life, or was I just a kid that didn't worry about my life when I was so young? I don't know Lord I haven't a clue to the puzzle. Maybe when I get home I'll find the answer to this life question or you'll answer it for me in your time. I guess I really am like a lot of the inmates here in prison and I'm sure they have asked themselves the same questions. Lord I guess for the time being I'll just let the past be just that. I can't go back and you have forgotten this garbage. Lord I'm thankful for the corrections that I've made in my life and stand ready to face a new day and a new future. Well Father I'm tired and I just needed to sound off. I love you Lord and always put you at the head of my table.

G.
Psalm 38:8

November 3

Father,

Lord today was a nice day. Today I got my test scores back on my Political Science course, and English Composition course. I'm proud that I aced them both, so my grade for each of the classes is an A. I will be finished at the end of November and I'll get about one month back from the time I lost earlier this year. Lord with your help I'll get 4 more classes in with the next two sessions and might get out in August of next year, hopefully in time for my 58th birthday, I'm praying Lord I know that you can make it come to pass. Lord this last year and a half has been anything but pleasant, but then again I guess it's not supposed to be pleasant. Lord when I arrived here at Hill I was at a loss for things to help get me out of here earlier and yet you moved another mountain for me. Praise you Lord! Praise you! Lord I thank you again for listening to me and listening to my problems you said you would and you have. I was able to go to commissary today and stock up on food stuff and other essentials. I thank my family for sending me some money to help my cause. I've been thrifty with what has been provided. I know that when I get out I don't want to see another pack of Ramen Noodles for a long time. Lord! Blessed be your name above all others. I will write you tomorrow; the weather is getting colder time to put on the thermals.

G.
Psalm 59:16

November 4

Father,
Good evening Lord it's been a very relaxing day and I thank you for that. Today was my first time at the gym for exercise and I actually had an opportunity to work-out on the weight machines. I spent time with J. and was given pointers on how to use the machines. After working on the machines I walked around the gym for about 15 minutes. When I got back to the cell it was time to chill for awhile before dinner. I've got two guys that I made friends with, J. a crack- addict from Lombard, and K. who's in for multiply D.U.I. from McHenry. Both of these guys are funny loving and laid back we seem to get along great. We have been playing a lot of cards together and that's been one of the few fun things to do here on the gallery. The one thing about the school wing is that everyone here has a desire to learn and that keeps the unit fairly quiet. The unit feels a lot safer than any of the other units I've been in since I've been incarcerated. I know that K. goes to Sunday service for Catholics and J. doesn't have any desire to go but I'm going to work on him. Lord give me the understanding and knowledge to present you to him; so he can think about a relationship with you. Father I give you all the glory for whatever takes place as I work for the Kingdom, you are my God and I love you so much. I'll write tomorrow.

G.
Ephesians 2:4, 5

November 5

Good morning Lord.
I got up early to go for breakfast and I think I would have better served myself by staying in. The temperature at 4:00 in the morning in Nov. is a little chilly; well maybe a lot chilly. Anyway I figured that as long as I was up I'd spend time studying in the word and communicating with you so here I am writing another letter. I know that I don't have to come to you with these letters but it's comfortable for me so here I am. I know that it's coming up on Veteran's Day real soon and I'm thinking about the

men I served with over in Viet Nam and the men who are in Iraq and Afghanistan at this present time. I know that no one in their right mind wants to be fighting a war and maybe there were mistakes made about fighting these conflicts but we are there now and should probably see it through. I figured that we as a country might have learned by our mistakes in Viet Nam not to do the same but we haven't, so there are men dying again to protect a people who would like nothing better than for us to leave them to their own affairs and not worry about the rights of others who look for independence. Lord I would like to pray for all the men over in the Middle-East that are fighting to help people obtain a free society, free from torture and oppression. Lord I ask that you keep our men safe and out of harm's way. Father I wish that men could look at history a little clearer and see that war and hate never win and only decreases the world population. Lord I'm sorry to be on my high horse about this but I feel I served and have a right to complain, I only complain to you because you are a captive audience. Well Father I'll write you after the Bears game tomorrow. I love you Lord and will write tomorrow.

G.
Psalm 18:25-27

November 6

Father,
Good evening Lord it was great to see the Bears hang on to beat the Saints and have won 4 in a row that makes them 5-2 for the season. I hope the rest of the season is good for the Bears and we go to the playoffs. I guess I'll have to wait. I had a good fried chicken dinner with French fries. The biggest surprise was that it was hot for a change and that makes all the difference in the world. I spent the rest of the day reading in the word, reading a Nora Roberts novel and playing cards with J. and K. I also got my English assignment done for class so I had a busy day. I am hoping for some mail soon it's been a while, so I hope soon. I think that since I am allowed to call home the kids figure that it's easier to talk with me than write, I still like to get letters though. I think we get done with class the second week of Dec. and if all goes well I'll get 18 days off my remaining

time so that would reduce it to Oct. 13, 2006. I hope I can get more time than that with the next two sessions of classes. Lord I pray that everything goes smoothly and I can get the good time so I might go home closer to my scheduled out date. I love you Father and am so grateful. I thank you for listening to this old man rambling and I'll write you tomorrow.

G.
Romans 1:9

November 7

Father,
Good evening Lord thank you for another day. Lord I am trying to come to terms with the people that I let down and it's very hard to let the guilt go. Lord I pray to you for comfort and then get attacked by Satan. I know that you have forgotten my transgressions but in my mind they are still there. I have tried surrendering my friend and families resolutions to you and I pray that it works for me. Lord I never realized how many people I hurt by my addiction. There was always the next high and the more I got the more I wanted. Lord my addiction was as bad or worse than drug addicts, and alcoholics, I just couldn't see it because my addiction wasn't physical in nature. I know that my addiction was wrong and against your commandments I just go progressively out of control. I was very adept at hiding it and was able to do what I wanted without ever leaving my house. I know that I hurt myself the most and I didn't know it until I was arrested. All I know Lord is that when everyone began to abandon me it was only the true Christians that were there for me. I think the fact that some of my so called Christian friends and family forgot that as you forgive so should they. Lord I know that I have a lot of rebuilding to do when I get out and I will need your grace when that time comes. So I pray Lord that you guide me in the right way to correct my many errors. I know that I'm feeling down today and will feel better tomorrow I just had to vent forgive me for my pity party. I love you Father and I'll write tomorrow. Blessed be your name and the name of my Lord and Savior Jesus Christ.

G.
Romans 12:17-19

November 8

Father,
I got a nice letter from my daughter K. today and she sent me some pictures of my granddaughters. I see by their pictures that they have grown a foot since the last time that I saw them. It is nice to get pictures of the girls this gives me the opportunity to see them as they grow. I have two adorable granddaughters. My other daughter sent me pictures of my grandsons about a month ago so I can see their growth also. When I'm out in the world I was able to see them enough to watch them grow gradually. I am looking forward to that happy day when I can give them a big hug. That is something that all parents and grandparents should always try to do is let the kids know that they love them because I can say by experience that they are missed terribly. I know when you don't see them for a while I'm afraid they have forgotten you. I hope that when I see them after I'm out that they will remember me. I guess that there is a season in one's life where the things that are most important slip by and as time goes by it is almost too late. I pray Lord that it's not too late for me. I remember when I was at Stateville all the kids sent me copies of their hands and I've asked that they send them again so I can compare them with the ones sent 6 months ago. Lord let me always remember my grandkids and be a good example as I walk the Christian life. I love you Lord and will write tomorrow.

G.
Hebrews 12:28

November 9

Father,
Lord you are the magnificent God of all creation. A God of wonders, a God of peace and love and I am glad I found you; Father. Please be with me and give me strength through Jesus Christ my Lord. Send your Holy Spirit to help me blot out all the temptations that are put in front of me. Help cleanse me and purify my thoughts, words, and deeds. Lord I am less lonely Father because I have you to fall back on. Praise you God for offering up your Son for my eternal soul. This was the greatest act of love that has ever taken place. "The greatest of these is Love." I petition you Lord for those around me who run this unit. Lord that they use fair treatment towards me and the other inmates. I know Father that I've been asking you for help and you have been giving it to me. Lord give me what I need to help glorify your Holy name. Lord I know you know what's ahead of me and I pray that it's all good I want so much to be a disciple of you Lord please let this come to pass. In the name of Jesus; your Son.

G.
1 Corinthians 13:13

November 10

Father,
Lord the butterflies are still there and I try to trust in you with what is to come. I don't know if it is fear of my new life, fear of failure or it's the excitement of the blessings that you have given me. Lord I don't know if I'm being tested or that Satan is attacking me with doubt. Lord I pray that you remove any doubt and give me peace of mind. Lord I know that when I pray to you it's exciting and I get goose bumps. My prayers are exciting because I get to commune with you daily and I can use my prayers for the ministry you have planned for me. I know that my time on earth could be short especially looking at the world today. So any time I have with you is a blessing. Lord I know that I made a mess out of my life and you have corrected it and I thank you. I am looking forward to heaven where I'll see Jesus and you in all your glory. I am sad that I always put anything and

everything in front of you Lord not realizing that you are the only love I'll ever need. I know that I will always be tempted and yet you will always be there for me to give strength and encouragement bless you Lord and thank you. Satan no longer has a hold on me and you have broken those chains and again I say thanks. Lord you have led me from the dark into the light. I know Father that where I'm going there is no dark because your light will always be a beacon. Lord I'm ready; I'm set and want to go just fire the starting gun or even a bolt of lightning. Lord I will endeavor to keep my heart and mind pure. I will write tomorrow, as always.

G.
Galatians 3:5

November 11

Father,
Lord I just want to pray for all my fellow Veterans because today is our day. I ask that you bless all Veterans who have served their country faithful when duty called. I ask that you bless the families of those Vets, who gave their lives protecting the freedoms most people take for granted. For the families of all the Vets who have passed from this life to the next. I especially want to pray for the new Vets who are fighting in the Middle East. Lord bring as many as you can home and protect them while they are serving in Foreign lands. Happy Veterans Day!!!! Lord I know that most of the year the Vets. Are forgotten or out of peoples mind and that's why Veterans Day is so important. It's an honor for the living as well as Veterans past. I know that if everyone was required to serve the attitude would surely change and Vets would be honored more. So I personally say thanks to all my brothers and sisters in arms. A. this day is for you see you when I get home. I'm proud to have served and glad I'm being served by a new generation. Today was a quiet day, had some fish and chips for dinner and it was good and hot for a change, I think that was because our unit was first to go to chow.

G.
Ephesians 6:13, 14

November 12

Father,
I struggle everyday to exist here in prison. This is not a place that I'd wish on anyone. There is nothing it this place that is positive for the men that reside here. I guess looking at it from the outside looking in, it might be said that the prisoners have been given too much leeway. Lord all I can see is that this is a prison; where there are controlled environments where men must obey without question or face corporal discipline. This control is paramount in the Illinois Correctional Facility. This control is for the safety of the officers guarding the prisoners. There is no sense of freedom in the minds of the prisoners, and there is strong dislike of the C.O.'s. The Correctional System was change in the mid 90's so the guards could have complete control of the prisons. I know that since these controls were instituted not one Corrections Officer has died at the hands of an inmate. I guess in retrospect this is a blessing for them. I know that this control also protects more fully the weaker prisoners from harm by the more violent and experienced prisoners. I hope that someday there will be no more repeat offenders and fewer men in prison. I do know that things are going to get a lot worse than better for the next several years. Lord you are my God and all I ask is to serve you. Use any way you see fit. I will write tomorrow as always.

G.
Luke 22:50, 51

November 13

Father,
Good evening. Another wonderful day for the Chicago Bears as they beat the 49ers; 17-9, that's 5 in a row. The Bears are starting to put things together. I pray that they keep on winning and maybe make the playoffs. I was thinking today about all the fantastic jobs I've worked at and I know I am blessed because I loved all of them. I remember back in the early 70's telling me that the best way to get rid of migraine headaches was to find a job I liked. I took him up on this advice and every job from that point in was one I liked and felt comfortable with, no more migraines and some very unique and enjoyable jobs. I was a policeman, a fireman, a lineman, a truck

driver, and I cleaned up disasters; like fires and floods. I know that the most enjoyable job was being on the fire department for 8 years. I fought fires and worked as an E.M.T. for the department. I was in a flash over once and got the hair on my head singed. I was piking down a ceiling and had a piece of sheet metal come down and slice my lip open, had 8 stitches put in by a plastic surgeon, even with these minor mishaps this was the greatest job in the world. Lord I thank you for all the wonderful jobs that I've had in my life and I am looking forward spending the rest of my life working for your kingdom and your glory and gain that I may make a difference in the lives of prisoners some way, somehow. I love you Lord as always.

G.

Philippians 3:10

November 14

Father,

I am feeling rather blue today and I need to come back to you. I know that Satan is attacking and giving me a guilty feeling. I feel lonely and depressed and I need you to help me. I have asked forgiveness for all the sinful things I've done and know that you have forgiven me and Satan still attacks. I pray again for you to lighten my load and keep me on the right path heading towards Glory land. I love you Lord and never want to be separated from you in anyway. I wish that all people could feel the love that you have waiting for them if they just come to you, the love that I feel everyday of what life I have left. Praise you Lord! You have taken care of my every need and I don't understand why I still have doubts, I guess Satan tries to make a person think that he's not worthy and yet I know I am. So I ask that you put a protective hedge around me to block out these attacks by Satan. Lord you can ease the pain and agony with one mighty thought and I need it now. Prince of darkness you have no hold on me, you have no control and I claim the blood of Jesus over you. I love my Father and your power is void Satan so depart from my life. Father as I pray for help I feel your loving arms around me and that gives me comfort. Hallelujah! Father I will write tomorrow and I thank you for your presence here in this time of need. I love you Lord and praise your Holy name.

G.

Ephesians 6:17

November 15

Father,
Lord I thank you again for the blessing of being able to commune with you daily. I am so grateful of the love you show me. I know Lord that I was heavily in despair yesterday but I also know that you comforted me in my time of need so I thank you. I was sad because I got to thinking that I always put everything ahead of you and never looked to you for the guidance I needed for that I'm sorry. I know that through the Blood of Jesus I cannot be harmed maybe a little singed but Satan can't do to me what he did before unless I allow it so I rebuke him. Lord I am standing by the river and wanting to get to the other side for your glorious reunion of the saints and the supper table of the Lamb. One day Lord I'll be able to say that I fought the good fight and claim victory for you my Father, in my race here on earth. Lord may I help in showing people throughout the world your glory. Lord I pray at this time for my best friend D.H. that through observing the suffering and pain that I've been through he might see the difference in me and come to accept you as his Lord and Savior. Lord I hope that when I get out I can help him see the light and correct the error in his thoughts about you, he is so stubborn. I am so looking forward to the time when I can see him again. I know that day will come and I will be patient until then. Lord you are my Savior and your Holy Spirit works within me. I praise and love you constantly as I walk down my path. I will talk with you tomorrow, as always.

G.

2 Timothy 3:24-26

November 16

Father,
Lord may your glory be shown to the world. I love you Father and I thank you for the grace you have shown me through your Son Jesus and the presence of the Holy Spirit. I pray Lord that all my family and friends take notice of the sin that brought me to this prison and that they bring themselves before you Lord to repent and find them a new love or to refresh the love that they might have had before and let it slip away at some point during their life. Lord I pray for the men in my Wednesday class that they may overcome their guilt and learn that you have relief for their suffering in accepting Jesus as their Lord and Savior. Lord help them see who you are and what you can do for them, Lord no one is beyond hope, and make them realize that they can have a life that they don't need to give up, there is a future. Lord I pray that T. can rebuild his relationship with his wife and family. I pray that H. can see that he is not alone in his suffering and that there is forgiveness if he asks. I pray for our group leader that he has the right things to stimulate the group in our understanding of what brought us to where we are right now. Lord I know that I can count on you for the help I need and you will be able to help those in my group if only they will get past their stubbornness. I thank you Father for your great mercy towards me and all mankind. I ask this all in the name of Jesus. I love you Lord and will write tomorrow.

G.
2 Timothy 3:16

November 17

Father,
Lord I pray that when I go out and present you to others that they have a heart to feel the love that you have given me and that they might have the same love beaming from within that I have. Lord as I get more into the Word I find out how much you love your people and about all the chance that were given to them. I know also that we as a people are stubborn and do not want to be told how to act or when to act. I know that we as a people living for ourselves and not you Lord and that's the grace of free will that you gave to all of us long ago. Lord I know that we have found it easier to abuse that gift for our own gain and benefit and not yours. Lord for myself I am sorry that I abused this right that you gave me. Lord may I always remember to put you first in all that I do, to remember that you can answer all my troubles and lift the burdens from me. I have given you my life and I am thankful for your forgiveness and the sacrifice of my Lord and Savior Jesus Christ. Father I know that I do not need to look back because all those guilty stains have been removed and forgotten and I am forgiven. Praise you Jesus! I am just so elated that you have washed me clean and I can look forward to eternity with you. Lord I ask that you continue to strengthen me and mold me for the tasks that you will give me in the future. I need your wisdom and understanding to help me in this journey so I pray for your deliverance. I know Father that every day that goes by I learn more and more about your love and I thank you for the life lessons you give. Lord I must always remain faithful to you when good things happen or when bad things occur in my life so I just want to remain humble in your ways and do the right thing for your gain and benefit. I love you Lord and will write tomorrow as always your trusting son,

G.
2 Timothy 4:12

November 18

Father,
Lord I want to say good evening and thank you for a very blessed meal. I always look forward to fish Friday because I know it's one meal that is real and not made up of vegetable by-products or processed meats. So it was a good meal even if it was only lukewarm. I wish that the Mac and Cheese had been a little bit thicker, but I'll take what I can get. I was able to trade a pack of noodles for an extra portion so I was able to have I respectable meal. Lord I am just so thankful for my family and their love for each other. I know that most of the men here have come from broken homes and not many have had a structured life and this might be a factor in why they have arrived at this place. I would hope that they could reach out to their family like I have been able to do. I do not want to see them abandoned. I am so thankful for the classes I'm taking it is nice to get out of the cell for extended periods of time. The classes I'm taking are going well and next month I should get some of my good time back, praise you Lord for making this all possible. I am so blessed that I have you in my life I really can't believe I was so dumb to have ignored you for so long.

G.
1 Peter 2:22

November 19

Father,
Lord I was watching the Gaithers and their Homecoming Friends and was thinking about their trip to Jerusalem, the city where my Savior your Son was crucified so that I might live. In thinking about this I had tears of sadness and tears of joy, sadness that my Savior Jesus died for me, sadness that his own people turned away for him, and sadness that I too spent much of my life turning away. Lord my Joy is knowing that I have been given eternal life from his great sacrifice. I know that when I am called home there will be a New Jerusalem waiting for me and all believers thanks to his blessing. Hallelujah Father! Hallelujah! Lord I'll hangout the banners and shout the "Good News" that Jesus Christ is my Lord and

risen King. Lord that we are set free from any hold this world or Satan may have had, death has no victory with me. Lord I'm on such a wonderful high knowing that I will always be with you as you will be with me. Thank You Lord! Lord you know that I have tears in my eyes for what's going on around me both the good and bad. It's the blessing that I no longer fear my surroundings, I no longer feel hate and disappointment with the inmates that I do not get along with because they have chosen their own path and I'm not responsible for their problems. Lord I know that you are in control of my situation and I never need fear. I know that you have given me the protection through you Holy Spirit. Praise you Father! Lord I want to pray for those inmates who do not accept the gift that you have given to all mankind. I pray that some day they wake up to the knowledge of your grace. I love you Lord and thanks, I'll write tomorrow.

G.
1 Peter 1:22

November 20

Father,
Good evening Lord. Bless you and praises to your name above all others. Bless you Son Jesus and the Holy Spirit that was given to me for all eternity. Today was a pretty good day in sports. The Bears beat the Panthers 13-3 and that makes 6 in a row. Go Bears! I got in to a few good games of cards, spent time working in Corinthians and Galatians furthering my knowledge of Jesus and his grace for me. Praise Jesus! I bring my sins to you tonight, the things that I might have said or done that offended you, to ask forgiveness for them. It's very difficult not to sin even when I'm trying so hard. I know I catch myself using curse words and think how stupid I've been or said something that might have offended one of the inmates I'd been talking to. I know that the Destroyer is always there to trip me up so he can attack my heart, he's not gaining much ground these days and I thank your Holy Spirit for interceding for me. I find that a lot of the guys in the cell block are trying to reach out for your love but get distracted and forget you Lord. Have pity on me as well as them, continue to show us the way. I know that there is power in that wonderful blood of Jesus. I've been talking with K. and J. trying to get them to understand all that you

did for me and that you would help them if only they would let you so I pray for them as well as the other inmates. I looked at myself in the metal mirror today and noticed that I am starting to age and am looking more like my dad all the time. I will write tomorrow Lord, I'm just trying to keep it real as always.

G.
1 Peter 2:1-3

November 21

Father,
Good evening Lord, today has been a day of quiet and peace. I guess I should be thankful that nothing is going on. I am really surprise I don't get to many days that are like this. It might be the peace that comes from studying you word and finding out all the wonderful things that you have promise to me as a follower of your Son Jesus. I really like the part about spending eternity with you. I can't wait to be called home. I will be so happy to have a perfect body, and a perfect voice. A voice that will sing praises to you in that great chorus on high. Lord I ask that you continue to draw me nearer to your grace. I never want to lose sight of your fantastic glory. I know that when I get out there will be skeptics and I'm sure many ups and downs. Lord with you as my rock I am on solid ground. Praise you Lord! Praise you! Thank you Jesus for removing all my guilty stains it is such a blessing to be a child of the Kingdom. I know that you will always love me through all my faults and frailties that may take place in the future. I know I can't worry about tomorrow because I'm only given the present. Lord I am not expecting to come home and I know that you have something special planned for my life. I just want you to know that my bags are packed and I'm ready to go when you call. Lord I know that I will one day make a difference in the lives of people who need a helping hand; as a beacon of light for the lost. I trust in you Lord and I thank you for giving me the opportunity to walk in your grace again. I will write tomorrow as always.

G.
Revelation 21:3

November 22

Father,
Good evening Lord today I have been reflecting on faith and it seems to me that a lot of people are afraid to take that leap. I know that behind these prison wall a lot of inmates have given up any hope of a new life when it is their time to get out so they will go back to their old ways and this makes me sad, as sad as I've ever been to see souls who are lost for all eternity and when they reach the end of the road that life will end forever. I myself know that a life separated from you for all eternity is not something I'd want anyone to go through no matter what they have done. I also can see where men have a hard time believing in someone or thing they can't see. Lord whatever you want of me let me do it with as much love as I can. Lord when Abraham was tested by offering his son Isaac as a sacrifice it was through his great faith that you made him the Father of all nations. It was by faith that Moses brought the nation of Israel out of Egypt, and by faith your son Jesus died on Calgary so all who accept him will have eternal life oh what a blessing these acts of faith in your Holy name must have been. I think this is one reason why my heart is touched and have tears in my eyes when watch biblical movies that show Jesus sacrifice on the cross or these movies show the sacrifices many went through for their part in the Kingdom. Lord there is no one or anything that is greater then you and I'm proud to be count in that number when I'm called home. Lord I will write tomorrow and we'll talk further.

G.
Romans 3:24

November 23

Father,
Lord I want to talk with you tonight about joy and victory. I read Psalm 98 and as it gave me joy I know it will give joy to others: Sing a new song to the Lord, for he has done wonderful deeds. His right hand has won a mighty victory; his holy arm has shown his saving power. The Lord has announced his victory and has revealed his righteousness to every nation! He remembers his promise to be faithful to Israel. The ends of the earth have seen the victory of our God. Shout to the Lord all the earth; break out in praise and sing for joy! Sing your praises to the Lord with the harp, with the harp and melodious song, with trumpets and the sound of the ram's horn. Make a joyful symphony before the Lord, the King! Let the sea and everything in it shout his praise! Let the earth and all living things join in. Let the rivers clap their hands in glee! Let the hills sing out their songs of joy before the Lord. For the Lord is coming to judge all the earth. He will judge the world with justice, and all the nations with fairness. Lord all I can say is wow! Lord this gives a great picture of the loving kindness the Psalmist felt for what you have done and how you will judge in the future. I know that I can claim victory and leap for joy knowing that Jesus gave it to me. I praise and sing to you oh Lord for my salvation. I will write tomorrow and give you thanks as always.

G.
Psalm 98

November 24

Father,
Happy Thanksgiving! Lord I give you thanks for everything. Lord there is nothing in this world past, present and future that is here by any other way than the way you have decided it. Lord your will is perfect and although much of what has happened, the cause of which may never be known I can be assured that it was and will be for the good and the right. Almighty, most Holy God as time has gone by you dwell within everyman and that indwelling Spirit is the protector of the faith and I am proud to be in that number. Praise you Lord. I think back on all the wonderful Thanksgivings and they were spectacular for the most part. I remember going to church and sing wonderful hymns praising your name for all that you have given. I remember the joyous time sitting around the dinner table and enjoying a great turkey dinner with all the trimmings, it was really great. I remember watching all the parades and football games that were on T.V. I remember going downtown to Chicago and window shopping preparing for Christmas. I know that some day that will happen again, thank you Lord. We had a pretty good dinner today, it may not be as good as family cooking but at least they gave us extra portions of food. We had processed turkey, and ham, real mash potatoes, sage dressing, cranberry sauce, cheese cake and pie. I give thanks Lord for these provisions, I give thanks for my family and friends, I give thanks for a calm and peaceful day here in our unit, most of all Lord I give thanks to my Jesus for his gift of life. I love you Lord and praise your Holy name. I will write tomorrow.

G.
1 Thessalonians 5:18

November 25

Father,
Good evening Lord, it has been a quiet day here left over from too much turkey and fixing's. I am sure that tomorrow the unit will be back to normal. The weather has turned cold and winter is in the air, fresh and cool. I am going to dread the super cold because the coats that we have are not very warm and do not keep out the cold. I know I will survive however, although I will have to suffer in the arthritis dept. Lord I ask for comfort and warmth this winter season, make the next three months as comfortable as possible, keep out the chill, thank you Lord. I think that the saddest part of holidays in prison is that everyone including me knows that our families on the outside are gathered together but it's the not being with them that hurts the most. I just have to remember that we did this to ourselves and we must take the blame. I know Lord that you are with me and will always be and that makes my holidays go by a lot easier. Lord I know that I will still have many holiday seasons ahead where I'll be able to commune in fellowship with my family and friends. I love you Lord and I'll write you tomorrow.

G.
1 Thessalonians 5:23

November 26

Father,
Lord I will thank you every day for the rest of my life and I will lift my eye up to you in heaven. Lord you are my shelter, my armor and my protector and refuge. I can feel safe in the shelter of your wings. Lord I know that you will rescue me when my enemies are upon me. Lord I honor your name above all others. Lord I am grateful for all you have helped me with here and throughout my life. Let me praise you for all eternity. Lord when called upon let me listen and do that which you have chosen for me. I know that you above all others will never desert me and I thank you. Lord my eyes have seen many things and nothing that I've ever seen compares to the visions of life you have shown me through your Word and I thank

you for that. Lord I know it took me a long time to come to you but then it took Abraham a long time to have an heir. It took Noah a long time to build an ark, and it took Moses a long time to rescue your children from Egypt so if it took them a long time I guess I can be glad you have me as one of your children too. I love you Lord and I just can't stop praising and glorifying your name. Lord you gave me a chance when many would have given up and I'm so grateful. I will write tomorrow as always.

G.
Hebrews 4:16

November 27

Father,
Good evening Lord, well it was another good day for the Bears they beat Tampa Bay making it 6 in a row. It's starting to look real good for a spot in the playoffs. Lord I know that I was a prodigal son. I know I took the long way home to get to you and I am sure happy that I did. There is nothing more exciting than to know that you truly love me and always will. There is nothing more wonderful than being in love and I am so in love with you Lord. Lord through all my ins and outs your there, and for all my short comings you never once gave up and I am so thankful today knowing that I will have an eternity to tell you. Lord I ask that you take this poor wretch and turn him into someone that you may be proud off I desire this of you in the name of Jesus I pray for this. Lord make yourself known to me and give me the wisdom to listen to the thoughts that you give me so I may be a better person in this world. Lord I hate evil and will always try to avoid those things that are evil in your eyes. I may fall down but I know that you will be there to pick me up and dust me off and I thank you. Lord I will write tomorrow as always.

G.
1 Peter 1:13

November 28

Father,
Lord I know that there will be a time when I'll be free of my bondage to this world and bind myself to your world and I feel blessed for that. Jesus take my hand and lead me, teach me, comfort me and have mercy on me. There is an old song that is used to call and draw people to you: "Just as I Am" and the first time I heard this song I was drawn down to the platform where Billy Graham had be preaching the blood of Jesus and first accepted Jesus as my Lord and Savior. I have traveled a long way since that day over 50 years of travel to be precise. I know that over this time period I did so many things that would have given many friends and family heart attacks, I do not think that many would believe these things I'd done were possibly true, you are the only one who knows all and you have forgiven me and I'm so thankful otherwise I would have been damned. Lord there will be a time of freedom and I am bound by love to do whatever you desire of me from this day until my end. I know that I have less than a year to go in this forsaken place and I will prevail with you by my side; who can be against me. Lord you are my God for all time and I am so honored to have come to your throne and present all my faults and sins for your forgiveness and grace. I am honored to serve the Kingdom. Praise you Lord. I'll write tomorrow as always.

G.
1 Peter 4:12

November 29

Father,
Lord I give thanks for your great mercy and the wonderful blessings that you have given me throughout my life. I just hope and pray that at some point in their lives that all the inmates here and in other prisons may come to know you like I have. Lord work on their hearts as they serve their time. I find great comfort reading Paul's journey on his path to your Kingdom. In Romans Paul submits to your will and considers himself a slave to Jesus Christ and apostle. I want what Paul has; such a love and dedication to Jesus. I know that like Paul I had helped put nails in the hands of Jesus as he died on the cross for me and all mankind. I know Lord that I've been

chaste and been forgiven and yet I still feel ashamed that Jesus had to die so I might live. Let me and men of every kind become stainless in your eyes forgive us Lord for our shortcomings. I eagerly await the tasks that you will give me when my name is called. Lord let me listen and learn what it is that I will be doing for the Kingdom. Lord we all have sinned and fall short of your glory, Romans 3:23. Lord I know that the wages of sin is death Romans 6:23, but Jesus has made the ultimate sacrifice for me and died for my sins Romans 5:8. Lord I believe that Jesus is my Savior and ask for forgiveness and trust that my Salvation is in Jesus Christ Romans 10:8-10. Father I have been given another chance don't let me blow it. Lord I love you and will write tomorrow as always.

G.
Romans 10:8, 9

November 30

Father,
Good evening. Well it's time to give you my monthly report. My classes have been going well and next month I will finish and find out how many days I'll have removed from the time I have left to serve. I hope it is a decent amount of days. I really want out of this place and the sooner the better. My empathy group is going well and the group is following a great format that will help us overcome when we are back in society. I know that for two years after I am out I will be on parole but after my stay here it will be easy to follow the rules that my parole will bring. November was good for the Bears and they didn't lose a game the whole month. I was able to make a couple of friends in K and J. We get along great and we can talk about our issues and support each other as each day passes. We will be getting out within a month of each other, and we all live within 50 miles of each other so we might even keep in touch. Lord I am just thankful for all the wonderful words that you have given me to live by. I love my family and am thankful that I wasn't forgotten on Thanksgiving and I appreciate the cards that they sent me. I am blessed to have such a beautiful family. Lord as the snow and cold of December arrive so does the year soon come to a close all in all it's been a very year. Lord I'll write you next month as always.

G.
Psalm 117

December 1

Father,
Lord I don't know where the following quote came from but it's interesting for me to note: "If you are to be used by God, he will take you through a multitude of experiences that are not meant for you at all; they are to make you useful in his hands and enable you to understand what happens in other souls so you will never be surprised at what you come across". I find this so true and have been there and done that. I know now that I am the clay and you are the potter. I ask to be molded to mirror the images of all the saints that have gone on before me that were in the fields or trenches of warfare against to powers of darkness. I want to be a prosperous farmer, a great warrior for your glory Lord. Lord I would like to think that I have a new nature and through your Word I learn so much of what you created and want to become a help in presenting you to others so that they might obtain the Keys to the Kingdom. Lord I take up my cross and I follow Jesus with total love so that I am worthy of a place near your side. I have had lots of problems and issue in the throngs of life and have had many experiences that may qualify me of the job. Lord I pray that you use me to the best of my abilities. Lord welcome to my December may it be fruitful for me in both my personal and Christian life. I will write tomorrow as always.

G.

Jeremiah 46:3-6

December 2

Father,
Precious Lord I give you thanks and glory for always being here with me. You listen to me without turning away. Lord you never desert me and always give me comfort I thank you for that. I know that when I listen to you things always go better than when I try to ignore you, I thank you for that. I was thinking about friends and how as the years go by my friends change. I realized that the people who were important forty, thirty, twenty, ten, and five years ago are different. As my life situation changed so did my friends. I know that every time I got an itch to do something new I would drift away from one friend and make another. I found that only one friend D.H. has always been constant and he has been a blessing. I know that he hurts over the fact that I'm here in prison and he can't understand why. Lord he like you has never abandoned me even when things in my life fell apart and disaster struck. I ask myself is it common for all of us to drift so far from one another that we forget the wonderful time we had with our friends in the past? Lord I know that you are my greatest friend and you and I will always have a friendship and I know that I can bring any problem I have or situation I get myself into and talk to you about it. Lord you don't get mad, you don't desert and you always give the right advice. I pray Lord that I always have an ear to hear. Father I pray that all the friends I've had over the years are doing well. I pray thank you Lord for always being my No. 1 friend. I will write tomorrow my friend.

G.
1 Samuel 3:9

December 3

Father,
It's Saturday and time to take it easy after a busy week in school. I had tests in both classes and I think I did pretty well. I know that in a couple of weeks that I will be eligible for some good time and that means I'll be going home sooner. Lord I was think back on my life and all the things that I've done and my greatest regret is abandoning you, I'm so sorry. Lord if I had come to you I would have had a more solid foundation and I would be looking back at three wives how stupid I was always chasing the perfect woman for me. I did not allow you to help in these selections and it cost me everything in the end. I was not faithful to them and I wasn't faithful to you. I know Lord that what I went through would have been unnecessary if you had been in the equation and I would have had a different outcome than the one I face these days. Lord let me learn from the mistakes of the past and guide me through the rest of my years. Lord I need you with me on my journey and I intend to be a better person then the one I was in the past. I will always try to put you first in all that I do as I walk along the path that you have chosen for me. Lord I just thank you so much for listening and your great understanding is appreciated. I love you Lord and will be a blessing for you in the time I have left on this earth. I will write tomorrow as always.

G.
Isaiah 48:17, 18

December 4

Father,
Good evening from Chicago Bear central 8 wins in a row and it looks like a playoff spot towards the Super Bowl. Today was a good day not because of the Bears win but just the comradely I've had with K. & J. The three of us are getting closer as friends and spend a lot of time together when we are doing the activities that we are allowed to do which of course isn't much but it still an opportunity to make some friends. I wonder when we all get out if this friendship will last. I guess only time will tell and

that won't happen for awhile so I'll won't worry about it until sometime next year. I've talked to my daughters and they asked what I wanted for Christmas so I gave them some ideas, basically money on my account and some new books to read. I asked that they send pictures of the grandkids and they said that they would so Christmas at Hill won't be as bad as Last year at Stateville. I look back at last December and think of all the hurt and pain I went through and am thankful to be where I'm at today. Lord I pray thank you for giving me life lessons throughout this year, for the teaching I've received in working in the Word, praise you Father for that blessing. I wish that others here in prison could understand how much more comfort they could have if they only started a journey with you. I pray that the people I have talked to start a relationship with you that will ease their suffering. I will write tomorrow as always.

G.
Proverbs 18:24

December 5

Father,
Good evening Lord, it's been a great day I aced my tests in my classes and even if I were not to pass anymore test I am assured of getting some time back thank you Lord for being with me as I took my tests. I am thankful for the wisdom that you have related to me through my studies in the Word. I am glad that you have given me a great foundation to build my new life upon. I need only to remember to continue to put you first and you will guide my every step thank you Lord. I had an opportunity to weigh myself today when I went for my yearly checkup and I have lost 60 lbs I weighed 170 lbs wow is all I can say. I feel healthier and less tired then when I first was incarcerated and that is a good thing especially in here. I still wish that I had a warmer coat because it's downright cold out today and with the wind it feels even worse. I am still thankful that we haven't had much snow because that would be a whole new ballgame. I know that gym shoes aren't the best thing to be walking in the snow with. I was able to pick-up a set of sweats to wear around the unit so even the drafts from the cold are less in here, thank you for your provision. Lord you are so

great and you are always on time I am so thankful for your blessings to a poor sinner like myself. Lord I know that I sound like a broken record but I can never seem to give you enough praise for all you do for me, I know you know my heart so I'll leave it at that. I will write tomorrow as always.

G.
Mark 9:35

December 6

Father,
Good evening Lord today I was working in Revelations and I thank Jesus I'm a believer. I know that the trials and tribulations that will be placed upon mankind is going to be horrific. I know that this earth has never seen what your wrath can do at least not for thousands of years and it seems to me this will be worse. Give it up for Jesus is my motto. Lord I am so thankful that Jesus died for me and I will not be in this world if I'm reading Revelations right. Psalm 23 says: The Lord is my shepherd; I have all that I need. He lets me rest in green meadows; he leads me beside peaceful streams. He renews my strength. He guides me along right paths, bringing honor to his name. Even when I walk through the darkest valley, (death) I will not be afraid, for you are close beside me. Your rod and staff protect and comfort me. You prepare a feast for me in the presence of my enemies. You honor me by anointing my head with oil. My cup over flows with blessings. Surely you goodness and unfailing love will pursue me all the days of my life, and I will live in the house of the Lord forever. Lord I think that sums it up for me. Thank you!!!!!! Lord I've given you my life and will always be thanking you I don't think you'll ever get tired of hearing it so if I say it often it's my praise to you. I love writing Lord and I will chat tomorrow as always.

G.
Psalm 23

December 7

Father,
Good evening Lord, today is the day that will live in infamy. Lord on this day the bombing of Pearl Harbor took place and thousands died at the hands of our enemies. The start of WWII. I wasn't around at the time but my father was and he enlisted in the Navy I'm proud to say. He didn't see any combat but where he was stationed he might have. He was on one of the peninsula islands close to Russia. I know he said it was quite cold. I pray thank you for his safety back then, he had a big part in me being born. Seriously I am thankful because I know lots of men gave their lives throughout the war and sacrifices were made by them, family and friends back home. I know it is easy to forget and I feel I should make an effort to remember them every day. Lord I know that everything in this world is yours and created with your ultimate plan. Lord there is nothing that you don't know in fact you know tomorrow. I am glad I don't know the future because not know is the challenge that keeps me going. Lord you know that I want to have the right relationship with you and live a life that you are proud of. Lord one of the things that has happened since February is being able to feel your presence and that comforts me in my daily life. Lord I know my time is brief here on earth so let me be all that I can be for the Kingdom. I love you Lord and will write tomorrow.

G.
Joel 2:11

December 8

Father,
Lord as I start looking back I go back to the time when at Mt. Sterling upon arrival I was placed in the Phase program, locked down only to go to the chow hall and back. I had lots of time for reflecting back on my life all the good, the bad and ugly that took place in my life. I think that it was during this time that I began to realize that a good majority of my life had been one lie after another. I didn't really like what I saw; my selfishness, my pridefulness and unnecessary wants. I think that everything was about

me. It was at this point that I really knew a change was in order. I started by releasing the anger I felt for all the people that abandoned me when I was incarcerated. I didn't really think about doing it for your sake at the time but for mine. Lord I know that giving my burden to you worked better when I became ready. Lord you lifted me up and made me new and I thank you for that blessing. Lord continue to educate me and mold this piece of clay. I am ready for your instructions and am listening. Lord let me work with the wisdom, knowledge and skills that you provide. Let me walk with integrity and honesty towards completion of the mission you give me. Correct my errors with kindness and love. Continue to grow in me and make me stronger every day. Lord I was damaged goods and you repaired me and I am like new and I thank you so much. Lord I will write you tomorrow as always.

G.
James 1:19, 20

December 9

Father,
Good evening Lord well tonight's dinner was another spectacular fish dinner, Mac and Cheese included. I have been given a list from one of the inmates that is working in your Word and came up with a list of words to live by: Romans 6:14 Sin must not be my master for I do not live under the law but under your grace Lord. Romans 2:6 For you will reward each of us according to what we've done. Romans 3:22 Lord you make me right in my faith through Jesus; you do this for all believers in Christ because there is no difference at all. Romans 4:7, 8 Happy are those whose wrongs are forgiven, whose sins are pardoned. Happy is the person whose sins are not kept account of by you Lord. Romans 5:8,9 But you Lord have showed how much you love us; it was while we were sinners that Jesus died for us, but by his blood we are now put right with you Lord. How much more then will we be saved by Jesus from your anger. Romans 6:22, 23 But now I've been set free from sin and am a slave to you Lord. Your gain is a life dedicated to Jesus and the result is eternal life; for the wages of sin is death, but you free gift Lord is eternal life in union with Jesus. Romans 8:1 For

there is no condemnation for those who are in union with Jesus. Romans 8:14, 15 For those who are lead by the Spirit are your children Lord. For the Spirit that you have given Lord does not make me a slave or cause me fear, instead the Spirit make me your child Lord and by the Spirit's power I call out "Father, my Father." Wow what a blessing these words are that C. put down on paper, true words to live by, thank you C. and thank you Lord for bringing C. to me with them. Well I'll write tomorrow as always.

G.
Romans 3:22

December 10

Father,
In searching through the Word Lord I saw a list that was created about our true identity is Christ and thought it to be pretty insightful, the following is that list:

- Romans 3:24, I am not guilty of sin, Jesus takes them away.
- Romans 8:1, No condemnation awaits us because we belong to Christ.
- Romans 8:2, I am set free from sin and death by Jesus life giving Spirit.
- 1 Corinthians 1:2, Made Holy in Jesus when I call upon him.
- 1 Corinthians 1:30, Pure and Holy in Christ with his wisdom.
- 1 Corinthians 15:22, I will live at the resurrection and there is not eternal death.
- Corinthians 5:17, I am a new person as a Christian, the old is gone.
- 2 Corinthians 5:21, I am made right with you Lord through Jesus sacrifice.
- Galatians 3:28, I am one in Christ with other believers.
- Ephesians 1:4, I am holy and without fault, before I was born.
- Ephesians 1:5, 6, I was adopted as your child through Christ's blood.
- Ephesians 1:7, Our sins are forgiven and taken away when we are with Christ.
- Ephesians 1:11, 12, I am brought under authority for you Lord because of Christ.
- Ephesians 1:13, I am marked and belong to you by the Holy Spirit.
- Ephesians 2:6, I have been raised with Christ to sit in heavenly realms.

Lord I was going to work through these truths tonight but I am exhausted. I love you Father and will finish them tomorrow, as always.

G.
1 John 2:27

December 11

Father,
Good evening Lord, I watched the Bears game today and I guess they had to lose eventually. I hate it when they lose to Green Bay. Oh well this happens. I got so tired last night that I couldn't continue the list a found while doing my studies so here are the rest of the thoughts on true identity:

- Ephesians 2:10, I am your masterpiece.
- Ephesians 2:13, I am nearer to you.
- Ephesians 3:6, I share in the promise of blessings through Christ.
- Ephesians 3:12, I can come boldly and confidently in your presence.
- Ephesians 5:29, 30, I am a member in the body of Christ. (The church)
- Colossians 2:10, I am made complete on Christ.
- Colossians 2:11, I am set free from my sinful nature.
- 2 Timothy 2:10 I have eternal glory.

Well that's the completion of the list and it gives me great comfort knowing that I am a follower of my Savior Jesus. I thank you Lord for your grand design. I know that when I fail I can always come to you in the name of Jesus. I am glad that I belong to you Lord. Lord you are present with me at all times. Lord if I seem distant I haven't forgotten, I truly love you. Will write tomorrow, as always.

G.
1 John 3:1-3

December 12

Father,
Lord I was thinking back on all the things that I did in the last 40 years and looking back I was for the most part selfish in my desires. My wants were always first in my life and I seemed to hurt others to get what I wanted. I tried to do well and get involved I even had thoughts about becoming a minister. I just didn't want to give up the good things I had. I was afraid of a total commitment and I thought only about myself. I used the church for appearance sake, I was involved and yet I don't know if my motives were right or not. I know that you know what was false and what was righteous I hope that I did some good. I know Lord that from now on what I do will be done to the glory of your name and I will give you that glory. I want nothing in return because your gift of Jesus gave me life eternal. I was lost and you found me in the barrel at the bottom. I know Lord that Satan has no hold on me anymore. I know that I can always ask for protection and you'll give it in the name of Jesus. Praise you Lord! Praise you! The good news is that when I feel guilty I can ask for forgiveness from the foot of the cross. There are times that I will feel ashamed and when I do I can bring that shame before you in Jesus name. I am so thankful and blessed. Lord I know I am rambling over the same things I've talked to you about before but I still have the need to reaffirm these thoughts with you. I love you Lord and will right tomorrow.

G.
Jude 22

December 13

Father,
I know Lord that sin is my prison and not these locked rooms I'm living in here. Paul writes in Galatians 5:1, Stand fast in the liberty where with Christ I am made free, and I need not be tangled with the yoke of bondage. What does this mean? It means that I am free because of Christ's death on the cross and as a free man I should not be a slave again to sin. In the Old Testament the laws you gave were past down from Moses to your chosen

people. What did people do? They continued to sin and brought down their faith when they turned their backs on you repeatedly. Lord you saw fit to punish them. I know Lord that only a few would have been worthy. We are free willed people and Lord you gave us your Son Jesus to pay the price and give all people the opportunity to be saved and enter into the light. Lord as it says in Galatians 5: For we place our faith in Christ Jesus, it makes no difference to you Lord whether we are circumcised or not circumcised. What is important is faith expresses itself in love. Walking out of the darkness and into the light has been a good thing for me. I pray Lord that I always walk in the light and never the darkness. Keep me safely in your arms on my journey. I love you Father and will write later, as always.

G.

Galatians 5:1

December 14

Father,

I pray Lord that some members of my family might find away to come down here to Hill before Christmas which of course is in 11 days. I have told my family what would be nice for Christmas and I hope that I might get a visit. I hope Lord that I might hear from my son. I think I only heard from him once in all the time I've been in prison. I don't know, maybe it's a guy thing or maybe he hasn't forgiven me yet either way I can at least hope. Lord I do know that I will have you with me at Christmas and we can celebrate the birth of Jesus on that day. I know that this is the day that men have set to honor your Son so I ask you Lord what is the real day? I know that I'll have to wait until I get to Heaven to find out the answer, I just thought I'd ask. Lord I know that your grace is sufficient for me and that's all I want forever and always; a guarantee of eternal life. Lord I once was that lost sheep and Jesus found me and brought me back to the fold. I thank you Lord Jesus for that blessing. Lord can't think of much more to write about so I'll talk tomorrow. I love you Lord as always.

G.

John 10:1-5

December 15

Father,

Lord until a person loses their freedom and everything is taken away the dynamics of life are always the same. The dynamics change drastically when one's freedom is lost. Lord when I uses to think of all that I had obtained I thought I was content; it wasn't contentment as much as it was security. My life was one of hard work, long hours and lots of overtime. Lord I never took time to stop and just enjoy life. In being confined here in prison I have the time and I know this time has given me the opportunity for study and reflection. Lord what I thought was important wasn't and what I thought wasn't important is and that's you my Lord. I look at the fast pace world that we are living in today and the direction we are going in is wrong, we are in worse shape not better, we are destroying ourselves. Lord when you are left out of the equation things literally go to Hell. The percentage of people that are Christian today are lower than they have ever been. The sad part is all the signs that you gave in the word are coming to light. I do not know how much time we have left on this earth but it looks like that time is short. I know no one knows the time or place but I know it will happen and it could be in my lifetime. I am just thankful that I know where I'll be going if the day comes while I am still alive. Lord I pray that all men and women make I sound decision and chose my Lord and Savior Jesus Christ. I pray for all mankind. I love you Lord and will write tomorrow as always.

G.

Revelation 6:12

December 16

Father,

Good evening Lord, another fish Friday which makes eating tolerable here. I got to thinking this morning on what causes your children to stumble? Lord is it a weakness in faith or is it a lack of understanding that you are our priority not things of this world? I know that if I abandon you Lord Satan will drag me back to this earthly world. I sometimes think we are like a horse with blinders on given a narrow path to travel upon. I know that we limit ourselves by how much we submit to worldly not godly thoughts. You gave to us your people free will to make choices, to come to you because we want to. Lord to defeat Satan you must be first. I know we must live in your Kingdom realm not Satan's. Lord it's a tall order especially when the pressures of this world are heaped upon us. I know that when this happens it's the best time to call upon you. Lord each generation has fallen deeper out of love for you Lord. I also know that the most devoted people drawn to yours are the poor, downtrodden, the ones that have hit rock bottom. Like me I had to hit rock bottom to seek out help and that help is calling upon your name. I know Lord that if you were my first priority when I started my journey things would have gone a lot smoother. This world has become so tolerant of immoral ways, very few people care and that is so sad. I would expect that over the course of the next 10 years our prison system will be very crowded with a lot of these lost souls. Satan owns this world but we have you to remove us when it's time to the next. I love you Lord and will write tomorrow as always

G.

Job 1:7

December 17

Father,

Lord to you be the Glory! Sacred is your name and the name of your Son Jesus above all others. Through my Savior Jesus and the Holy Spirit I come to you this Saturday. Lord I know that your Kingdom is at hand. Lord it soon will be time for all to answer and be accountable for the time we spent here on earth. I am a sinner Lord and have been unworthy, unworthy by all I've done in my past. I let myself be taken in by the great deceiver. I used the gift of free will to make wrong choices. Lord I took the easiest path, the path of least resistance. I choose to live my way in Satan's realm not yours. In my time here on earth I have done so many shameful things. I was weak and made choices of earthly pleasures. I choose the quick fix, temporary enjoyment, enjoyment with no meaning. I know that there were times where my heart was touched by the Holy Spirit and I did things for the Body of Christ. I look back and I wonder if it wasn't just done for show? Maybe it was the guilt and conviction of the Holy Spirit I don't know, it makes no difference now because I'm in Christ and where I always want to be. My faith was weak and you gave me strength, you took away all the hurts and pain I carried throughout my life and made me new. Lord I pray that all men come to you with their burdens and surrender them to you. Lord you are the great healer and I know they can be healed by your grace. I love you Lord and will write tomorrow as always.

G.

Matthew 17:5, 6

December 18

Father,

Good evening Lord well I have good news the Bears won and they are getting close to the playoffs. My cellie went home today so I have the cell all to myself for a little while. Lord I pray that you watch over my cellie on the outside. Lord I pray that he doesn't get involved with the crack cocaine again and find himself back in prison. Lord keep him safe and maybe he will be able to turn his life around. I think one of the saddest things is knowing that he has a 73% chance of coming back so I pray that he beats the odds. Last night I trying to get some sleep and thought about how you will give me what I need to make it when it's my time to go home and I thank you. Things were placed on my mind about using my story to tell people about my fall and how you changed my heart and gave me a new life. I hope that my story will give them hope and lift them up. If I could prevent one person from their self-destructive nature then I would have been successful. I know that I haven't been given any details yet but I am ready to do your will. Lord I pray for your wisdom and guidance. Lord provide me with the right tools to do your work. Lord give me comfort and peace about doing what you want me to do. Lord I want what you want so let me help where I can. Lord I know that I will probably be scared to get involved but I know that you will get me through. Praise you Lord! Father I love you and will talk tomorrow, as always.

G.

Luke 6:40

December 19

Father,

I ask you to forgive me for thinking evil thoughts wishing that something bad happens to one of the inmates in my cell block. I pray that you protect C. from this angry inmate. Lord I do not know what happened but let cooler heads prevail especially this close to Christmas. All the inmates are looking forward to Thursday when we get to go to commissary for our Christmas shop. I found out that we can double up and the limits have been lifted. I will be able to get 12 Snickers instead of 6. These are my energy bars or should I say feel good bars. I've got a substantial amount on the books and expect more before Thursday so I should have a good shop. My classes are over this week and my final tests are on Thursday also so it's looking like a pretty good lead in to Christmas. I know I will pass the courses and I think with straight A's. I just won't know how much good time I'll get back until next week. Lord I pray for a better December than last year when I ended up going to Stateville. Lord keep the cell block peaceful during this important time of the year. Jesus you are the reason for the season and I'm looking forward to the coming celebration. Lord I love you and will write tomorrow, as always.

G.

Luke 1:78, 79

December 20

Father,
Lord as I approach Christmas I think back to better times, times of Christmas past. I remember the fun of taking my children out and cutting down a fresh Christmas tree. I remember the excitement in their eyes. I remember the struggles trying to find the right Christmas gifts. I remember buying in on the latest toy like everyone else. I remember the look in their eyes when they opened their presents. I know that those days are gone but next year I'll be able to see the joy in my grandkids eyes as they continue the tradition. Had my last tests yesterdays and now it's a waiting game to find out how I did. I see where C. and the other inmate shook hands and made peace with each other, this is good, good for the whole prison. I really thought there would be a fight and we would end up in lockdown again. Lord I thank you for answering my prayer it will mean a nicer Christmas for all concerned. One of things I'll be doing on Christmas is watching the Bears play Green Bay so that outta be fun. I am hoping that my daughters K. & H. will send some new books for me to read. I am looking forward for some new hands prints form the grandkids so I can compare them to the last ones I got. I know that this will be my last Christmas in prison and I have learned so much, and become aware of the bad situation that the inmates have. Someone once said that the prisoners had it made and it was like spending time at a country club. I doubt they have ever seen the inside of a prison or they would know that this is not true. The inmates are not treated any better than a herd of cattle. Movement is restricted and our every move is observed with constant scrutiny. I remember back when the students for a criminal justice course came to Stateville and I could see the surprise look on their faces as they observed the harsh conditions that we, the prisoners were in. I do not think they were prepared for that, looking at the fear and apprehension on their faces. I know Lord that all of us here did something illegal and we must pay the price for our mistake I would just like to see a little more caring from the staff. I will write tomorrow Lord, as always.

G.
Hebrews 13:3

December 21.

Father,
Lord I want to thank you for the naturing you gave me. I seem to be able to get along with all of the other inmates that I am around and let me tell you that is a blessing. I think besides your grace my age has a lot to do with it. I look a lot older than I am and I mind my own business. My dayroom time is spent in playing either pinnacle or spades and we always have a crowd of guys wanting to play pinnacle with us so there is never a table empty. I have a guaranteed spot because I own the game cards. I have found that a good card stimulates conversation and I learn a lot about the guys I'm playing with. Take for example B., he is spending time in here for selling stolen guns and says he has a stash of guns to sell when he gets out. If it were me I don't think I would be bragging. A. is a member of an Aryan gang and he talks about the hidden caches of weapons that his group has store for the time when something needs to be done, and uses the Constitutional rights he's been given to keep weapons; for protection. I think that there is only one problem being a felon he is not allowed to own a gun. Then there was the time that one of my cellies talked about the robbery he committed while we were playing cards. He was sent up for having stolen merchandise in his possession but not for the robbery. He told me how he pulled it off and where the stuff he stole was taken to for safe storage. I have found all sorts of interesting things out and true confession is good for the soul. I guess these guys need to get their problems off their chest; or can't stand the fact that no one knows about what crimes these guys committed and they feel comfortable sharing. I can't change what was all I can do is listen and give sound advice; shut up and keep quiet. Lord I want to pray for my cousin L. in her struggle with the pain in her body that disables her so badly. I feel so sorry for her pain and I pray Lord that you cast the pain out of her. In the name of Jesus, I thank you Lord. I'll write tomorrow as always.

G.

Mark 1:5

December 22

Father,
I got a letter from my daughter today and she sent me a poem she had written back in 1997, she was about 19 years old. I thought I let you see it and keep this memory for myself. The poem is entitled: THROUGH THE DARKNESS:

> Through the darkness there is light that shines so bright.
> It comes and goes with the blowing wind.
> It's the kind of light that settles deep in your bones
> And warms you up from within.
> It brings you places you've never been.
> It gives you hope and takes away your fears;
> It brings you laughter when there are tears.
> It digs down further into your soul;
> Just to let off that special glow.
> Make yourself move into the light;
> Through the darkness out of the night.
>
> KER 1997

The poem is such a special gift to get for Christmas I only had a glimpse of some of her poems and they are so insightful. She wrote these almost 9 years ago that would have made her around 18 or 19. I am so proud of her. I can feel my heart bursting with pride. There are special moments in life and receiving this poem is one of them. I pray Lord that she is able to continue writing poems she has such a talent. Well Lord I'll write tomorrow thanks for being with me. I love you Lord as always.

G.
2 Corinthians 4:26

December 23

Father,
Good evening Lord, well we had a good dinner Friday night fish and chips. Shop went very well yesterday and I was able to stock up on plenty of food stuffs and was even able to get a nice pair of gym shoes in trade for some of the supplies I got. Lord I want to pray thank you for the need of better shoes and the provision that you gave. I was talking to one of the inmates about giving his life over to Christ and at this present time he said no, I was frustrated and disappointed. I know Lord that I must remember that it's the Holy Spirit that must convict him and save him. John 3:5,7; says we cannot believe for him or redeem him, That the Spirit convicts him of his sin, forgives him and gives him new life and all I can do is pray. I pray Lord for the soul of this young man who is searching for a better way and life. I know I just have to remain faithful to your word, bless you Lord. I got a new James Patterson book today for Christmas from my daughter. The book is a new Alex Cross novel "Brooklyn Bridge" I can't wait to get started reading it. It this crazy world of prison it is great to escape from the dreariness in one of James Patterson's books. Patterson is a very popular read here in prison, along with Tom Clancy, John Grisham, and John Sanford. I also got my grandkids hand prints and can see how much they have grown since the last ones I got earlier this year. Lord I thank you for my children and family who did not forget me this Christmas. I know I'll be with them for Christmas next year away from this place. I love you Father and will write tomorrow as always.

G.
John 3:5-7

December 24

Father,
Lord tomorrow is Christmas and I can't wait for the day of rest. I know that things have been tense here mostly because a lot of inmate will get no letters or be unable to contact their loved ones by phone for lack of money on the family's part to accept a charged phone call. The average phone call cost about $25 to place from here to home. At least this privilege is granted to be able to call home if you can afford it. I pray Lord that the inmates that are having a rough time dealing with this holiday season get some type of blessing from home. I think of all the Christmas candlelight services I've gone to in the course of my life and wish I was at one this evening. Next year I will be going to one for sure. I was writing a list of things to do when I get out and it seems pretty lame. Plant a garden, both inside my place and outside. Learn to make homemade recipes; Spaghetti sauce, Mac & cheese and Fettuccine Alfredo. I want to be able to fix Blackened Chicken and how to marinate steaks for cooking on a grill. I want a simple life surrounded with your love and the bounties that you provide. Lord make me into a better person, and one who keeps Christmas in my heart all year long. Father tomorrow would have been rough on anyone if their son was born into this world and knowing that his death was coming around 33 years later, but you gave him up so that all mankind would become your Sons and Daughters and we should all thank you for that. Lord I love you; and will adore you forever. Happy Christmas Eve.

G.
2 Thessalonians 1:4

December 25

Father,
Merry Christmas Lord, peace on earth good will towards men. Lord today celebrates the birth of my Lord and Savior Jesus. Lord he came into this world to give us lessons to live by. He came into this world to bring and show love. He came into this world because we were sinners in your eyes and no way to reach you. Over 2000 years have passed since the baby Jesus was born into this world laid in a manger. Today we had another feast at chow, Pressed Turkey with all the trimming. This was the same menu that we had for Thanksgiving. Spent time talking to my kids this evening and it was nice to hear their voices and I even got to say hello to all my grandkids. I thanked them for the gifts and checked on what they were doing and what they got for Christmas. The conversation was bitter sweet knowing that I wasn't there to give them a hug. I found out that this coming week I'll be getting my grades for the classes I took and also how many days I'll get taken off my time here. Lord it has been a good Christmas, even the C.O.'s have been nicer a blessing in itself. Jesus I wish you a Happy Birthday and thanks for your birth for without you I along with all others would be lost so thanks again. I look back on this past year and it's hard to believe that it is coming to an end. Another good thing that happened today is that the Bears beat the Green Bay Packer. I am so glad that the Bears will be going to the playoffs. Tonight is a silent and Holy Night. I love you Father and know that I am totally blessed. I pray for the world to feel the same. I will write tomorrow as always.

G.
Matthew 2:6

December 26

Father,
Good evening Lord. For the wages of sin is death and all fall short of the glory of God. (Romans 3:23) When you created the world it was a perfect place. Man was created in your image and was without sin. Lord you asked one thing of man and thanks to the great deceiver sin came in to the world. The original sin that all mankind were to fall under. Lord in your infinite plan it took thousands of years of patiencs before you gave your people the only way to gain eternal life and not live separate from you. Jesus was born in perfect harmony with your plan. Lord you could have at anytime totally destroyed your creations and started over, you didn't and for that all mankind should be thanking you. I find it so difficult to understand people who are given a chance to have this wonderful gift of eternal life and then watch them turn it down. I know that I can never be ashamed of Jesus and his sacrifice on the cross, if I was I wouldn't be writing you everyday that's how much I worship and adore you. Lord you guaranteed me eternal life and I'm taking it all the way. My life was just plodding along and having no direction I let Satan slip into my consciousness leading me away from you and continuing to make me feel guilty until I finally was lured into illegal activities. I paid man's price and gave the most important part of that consciousness to you, sin. Father I am saved because of my Jesus your Son and thanks be to your name. I will write tomorrow as always.

G.

Romans 3:23

December 27

Father,
I was going over 1 John 1:7-9 it says if we say we have no sin we deceive ourselves and there is no truth in us. But if we confess our sins to you Lord you will keep your promise and do what is right; you will forgive us of our sins and purify us of any wrong doing. The thing that amazes me is that everyone who hears the message of salvation do not want to be saved. Some people don't take the time to think others don't listen and still others think that the Word doesn't affect them. The most difficult non-believer doesn't think that their sins can be forgiven. All these people have no clue

as to your power and that in itself is extremely sad. I look upon these decisions that they make as pure laziness. I also think that if they have never read the word they will have difficulty forming a right decision. Lord maybe I'm off base here and maybe I've become jaded especially with the studies that you have laid upon my heart, I don't know. I pray that you help me find the right answer. Let me do the work and teach me with love how to present the right answer to their questions. I just pray that anyone who has heard the message of forgiveness comes to know the Holy Spirit. I love the gift Jesus gave to me and I sincerely hope others might too. I pray that I may use what you have done in my life to affect change in others.

G.

1 John 1:7-9

December 28

Father,

Praise you Lord have I been blessed today! I got my grade sheet back today and my good time has been calculated. I got A's in both classes and received 28 days off my time. I thank you Father for helping me get through these courses and for the amount of time knocked of incarceration. Oct. 2, 2006 is now my out date, Hallelujah! I am looking at the calendar and I think I will be able to take 4 more classes, if that holds true I could be out sometime in August and home in time for my birthday. I know I have no idea where I'll be going but I'll let you help me find the right place when it's time. Lord the weather is getting colder but I am feeling super warm right now. I will not miss the cold weather when I'm gone from this place and I know I'll have a much warmer coat for next winter. I want to thank you for listening to me and my ramblings. You said that I could come to you any time and that's what I've done. I just feel so comfortable with writing to you because I know that you are here with me. Lord when I pick up the Bible and read it I thirst more and more I am so hungry for your Word. The more I read the more questions I have to ask. The more questions I ask the more informed I become. I am thankful for all the knowledge and wisdom that you impart. I think of all the time I wasted in my life and am thankful now for the time to catch up. I love you Lord.

G.

Psalm 145:16

December 29

Father,
Most precious Lord I come to you tonight to pray for all the inmates here at Hill. I pray also for their souls, that they take a leap of faith and bind themselves over to your love and grace. Lord I pray for my family and friends and the family and friends of the other inmates that they reach out to assist and aid their people that are here with me. Lord we are all your children whether we all know it or not, and all it takes is an open heart to come to you. Lord let me be the aorta, pumping fluid to that heart so the Holy Spirit can make that heart beat and grow stronger. I know Lord that you can do anything so let it be done by your will and the power of your name. Lord I read a piece on loving thy neighbor and I've had it since I was in Stateville back in February of this year. It was published by Rainbow Publishing in Mesa Arizona and it goes like this:

> *"Lord be gracious and gentle to me. May your face shine upon me. Light my path as I go throughout the earth. Keep my hands in yours, guide my thoughts, guide my ways, guide me Lord all my days. Steer me right when I walk by day and sleep at night. Bless my going out and coming in. Bless my every step keep me from sin."*

I found this piece very meaningful on my walk this year; so I thought I'd write it down. Lord you are my first love and there is no other, three-in-one; Father, Son and Holy Spirit. I will write tomorrow as always.

G.
Mark 16:15-17

December 30

Father,
Good evening Lord. Today was a fairly quiet day, one of thought and contemplation. This has been day to reflect on my future and where I'll be going. I had some thoughts and I came up with Dupage County. I was thinking that it's time to go back home. I know that all my children are there and if they want to be close to me that this is the place I outta be. I left there in 1999 and went out to northwestern Illinois in Stephenson County. I loved it out there but I only have one friend and that's my former boss R. I love him very much but then again family is family. I know that one of the things that will need to be done is for my family to find a place I'll be able to afford. I will need to find a job as soon as I can to pay for the place that they will find. In 1999 I was running away from the life I had and taking a chance on a new and different lifestyle. I liked it in northern Illinois and the pace of life was a lot slower. I know that after I got use to the slow down place things were working out great. I know that at this time in my life family is so important and my biggest concern. I had hoped for some type of resolution from my family and got it with the outpouring of love I received from Christmas, the healing has begun and I now think it's time for me to go home. Lord I need family around me and I pray for a positive resolution when the time comes and I can go home. Lord lead me and guide me to the proper place. I love you Lord and will write tomorrow as always.

G.
Galatians 5:16

December 31

Father,

Good evening Lord, it's 11:15 P.M. And in 45 minutes we will begin a new year, 2006. I look back on this year and have very mixed feelings. The year began for me in the worse possible spot a person could be in segregation unit at Stateville Correctional Facility, a Maximum Security Prison. This was one experience that helped define who I will be. Lord you removed the pain and suffering by a blow from your breath. You brought me from the darkness into the light. You gave me the choice to serve you and only you. Lord I will be forever grateful for that chance. Lord you put me on the right path a path that in the end will lead me home to live with you forever. I know that lots of people don't want to understand this concept but I can only present and you will do the rest putting these people on the right paths. Lord as this year has progressed I have been nurtured and taught the ways of life through your eyes. Lord the foundation is there and I still have 9 months to go; work in me Lord during this time. Lord as I cast out the old and bring in the new I get a little nervous and scared. I do not know what the future holds only you do and I will give you the lead. Lord I pray that everyone everywhere may come to know you the way that I have. If anyone prays to you for forgiveness, forgive them for what they did, and grant them the keys to the Kingdom. I will hopefully be a beacon for many and maybe my story on the life I renounced will bring some light to those who live in darkness. Lord all the programs on T.V. are touting the New Year and the ball has dropped in New York. In one minute the New Year will be upon us here. Lord let this coming year be a blessing for me and may it begin with love. Happy New Year! Lord I love you and welcome this New Year. Lord it's time to look ahead and not behind. I will write later today, January 1, 2006, as always.

G.

Matthew 25:21

A New Resolve

The book that you just finished reading is a journal of 12 months out of the 28 months I spent incarcerated. Out of those 28 months, the first 7 1/2 months were in Stephenson County Jail and Western Correctional Center in Mt. Sterling. The next 6 months of this journal was spent locked down 24 hours a day, seven days a week in Stateville Maximum Security Prison near Joliet Illinois. The other 6 months of this journal was spent at Hill Correctional Center, a medium maximum prison at Galesburg, Illinois, where I spent the rest of my prison term. I was also locked down 24 hours a day at this prison for about 2 months on and off as the Correctional facility saw fit. (When there is a serious disturbance either at the facility I was at, or any other prison, all Correctional facilities get locked down.)

I wrote my daily prayer journal during the 12 months of 2005, until the end of my prison term. Who I had been passed away and a new person was born during this time. I started the journal just to document the harshness of the prisons and write my prayers to God. I had no idea that my time there was as close to hell as I ever want to be. To survive my time in this hell-hole I started seeking answers to my situation. When I started to read the Word of God in earnest, I started to find some resolutions toward my situation. As time passed and things started to get profoundly worse, I went to the Word more and more. I had a thirst to learn. I asked God to lead me in my studies and give me the knowledge and wisdom to understand who He is and who I am. Both questions were answered when I surrendered totally on February 9, 2005. My heart and mind were at peace for the first time in my life. All negatives were turned into positives and I was able to obtain peace both inwardly and outwardly.

The Lord was my protection and comforter. In my time in prison I realized that sometimes good can come out of adversity when God is in control. My life since prison has been blessed and God has provided me with all I need. I want for only what God wants to give me. I let God take the lead and try to spread God's love for everyone and to as many people who choose to listen to my story or observe the person I am in my daily life. I am not perfect and never will be, but I think I have a good start on my path to eternity, to be with my Lord and Savior Jesus Christ and my

Father God is the race I'm in. It is my prayer that all who read this journal, reflect on their lives and that they find truth in knowing that God will always be there no matter what someone has done. There is no problem too great that God can't solve. The hard part is to give God control over our lives. May the promises of God be a blessing to all of us forever and always.

I know that people might ask why they should read this prayer journal and what makes it different from other journals of prayer? I can only answer by saying this is a journal I wrote about coming to God through my thoughts and writings. The journal gives the reader a little bit of what it was like inside prison walls, and what daily life holds for anyone who may end up here. I also have hope that men who are in prison might read this prayer journal and start to heal their pain and agony by going to God. Prison life is not easy and the one thing that is for sure is the loneliness, that no matter how tough we think we are we will still get lonely. I had a choice to be lonely or talk to someone I could count on to aid me in getting through my stay in prison. I chose to have God as my companion, my friend, and my comforter. I know that without God my time in prison would have been unbearable.

I hope you enjoyed the journey.

G.

Acknowledgements

I would first like to thank my Father in Heaven, my Lord and Savior Jesus Christ, the Holy Spirit that guided me in writing this book.

I would like to thank my wife Carol for her patience and understanding while I wrote this book. I thank my earthly Father and Mother for giving me the life skills needed to survive in this world.

I thank my children; Eric, Kristen, and Heather for their love and support, and my family and friends who helped me during my incarceration and beyond.

I thank Pastor Steve Barr for mentoring me, and Pastor Burless Parker and his wife Dawn for their encouragement.

I especially thank Pam Wool and her husband John for reading my book and giving me their thoughts and loving criticism, to Russ and Connie for standing by me and giving me a chance.

I love you all very much.

Made in the USA
Lexington, KY
07 April 2012